SENTINEL

HOME-ALONE AMERICA

Mary Tedeschi Eberstadt works from home as a research fellow for Stanford University's Hoover Institution. She is consulting editior to *Policy Review,* the critically acclaimed journal of conservative thought. Her essays and reviews have also appeared in the *Weekly Standard, The Wall Street Journal,* and *Commentary.* She and her husband, the writer Nicholas Nash Eberstadt, have four children and live in Washington, D.C.

HOME-ALONE
AMERICA

*Why Today's Kids Are Overmedicated,
Overweight, and More Troubled Than Ever Before*

Mary Eberstadt

SENTINEL

To the memory of my mother,
Kathryn Savoy,
and to my stepfather,
William Royal Savoy

SENTINEL
Published by the Penguin Group
Penguin Group (USA) Inc., 375 Hudson Street,
    New York, New York 10014, U.S.A.
Penguin Group (Canada), 90 Eglinton Avenue East, Suite 700,
    Toronto, Ontario, Canada M4P 2Y3
    (a division of Pearson Penguin Canada Inc.)
Penguin Books Ltd, 80 Strand, London WC2R 0RL, England
Penguin Ireland, 25 St. Stephen's Green, Dublin 2, Ireland
    (a division of Penguin Books Ltd)
Penguin Group (Australia), 250 Camberwell Road, Camberwell,
    Victoria 3124, Australia (a division of Pearson Australia Group Pty Ltd)
Penguin Books India Pvt Ltd, 11 Community Centre, Panchsheel Park,
    New Delhi–110 017, India
Penguin Group (NZ), Cnr Airborne and Rosedale Roads, Albany,
    Auckland 1310, New Zealand (a division of Pearson New Zealand Ltd)
Penguin Books (South Africa) (Pty) Ltd, 24 Sturdee Avenue,
    Rosebank, Johannesburg 2196, South Africa

Penguin Books Ltd, Registered Offices:
80 Strand, London WC2R 0RL, England

First published in the United States of America by Sentinel, a member of Penguin Group (USA) Inc. 2004
Published in Sentinel 2005

10 9 8 7 6 5 4 3 2 1

Copyright © Mary Eberstadt, 2004
All rights reserved

THE LIBRARY OF CONGRESS HAS CATALOGED THE HARDCOVER EDITION AS FOLLOWS:
Eberstadt, Mary.
    Home-alone America : the hidden toll of day care, behavioral drugs, and other parent substitutes /
Mary Eberstadt.
        p.   cm.
    Includes bibliographical references and index.
    ISBN 1-59523-004-1 (hc.)
    ISBN 1-59523-015-7 (pbk.)
    1. Children of working mothers—United States. 2. Parenting—United States.
3. Parental deprivation—United States. I. Title.
HQ777.6.E24 2004
306.874—dc22   2004054731

Printed in the United States of America
Set in Adobe Garamond

ACKNOWLEDGMENTS

TO BORROW A PHRASE, IT TOOK A VILLAGE TO WRITE THIS book. Thanks first to its farthest-flung member, Bernard Goldberg, whose 2001 *New York Times* number one best-seller, *Bias*, unexpectedly devoted several pages and some very kind comments to a *Policy Review* essay of mine called "Home-Alone America." That act of wanton generosity first set the process of this book in motion.

Thanks also to another unanticipated benefactor, John Raisian, director of the Hoover Institution at Stanford University. Two years ago, he unexpectedly honored me with an appointment as part-time Research Fellow, and he has supported my efforts ever since. If this book redeems even part of the debt I owe him and to Hoover, it will have paid at least some of its moral freight.

Several magazines and editors have published essays of mine generally relevant to this book, including *Public Interest* (Irving Kristol), *Commentary* (Neal Kozodoy and Norman Podhoretz), *American Spectator* (Bob Tyrrell and Wlady Pleszczynski), and *Weekly Standard* (Bill Kristol and Richard Starr). One journal in particular, *Policy Review*, where I am consulting editor, contributed directly to some of these pages. Both "Home-Alone America" and "The Child-Fat Problem," a 2003 essay of which chapter 3 is a revised version, appeared first in *PR*'s pages. My thanks to the magazine's staff for enabling my ghostly presence in the office, in particular stalwart Kelly Dillon. Former assistant editor Steven Menashi has kindly improved several points in these pages.

Numerous friends and acquaintances have helped with this book whether they wanted to or not: Douglas Besharov, Karlyn and Jim Bowman, Tom Cannell, Kate Chieco, Christopher DeMuth, Maura and Daniel Mudd, Karen and Michael Novak, Donald Page, Rhoda and Jeremy Rabkin, Sharon Savoy, Samantha Savoy, Judy Kelly, my father, Victor Tedeschi, and former *Policy Review* assistant Maureen Sirhal, who taught me in the late days of 1998 how to use e-mail and a computer. Anyone now cursing their inboxes on account of me has her to blame. Thanks also to Reverend William Ryan for his indispensable counsel during the past year and otherwise. As to other experts, my gratitude again to the professionals who have patiently explained various aspects of the medical vocation, again without implicating them a whit in this book's thesis: pediatrician Ronald Bashian, pediatrican Howard J. Bennett, pediatrician Susan De Muth, psychiatrist Anne Sagalyn, psychiatrist Sally Satel, and clinical social worker Frederick Eberstadt, my father-in-law.

Two people forced this book into being: my friend Tod Lindberg, *Policy Review*'s editor, and my sister, Eileen Page. Midway through the writing last year, my mother died, and I decided to abandon this project. They insisted otherwise. Had it not been for their nagging, the original manuscript would still be sitting in the basement.

To appease them, I sent my work off "blind" to Washington literary agent Raphael Sagalyn. Rafe not only believed in the project from day one but also worked the kind of agent magic that first-time book authors dream of by connecting me with Penguin's new imprint, Sentinel. My thanks there to Adrian Zackheim, the imprint's founder; utility infielder and assistant editor Megan Casey; copy editor Rose Ann Ferrick; and above all, my gifted editor, Bernadette Malone, who has passionately shepherded and improved this book with each go-round. All have my deepest gratitude.

Four personal friends deserve special mention for their many contributions to this book: Denise Ferguson, Tina Lindberg, Tina O'Rourke, and, again, my sister, Eileen Page. All have stood shoulder to shoulder (sometimes sandbox to sandbox) throughout our simultaneous adventures in motherhood. None of them had to read a word to know what was in these pages, because all of them have heard it from me ad nauseum.

Thanks of the humblest intellectual sort go to the friends who read and commented on chapter drafts. Francis Fukuyama and Leon Kass both made critical contributions to the chapters on mental health and psychotropic drugs. Longtime comrade Andrew Ferguson brought such clarity to his close readings that I'm still wincing from the experience. Tod Lindberg read every word and offered the kind of insights that explain why writers from all over now compete for his red pen at *Policy Review.*

As to other readers: P. J. O'Rourke, who has egged me on in expounding the ideas behind this book through numerous dinner hours and after-dinner hours, also ran his sharp editorial eye over lots of it and thereby deserves a double thanks. Special thanks are also due to one other exceedingly dedicated reader and friend, former Harvard anthropologist and current Hoover Fellow Stanley Kurtz. An intellectual empath, he has tirelessly improved these pages with insights, references, and other contributions to its argument.

In short, with a roster of readers like those, I am not only tempted to ascribe any errors to them rather than to me, but would be doing them an injustice by not insisting on it. Even so, I herein take the blame for any literary faults.

Included in the village that it took to write this book are those at home. Thanks to those who have helped with the children or house over the years—most recently Nicole Scouten and Kathy Medina. Thanks to my brothers, Bill, Steven, and Michael Savoy, for their moral support over the years on the adolescent male psyche. Thanks also to my stepfather, Roy Savoy, to whom this book is dedicated along with my late mother. He not only lovingly encouraged it, as he has encouraged my scribbling since childhood, but also made extra trips to Washington to help with the babysitting and household chores during the crunch times.

Both my sister-in-law, novelist Fernanda Eberstadt, and her husband, writer Alastair Bruton, have encouraged this book with insights and sympathy. My mother- and father-in-law, Frederick Eberstadt and Isabel Nash Eberstadt, also writers, have been the soul of tolerance and aid throughout this effort. They, too, have read and commented on the book's contents with wisdom and wit.

The youngest members of the village behind this book, my three older children, put up with everything it required with a most unchildish grace. I hope they will consider these pages a kind of nerdy valentine to them. In order of earthly appearance: Thanks to Frederick William Eberstadt for his intellectual and spiritual contributions and for his wide (if unconscionable) knowledge of contemporary popular teenage culture. Thanks to Catherine Nash Eberstadt for her moral rigor and inspiring dedication to scholarship and, above all, for her technical assistance in the writing hole whenever it was needed—which was a lot. Thanks to Isabel Eberstadt for her unflagging faith in Mom and her enthusiasm for this book, right down to the lucky mouse pad she made. Further thanks to all three children for their help with one another's homework, or whatever they were doing when they were supposed to be doing that, and also for their creative assistance in amusing and distracting Alexandra, light of the household.

Finally, to Nick, my husband. Known elsewhere and to erudite people as scholar, author, and intellectual in residence at the American Enterprise Institute, he has also shared his great gifts by reading every word of what follows several times over and by helping with every snag and hurdle in the writing. No one has done more for these pages or for me. This book is just one of the many adventures I am privileged to share with him.

CONTENTS

PREFACE

I AM GRATIFIED TO RELATE THAT SINCE ITS APPEARANCE IN hardcover in late 2004, *Home-Alone America* has been widely dispersed and discussed, both in the United States and elsewhere. This preface to the paperback edition offers an opportune moment to reflect briefly on the public reaction.

First, let me reassure first-time readers that, contrary to what some critics have intimated, this book was not written in the hope of catapulting the talented and educated women of America back to the Stone Age. Neither was it written in the hope of catapulting them back to an era regarded by other critics as perhaps even more oppressive and horrifying—i.e., 1950s America.

As anyone actually reading the book will know, *Home-Alone America* was and is something different from such distortions: an honest attempt to address an outstanding social puzzle of our time. On the one hand, the children and teenagers of today's advanced societies—like the adults of those same societies—are materially better off than ever before. Yet on the other hand, those same children and teenagers share acute problems that either did not exist before, or did not exist in anything like today's proportions.

Juvenile obesity, for example, has tripled since the early 1960s. Sexually transmitted disease is epidemic among teenagers and young adults (of some 19 million new cases of STDs reported in 2000, say the Centers for Disease Control, half were found in people between fifteen and twenty-four). Diagnoses of juvenile psychiatric problems like depression, anxiety, and "behavioral" disorders have skyrocketed during the last twenty years—and so too have prescriptions for the psychotropic drugs used to treat them.

Other sources too suggest a downward slide. Many adults who are actually around children and teenagers day in and day out—meaning teachers and other school authorities—believe that their students truly are angrier, more violent, and less civilized than before. Then there is evidence of an especially revealing sort, namely adolescent popular culture, in particular contemporary rap and rock music. As many adults have complained, that music is indeed darker and coarser than what came before it. What is even more important, as the lyrical record shows, is what is *in* this music—namely, repeated recourse to the themes of abandonment, longing for responsible mothers and fathers, and rage at the absence of the nuclear family.

In sum, a variety of evidence affirms that for some significant number of today's kids, life is actually experienced as worse—meaning riskier, sadder, and more problematic—than it was for their parents' generation. This book tries to understand why. It argues that these troubles are in large measure the unintended fallout of a world in which children are more separated from their families, including but not limited to their parents, than they used to be.

To say that this message goes against the contemporary popular and expert grain is something of a gross understatement. For decades now, two very different ideas about nurture have ruled the public realm—meaning not only the popular media, but the medical and psychiatric and other professional literature as well.

Proposition One can be phrased something like this: *however much we think children need from their mothers and fathers, it is less than we used to believe.*

Over the past few decades, for example, every leading child care expert has curtailed the amount of time that young children are thought to need from their parents, especially their mothers. Meanwhile, whether the litmus test was the Moynihan Report in 1964 or the television show *Murphy Brown* over a quarter century later, the question of just how much children might need their *fathers* has similarly been ruled off-limits among polite, progressive people. Thanks to path-breaking scholarly exceptions including James Q. Wilson, David Blankenhorn, Barbara Defoe Whitehead, and others, that taboo has finally started to crack. Even so, the social damage remains. Whether the subject has been mothers or fathers, the trend in expert opinion for decades now has been strongly biased in one direction: toward *maximizing* adult freedom and *minimizing* child and adolescent needs.

The second proposition dominant in mainstream opinion comes from the long line of anguished and ambivalent feminist-dominated literature complaining about modern motherhood. *The Bitch in the House, Myths of Motherhood, The Myth of the Perfect Mother, The Mommy Myth,* and most recently, *Perfect Madness*. As the dour titles suggest, these and many, many other books and articles from the last decade or so share nearly interchangeable theses. They depict modern American mothers as quintessential and pitiable victims of the maternal condition. The consensus "solution" to this supposed problem is, of course, even more mother-child separation: more preschools at earlier ages, more government policies aimed at facilitating separation, and above all, more and ever-longer day care.

Thus, the popular complaint—that *modern motherhood is a headache whose treatment lies in more parent-child separation*—joins the expert proposition—*children need less of their parents than we think*—in the same back-patting camp. Both are crowd-pleasing, adult-exonerating understandings of exactly how much time and attention children and teenagers will be allowed to require.

Home-Alone America rejects those grudging and minimalist views of nurture. It asks readers to step back from their own personal stories and those of their adult peers and to look instead at contemporary children and teenagers, whose problems appear to tell us something important about what *those* human beings want and need—desires often hard to square with minimalist notions such as "quality time" and chronically rationalized, extended separation from parents and other family.

Not surprisingly, given the currents of the time, that proposed change of focus has generated a certain amount of resistance both expert and otherwise.

Some critics, for example, have tried to circumvent the evidence with what might be called the "yes, but" train of objection. *Yes,* this line of resistance goes, *we grant that today's kids have problems that others didn't. But what about all the good news out there about today's kids? Isn't juvenile crime falling? Aren't teenagers smoking less? Isn't the teen pregnancy rate down, and isn't that a good thing?* In short, they have sought to dodge the darker issues examined in the pages of this book by pointing to isolated patches of brightness instead.

The answer to their rhetorical questions is of course yes—and, so what? That there is also good news about today's juveniles isn't in doubt. But it is irrelevant to the inquiry of this book. My purpose is not to exhaustively catalog the state of today's American children, an inquiry better suited to the research apparatus of, say, the Rand Corporation, the Brookings Institution, or any of a number of government agencies. This book zeroes in on a different question; namely, just *where* are the problems peculiar to this generation coming from?

Other critics have proved especially resistant to the book's examination of two closely related phenomena: the explosion of psychiatric and behavioral problems among children of all ages, and the simultaneous explosion of the medications used to treat those troubled kids. I argue in part what is evidently a controversial idea—that perhaps some juveniles are sadder and sicker and angrier today because changes in family life have given them more to be sadder and sicker and angrier *about*. In other words, readers are asked to entertain the thought that at least some of the record numbers of psychiatric "problem cases" among today's kids are about something other than inborn neurological defects. Rather, my book suggests, at least some of those objectionable behaviors and attitudes might be *legitimate emotional responses* to the disappearance from many kids' lives of loving, protective adults.

Some have found this line of thought particularly heretical, and in a way, it is. Yet contrary to the objections of some, my point in raising the question of environment was not to deny the terrible reality of, say, genuine autism. It is rather to observe what no critic has answered or in most cases, even addressed: that the independent existence of obvious cases of childhood mental illness *cannot possibly explain the explosion* during these last two decades in both diagnoses of psychiatric trouble and the simultaneous huge leap in prescriptions given to kids for mind-altering drugs. Millions of children and teenagers in this generation have been labeled defective and put on psychiatric drugs to alter their behavior—kids who a generation ago would have been considered normal. Is this a problem? I suggest that it is, and further that it is just one of several signature problems of this generation.

In the end, reflecting on the public reception to these and other countercultural observations, two observations continue to encourage. First, the harshest words for *Home-Alone America* have come from people furthest removed from actual children and teenagers—mainly, from critics who have made a profession of celebrating parent-child separation. By contrast, the firmest endorsements have come from those closest to the world inhabited by actual children and teenagers—including former and current troubled juveniles.

It is heartening, for example, to know that many, many readers and listeners with hands-on experience of children—particularly at-home mothers and teachers—have reached out through e-mails, letters, blogs, and radio shows to verify one or another aspect of the book's thesis. Equally moving, and even more unexpected, has been the passionate reaction of assent among teenagers and young adults to the book's chapter on contemporary rock and rap. It's not every day that a Hoover Research Fellow finds an argument affirmed on the fan Web sites of Tupac Shakur, Eminem, Pearl Jam, and Nirvana. But the authenticity of their endorsements speaks for itself.

Many other people, adults and teenagers, made a point of getting in touch to deliver eloquent testimonies of their personal experiences of the trends described in the book—how shared custody worked in their own cases or how their own adult-empty home was Party Central every day after school or what it felt like to be a latchkey kid waiting hours for a reassuring grown-up face. And so reaction would go. For every missive from a credentialed adult critic accusing the book of one ideological misdemeanor or another, many more impassioned testimonies have flowed in affirming one or another aspect of the argument. I am grateful to all those readers, and more moved by their stories that I can say.

No work grounded in empirical research stands or falls by the emotional response to its pages, and *Home-Alone America* is no exception. Yet what the personal stories inadvertently affirm is the positive side of the empirical record assembled in this book. Mothers and fathers and other family members don't have to be perfect, fortunately for the mortals among us. The mere *presence* of their parents and other relatives matters more to children and teenagers than many adults realize—again, not only to their long-term success in life, but to their immediate happiness and security in the here and now.

Home-Alone America is in part an attempt to dignify that question of their immediate emotional well-being, to rescue it from ideological oblivion and put it back into enlightened discussion where it belongs.

Mary Eberstadt, February 2005

INTRODUCTION

THE ARGUMENT OF THE PAGES THAT FOLLOW COULD SCARCELY be more controversial to many contemporary readers. Of all the explosive subjects in America today, none is as cordoned off, as surrounded by rhetorical land mines, as the question of whether and just how much children need their parents—especially their mothers. In an age littered with discarded taboos, this one in particular remains virtually untouched.

This book challenges that social prohibition. It strives to shed light on one of the fundamental changes of our time: the ongoing, massive, and historically unprecedented experiment in family-child separation in which the United States and most other advanced societies are now engaged.

Whole libraries have already been devoted to one side of this experiment. For decades everything about the unfettered modern woman—her opportunities, her anxieties, her choices, her having or not having it all— has been dissected to the smallest detail. From Simone de Beauvoir to Betty Friedan to any number of other recent feminist-fueled writers, the ideological spotlight remains the same: It is on grown women and what *they* want and need.[1]

Much the same is also true of the vigorous recent literature running counter to feminism.[2] Woman in her own right is also the focus of a recent boomlet in popular literature emphasizing the benefits to mothers of nurture.[3] Even in fictional treatments of the having-it-all question, it is women once again who are the main narrative event.[4]

In other words, to invoke a suggestive phrase from years past, the "mommy wars" have so far been about just that. Whether celebratory or critical, left wing or right wing, fictitious or factual, most of the literature devoted so far to this great social experiment has one critical common denominator: It is all about the adult side, and particularly the female adult side, of the absent-parent home.

Yet very little has been committed to print about the darker side of this massive experiment: namely, the sharp rise in child and adolescent problems that has occurred alongside this increasing adult, and particularly maternal, exodus from home. As the pages that follow show, to ask what scholars and researchers are turning up about the state of American youth is to invite a barrage of depressing information on mental problems, behavioral problems, sexually transmitted diseases, educational backwardness, and more. As William Damon, one of the first writers to have apprehended this empirical slide, put it in his book, *Greater Expectations*, in 1995, "Practically all the indicators of youth health and behavior have declined year by year for well over a generation. None has improved. *The litany is now so well known that it is losing its power to shock* [emphasis added]."[5]

Like Damon, some other observers have also commented on one or another aspect of this deterioration. Both rightward-leaning Francis Fukuyama (*The Great Disruption*) and leftward-leaning Robert D. Putnam (*Bowling Alone*) have noted independently that one factor driving the lessening of "association" in American life is the reorienting of adult attention, particularly women's, away from the home and neighborhood and toward the workplace. Numerous other writers have made a different broad sociological point—that what advantages the modern adult often *disadvantages* the modern child: Midge Decter (*An Old Wife's Tale*), David Ellkind (*The Hurried Child*), Arlie Russell Hochschild (*The Time Bind*), Barbara Defoe Whitehead (*Dan Quayle Was Right*), Christina Hoff Sommers (*The War Against Boys*), and Kay S. Hymowitz (*Ready or Not*), among others. Perhaps most important, in his 1995 book, *Fatherless America*, David Blankenhorn broke critical ground by drawing attention to the empirical correlations between troubled children and one particular subset of the adult-emptied world, i.e., absent fathers.

And so the time seems ripe to examine at book length these two established facts of our world—absent parents of both sorts and contemporary child problems of all sorts—and ask some obvious, if necessarily blunt, questions about the relationship between the two. Why are millions of American kids—almost one in four boys, according to the latest estimates—taking drugs to alter their behavior, with millions more said to stand in need of that same regimen? Why, to take numbers from elsewhere in the field of psychiatry, are depression, anxiety, and behavioral disorders apparently skyrocketing among children and teenagers? What might help explain another major health problem unknown until recently: namely, the millions of American (and European) juveniles now at risk for overweight and obesity? What does the epidemic of sexually transmitted diseases—some of them incurable—mean for the present and future health of today's teenagers? And to reach beyond social science, what exactly is at the melancholy core of current popular juvenile culture, especially what is dearest to them of all—their music?

These questions and others like them are the detailed stuff of this book. It is my hope that readers of varied political persuasion will hear the answers out. I believe many of us sense already that it is time for a turn of debate, that there is more to this brave new domestic world of ours than just the latest juggling act of modern Woman or the latest polemical lament that men cannot be made to do their share of the housework. And many people, especially many who are parents, compare their own childhoods to those of their offspring and worry about what the pages ahead illustrate—that there *is* something new under our bright material sun; that the kids aren't, in fact, all right.

In his recent book, *The Progress Paradox*, Gregg Easterbrook asks a question that seems to be on other American minds lately: Why is it that our unprecedented material abundance and our extraordinary leaps in health and longevity have not been matched by any related leap in morale? Similarly, in *One Nation Under Therapy*, Christina Hoff Sommers and Sally Satel address a version of the same problem: Why is it that so many Americans, against the evidence, think themselves to be in parlous psychological shape? Also in 2004, researchers from Duke University led by Kenneth C. Land unveiled a major study of children's well-being that was begun in 1975 and used twenty-eight different measures.[6] They expressed their surprise at how stagnant the overall score appeared; indeed, were it not for the decrease in juvenile crime, the composite score for 2003 would have been *lower* than that in 1975. If things are going so well, these and other voices have lately come to ask, then why don't we all feel better?

I believe the answer to that question is clear. Life *is* better today for many American adults; they are freer in all kinds of ways, including freer from social stigma in their personal moral choices, than any generation that preceded them. But life is *not* better for many American children, no matter how many extra Game Boys they have, no matter how much more pocket money they have for the vending machines, and no matter how nice it is that Dad's new wife gave them their own weekend bedroom in his new place. In fact, for a significant number of today's kids, life is worse in important ways than it was for their parents. And somewhere inside many of us adults know it.

And now a word about what this book is not. It is not an exercise in systematic social science by a card-carrying social scientist. It does not pretend to cover exhaustively the many criteria by which the well-being of children and adolescents may be judged—as the Land et al. study mentioned earlier sought to do and as numerous other statistical compendia assembled by armies of data-crunching researchers also attempt. Instead, this book singles out a number of particularly elemental subjects of concern to parents everywhere—among them day care, sex, music, and mental and physical health—and explores each one through a variety of evidence, from conventional social science and medical studies to books and TV shows and music videos and other unconventional measures of kids' inner lives. I do not pretend that this list of concerns is exhaustive, but I do think it is fundamental in the sense that most American parents worry about exactly these things. They are what might be called the apples of the book—meaning that while oranges might also exist, it is by the apples that the argument of these chapters should be judged.

Such is one summary of this book's message. As to the question of messenger, I am an at-home mother of four whose "fieldwork" consists mostly of fifteen or so years spent around sandboxes, schools, carpools, baseball games, and the like and whose intellectual work is conducted by fits and starts and at odd hours in the basement, one wall over from the washing machine and another removed from the Nintendo setup. I am an Ivy League graduate and former State Department speechwriter, and I haven't had a "real" office in more than twelve years. Until very recently motherhood meant that I did little writing apart from the occasional essay or review. Today things are different. Three of my children are in school all day long and the youngest is on the verge of it, so there is more time for reading and writing than there has been for years. I have a part-time paid babysitter who is upstairs with my youngest while I'm down, a husband who often works at home, and older children who also help out. Thus the "how" of this book.

I say as much to signal that I do know by raw experience a thing or two about what other writers have belabored, that is, the financial and other "trade-offs" of motherhood, including the penalties. The writing and editing that are my avocations have been made possible only by the alignment of figurative stars detailed in the acknowledgments. If any one of these fixed points had been otherwise, these chapters could not have been written—and I do not mean that as the usual authorial throwaway but as literal truth. This is in that sense an unlikely book.

And I am in some ways an unlikely author. *Who does this woman think she is?* a friend says people will be wondering. *Doesn't she know what planet we live on, what real life is like?* Well, yes. In particular I know certain of the trends singled out in these pages the same way other readers will know them: by experience. My own parents divorced when I was young, my mother (a nurse) worked out of the house frequently, and I was raised for the most part in a large—and, as it turned out, happy—blended family of siblings, half-siblings, and occasional stepsiblings (my stepfather, a widower, had older, mostly grown children who also came and went). In other words, my personal experience for the most part was not of the catastrophic kind that shows up over and over in the statistics on divorce, single motherhood, and the rest of the broken-home track record—statistics that play a serious part in the pages ahead. So a second reason that this book might seem unlikely is this: My own personal history runs somewhat counterclockwise to parts of its argument.

But this is exactly why I bring these facts up—because if I can put my own autobiography aside in judging evidence, then so can this book's readers, no matter what personal experiences they might also have in tow.

For unlike most of the adult-focused literature alluded to earlier, this is not, in the end, a personal story. It is not about me, it is not about you, and it is not about my cousins in New York or your neighbors down the street. It could have been written by anyone, married or not, parent or childless, in possession of the same empirical and other evidence. The purpose of these pages is not to ask what any *one* woman or man or family has decided to do. It is rather to ask what the *accumulation* of many millions of such decisions is doing to the children and adolescents of this society.

Consider a few examples taken from the pages ahead, of how this distinction plays out. It was one thing when teachers could count on large numbers of parents to help with volunteer work, because there were enough intact families and mothers at home. It is quite another—to cite recent reports in the *New York Times*—to have only two or three in any given kindergarten class who will pick up the slack for any event. Any *one* mother or father unavailable during the day is not a problem in the first instance; multiplied by many as it is today (ask any elementary school teacher), it is a problem.

But the multiplication of the effects of absent parents goes well beyond the solitary teacher now shorthanded for field trips and spelling bees. Some of the latest data on children's mental and behavioral problems are simply amazing—amazingly bad, that is. Violent crime by teenagers is down, and that's great. Yet as chapter 2 indicates, none of the explanations for *why* crime is down point to any general increase in mental or other stability among kids. Meanwhile, behavioral "issues" of all kinds are *up* in another segment of the population—the diapered, the preschooled, the kindergartners. Clearly, they are learning this feral behavior, at least in part, from one another, whether it is biting in day care or kicking and hitting later on. In other words, though your child might not be the offender on the playground, because you have taught him, say, that bricks aren't supposed to be projectiles, plenty of other children haven't learned that lesson at home—and their parental abdication affects not only them but you and your child, too.

Consider a third example: It was one thing when there were enough mothers, siblings, and others around after school to allow easy access to playgrounds, parks, and one's own or other backyards in the afternoon. In that world, as Alan Ehrenhalt observed in *Lost City*, there were enough "eyes on the street," enough informal networks of adults, to make outdoor play (among other child and adolescent amenities) a regular feature of life after school.[7] But the situation today is something else again—with neighborhoods so emptied of adult presence that even the richest kids just go home, throw the deadbolt, and get no exercise more strenuous than walking from the video game to the refrigrator (in fact, better-off children are more likely to be "caring for self" after school than others further down the economic ladder). And the unintended consequence of that new norm is something we hardly need social science for at all, because the evidence of our senses is trustworthy enough: Time in front of the screen is up; exercise and outdoor play of any kind is down; and kids, in the United States and almost all comparable countries, are fatter than ever.

None of these adverse outcomes was intended, of course, by the adults whose individual decisions ended up contributing to them. But that difference between action taken and action multiplied—between microcosmic intention and macrocosmic effect—is part of what this book is all about. It asks a question that has not been asked satisfactorily or answered so far in our literature on the modern family: Has the United States already reached a "tipping point" in this society of unattended children and teenagers? It also asks whether millions of individual decisions, taken for millions of individual reasons, have cascaded over the social cliff to our larger detriment.

It will be said—it was already said by would-be critics months before my writing was finished—that this book is too hard on women, especially the modern working mother. That is an erroneous characterization of its thesis.

There are two main engines of the empty-parent home and its fallout. The first is the divorce/illegitimacy explosion—or what might be called the absent-father problem. The second is what is often the flip side of that explosion, working motherhood—or the absent-mother problem—which is sometimes a real choice and sometimes not. To these I would add a slightly less powerful but still significant force: smaller and geographically scattered extended families—or what might be called the absent-grandparent and -sibling problem. These are the rulers of the empty hearth—not one single social force ("working women") but three.

The literature gathered so far about our experiment in family separation makes one thing clear: From the point of view of a great many adults, the trade-offs among contemporary adult freedoms, and particularly the gains made by women in the paid marketplace, are definitely worth it from the point of view of those free to choose. Whether they are also worth it from another perspective—that of the children and adolescents left behind by the adult exodus into freedom—has not yet been answered, in large part because the adult voices dominating the discussion have been reluctant to ask it.

This book seeks to open that question. It seeks to get adults offstage for the duration of these pages and put children and adolescents front and center instead. It is an effort to ask what the empirical and extra-empirical record shows so far about this relatively new and unknown world in which many parents, children, and siblings spend many or most of their waking hours apart. The essence of home-alone America is just this: Over the past few decades, more and more children have spent considerably less time in the company of their parents or other relatives, and numerous fundamental measures of their well-being have simultaneously gone into what once would have been judged scandalous decline. It is the argument of this book that the connection between those two facts cannot possibly be dismissed as coincidence. At a time when roughly half of all children will have no biological father in the home at some point, and well over half of all mothers with children under the age of six are employed, it is time to stop talking of mere "correlations" and start asking some questions about cause.

1

The Real Trouble with Day Care

NOT TOO LONG AGO—IRONICALLY, ON A DAY I HAD SPENT buried under just a little of the vast literature on what is called "early child development"—our ten-year-old daughter skipped home from school with some unexpectedly apt news. Her class would soon be volunteering some time at a local day care center—and not just any day care center, but the snazziest of several in our Washington, D.C., neighborhood, a cheerful and inviting high-end sort of place much prized by the parents whose infants and small children spend their weekdays there.

Like most girls her age, this one adores babies and toddlers, so she was elated at the idea. It was all the more surprising then when she returned home on the day of her visit with a long face. As things turned out, the day care center had not been the fun she had expected, and the reason was this: "There was a boy, a little boy, who was really sick and cried the whole time. His ear was all red, and he shrieked if they even touched it. The day care ladies were nice and everything, but he wouldn't stop. It was just so sad. All he did was keep screaming the same thing over and over: *Mommy! Mommy! Mommy!*"

In this way a distressed ten-year-old, empathizing with an even more distressed two-year-old, captured something I had been struggling to formulate for weeks—namely, exactly what our long-running national controversy over institutional child care is *not* about. It is not about that screaming toddler. It is not in fact about the immediate emotional experience of any toddlers or babies who spend most of their waking hours out of their homes and in nonfamily care. That is to say, for all the many things our discussion *is* about, it is not about this perhaps most prosaic of facts: institutional care as it is experienced by real, live, very small children.

No, our ongoing national child care debate—and it is a real enough debate, among the most heavily documented controversies of our time—is a more sanitized, abstract, at times even a fastidious thing. It is told of, by, and for educated adults, and its vernacular is that of scholarly social science. Does day care affect long-term "personality development"? "Cognitive ability"? "Educational readiness"? Is "attachment theory" out and "early socialization" in? Where are the "longitudinal data" in all this, and just how "statistically significant" are those sample sizes? These are the sorts of things that we talk about when we talk about day care, whether we ourselves are "for" it or not.

And just as the argument over institutional care is dominated by talk of outcomes and effects, so also is it advocated on the same basis: *results*. "My kids got dropped off at day care," as a feminist put it one Mother's Day in the *New York Times*, "and one is now finishing up at Brown, and the other went through Harvard and Oxford." "Our son," parallel-bragged another in the *Washington Post*, also that Mother's Day, "got a 3.6 grade point average in grad school and was the valedictorian of his class"—and in addition, "Our daughter [is a] Shakespearean actress." The day care proof, as advocates see it, is in the achievement pudding. In a 1997 book called *When Mothers Work: Loving Our Children Without Sacrificing Ourselves*, Joan K. Peters summarizes some of the research behind such boosterism: this British study argues that children of employed mothers read better than those of at-home ones; that American study claims that children left in day care from one month on develop higher cognitive and language abilities; and Alison Clarke-Stewart's work argues that day care children are more confident and "socially skilled" than others.[1]

It is not only advocates who think that institutional care rises or falls by the standard of outcomes, but also, for different reasons, the critics of institutional care. For the most part these writers make the opposite empirical point—either that data do not suggest the rosy outcomes advocates believe in or that the "good" data on cognitive and language skills are outweighed by the "bad" data on a variety of behavioral problems. The work of Jay Belsky, perhaps the best-known authority to raise questions about day care's possible negative impact on some children, exhibits both lines of empirical criticism. So does researcher Brian C. Robertson's 2003 book, *Day Care Deception: What the Child Care Establishment Isn't Telling Us*, which uses the "bad" data to argue that if parents knew more about the real facts of day care, they would try harder to avoid it.[2] Moreover, even critics who have made nonempirical arguments against institutional care tend to invoke the long run—that is, the imagined effect on such protocitizens down the road. One particularly interesting recent example is a 2003 essay called "A Schoolhouse Built by Hobbes" by Bryce Christensen, which argues against day care on the grounds that it weakens the attachment to family necessary for later character formation, thus contributing to the overindividuation of American society.[3]

Generally speaking, then, both the critics and the advocates of institutional care agree about one thing: It is the effects, whether behavioral or cognitive or other, that make or break the case for day care. This emphasis on the long run is only natural, of course; parents do indeed care very much about results of all kinds. In fact, as the ones most likely to have the long-term interests of the child at heart, parents by definition must care about such things; it would be perverse if they did not.

Yet this focus on the long term, natural as it may be, has also obscured one important related point: To say that day care should be judged on the long-term results is not to say that those results are the only measure by which to judge this experiment. Here, as in other serious arguments, ends aren't everything; the question of what happens in the here and now also needs to be factored in.

Let us momentarily grant for the sake of argument that most children who grow up in institutional care turn out fine. To advocates this is where the controversy over day care begins and ends; case closed. But they are wrong. The notion that "most kids will turn out fine anyway" does not end the question of whether institutional care is good or bad; actually, it should be only the beginning. That other question, about immediate effects, demands to be answered, too. It is not about whether day care might keep your child out of Harvard ten or twenty years from now or launch him into it, but, rather, about the independent right or wrong of what happens to him day to day during the years that he is most vulnerable and unknowing. Reduced to its simplest form, that inquiry goes something like this: *What about the way this radical change in care is experienced by babies and young children? Do we know anything about that, and, if so, does that knowledge deserve any moral weight at all?*

This chapter is an attempt to answer that question about contemporaneous as opposed to long-term harm. It argues that institutional care is a bad idea for parents who do have a choice because it raises the quotient of *immediate* unhappiness in various forms among significant numbers of children, and the continuing ideological promotion of such separation causes the related harm of desensitizing adults to what babies and children actually need. Yes, many parents have to use day care. But there is a difference between having to use it and celebrating the institution full-throttle. What follows is an argument about why that difference matters.

DAY CARE AS GERM FACTORY

The reason for beginning with institutional care, as opposed to other forms of substitute care, is simple: That is the chosen battleground of advocates who have argued over the years that such care is as good as or even better than maternal care or nonmaternal care in other forms—an older sibling or grandparent, a babysitter in the home, a turn-taking arrangement with the mother next door, and so on.

This ideological defense of mother-child separation is not new, of course. As Allan Carlson showed recently in an interesting essay on the history of such attempts, its pedigree stretches all the way back to Plato and includes many other thinkers through the centuries.[4] In our own time such advocates generally have been dubbed "feminists." I will refer to their ideology instead as "separationism" and to its advocates as "separationists," for that is what they are—thinkers who urge institutional care not as an inevitable practical choice for some, but as a theoretical choice that allegedly advances higher personal or social goals. This is how institutional care has come to be rationalized and promoted.

One immediate harm of such care—or at least what some people would regard as harm—is familiar to all pediatricians and many parents. Day care centers literally make children sick, and they do so a lot more efficiently than care at home. The screaming toddler with whom I opened this chapter is not the exception but the norm; he is perhaps on the extreme end of pain (of course, not all children in day care spend their days this way), but it is the norm nonetheless. He represents the truth that just being in day care increases the likelihood of physical distress. That is because infections are more likely among babies or toddlers tended to in an institutional setting—for three rather obvious reasons. First, infants in full-time care are almost certainly not being breast-fed, or not much at any rate, so the immunological benefits of human milk are not being supplied to them. This raises the risks of their contracting ailments no matter where they are. Second, certain specific things about babies and toddlers, such as diaper-wearing and constant hand-to-mouth contact, make them germ carriers beyond compare, especially germs transmitted by saliva or feces. Third, the sheer number of children encountered every day in such institutions—which is far higher than for children at home even in large families—further and dramatically raises the likelihood of infection. It is like playing pathogen roulette with five bullets instead of two.

In a medical nutshell, and as parents who use day care already know, children in it tend to be sick more often than others. Consider the example of otitis media, commonly known as an ear infection and the single most common complaint that brings children to the doctor. Otitis media itself is not contagious but is caused by upper respiratory ailments (URAs) that are. Over the past couple of decades, as any pediatrician can tell you—to say nothing of those millions of parents still harboring a sticky pink bottle of antibiotic somewhere in the refrigerator—ear infections in children, especially young children, have risen dramatically. Why? For the same reason that Dr. Charles Bluestone, an otolaryngologist (ear, nose, and throat specialist), told one newspaper: "Virtually every study ever done on the increase in otitis media has shown that day care is the most important difference."[5]

And otitis media is only the beginning. One current American Academy

of Pediatrics fact sheet on "Controlling Illness in Child Care Programs"—
the title is suggestive in itself—enumerates a number of other infections that are spread more easily in day care, from the common cold to
gastrointestinal problems to any number of skin and eye infections (im-
petigo, lice, ringworm, scabies, cold sores, and conjunctivitis, or pinkeye).
In fact, hepatitis A, which can be transmitted by contact with feces and
is actually more serious for adults than for children, is such an issue in
center-based care that this paper further recommends vaccines for "high-
risk occupations"—that is, day care workers.

Medically speaking, the story of day care as germ central is relatively
old news; it has been more than ten years since *Pediatric Annals*, an authoritative source for pediatricians, devoted a special issue to the subject—
and titled its editorial "Day Care, Day Care: Mayday! Mayday!"[6] But what
has lagged in the popular understanding, at least to judge by the relative absence of writing on the subject, is what might be called the phenomenolog-
ical face of all this—that is, what numbers like these mean in real life for
people, including babies and toddlers.

Something like that need has lately been supplied by Harvard professor
Jody Heymann who devotes considerable space to examining real-life case
studies of contemporary family life in her 2000 book on inequality, *The
Widening Gap*. (It was based on extended interviews with more than eight
hundred individuals, including workers in the child care industry as well as
parents.) The day care employees repeatedly emphasize the problems of
having to work not only around sick babies and children, but also around
desperate parents who drop off those babies and children at day care rather
than miss a day of work. One center worker even coined the term "Tylenol
signs" to describe what is evidently common practice: dosing a child with
fever-lowering medicine at home or in the car just before drop-off, with the
result that the caregivers do not realize the child has a fever until several
hours later when the effects wear off and the child's temperature goes back
up. Of course this is contrary to the rules of most centers; since fevers
usually mean that kids are contagious, they are supposed to stay home when
they have them—but this apparently is a rule parents frequently breach. In
fact, on account of this "Tylenol" practice, some caregivers also routinely

interrogate children about what happened at home—specifically, whether or not they have had any "pink medicine."

As anyone who has attended even one sick child can attest, the physical and emotional demands of several at once can strain many a "caregiver ratio" to the breaking point. "[M]any of the child-care providers we spoke with," Heymann summarizes, "described having received children whose acute health problems *made it impossible to provide adequate care either for them or for the well children under the child-care provider's supervision*" [emphasis added]. Problems arose, for example, because the child-care providers could not keep clean and well hydrated the sick children who were vomiting or had diarrhea, give sufficient attention to the sick children's other needs, and curb the spread of infectious diseases while also trying to care for the healthy children."[7] Moreover, many parents further confirmed these negative findings to the research team. "Overall," Heymann reports, "41 percent of the parents we interviewed extensively . . . said their working conditions had negatively affected their children's health in ways that ranged from children being unable to make needed doctors' appointments to children receiving inadequate early care, which resulted in their condition worsening."[8]

Heymann's account, sad and all too real, is one of several in recent years to have drawn attention to the poor quality of care in many centers and to infer the need for some national "solution" (paradoxically, more and also better day care). Like most other such advocacy, Heymann's emphasizes how emotionally difficult it can be for the parents who must manage all these competing claims at once. And who cannot feel for a stressed-out mother torn between an unforgiving workplace on the one hand and a sick baby on the other? To avoid that, as discussed by Arlie Russell Hochschild in her book *The Time Bind*, increasing numbers of corporations have devised ways to keep parents at their desks, including flex time and other leave arrangements as well as in-house care centers.[9]

Yet like most of the day care literature, Heymann's explains the sick child problem from the adult point of view—that is, the stress that a sick child adds to an already hectic schedule. As such, it is of limited moral utility. To get the full measure of the harm possibly transpiring, one must look at it from the point of view of the miserable ailing child in institutional care who is not only being deprived of the familiar people and things that might take the edge off his discomfort, but is also too young to understand where everyone else is and why he feels so bad. Shouldn't his unhappiness and confusion and lack of fulfillment count for something in the day care calculus, too? Life is indeed hard and misery abundant for all of us, and as some separationist literature reminds us, kids do have to get used to it. But why don't advocates answer this question: What age, if any, is too young for induction into the school of hard knocks?

HOW DO YOU SPELL "AGGRESSION"?

Another immediate harm caused by institutional care, well documented if still bitterly resisted, is that day care makes some children more belligerent and aggressive—and we are talking not only about the longer term here, but also about the here and now.

The latest evidence to back this claim, well publicized by all sides during the last two years, comes from lengthy investigations by the National Institute of Child Health and Human Development (NICHD), one subset of the National Institutes of Health (NIH). Beginning in 1989 a team of researchers began tracking children at ten different sites to determine what effects, if any, day care was having on them. Over the years various adverse findings have been thrashed out in the media and elsewhere—for example, that babies and toddlers at various ages appeared less attached to their mothers depending on the amount of time spent in nonmaternal care.[10] Even so, perhaps nothing about the NICHD project has proved quite as incendiary as the lead article published in the July/August 2003 issue of *Child Development* that asked, "Does Amount of Time Spent in Child Care Predict Socioemotional Adjustment During the Transition to Kindergarten?"

Yes, said the research, and not in a good way, at least for some. "The more time children spent in any of a variety of nonmaternal care arrangements across the first 4.5 years of life, the more externalizing problems and conflict with adults they manifested at 54 months of age and in kindergarten, as reported by mothers, caregivers, and teachers" are perhaps the most quoted words of their report. "More time in care not only predicted problem behavior measured on a continuous scale in a dose-response pattern but also predicted at-risk (though not clinical) levels of problem behavior, as well as assertiveness, disobedience, and aggression."[11]

As Jay Belsky, one of the lead researchers, explained elsewhere, the criteria for these problem behaviors were quite specific: aggression meant "cruelty to others, destroys own things, gets in many fights, threatens others, and hits others"; noncompliance/disobedience meant "defiant, uncooperative, fails to carry out assigned tasks, temper tantrums, and disrupts class discipline"; and assertiveness meant "bragging/boasting, talks too much, demands/wants attention, and argues a lot." All three behaviors increased alongside the amount of time in nonmaternal care. The effect did not hold for most of the children; Belsky stressed repeatedly that it was "modest."

He also stressed, however, that even modest negative findings are important for this reason: "In the U.S. more and more children are spending more and more time in nonmaternal care than ever before." Thus, something that has "a small effect on lots of children" can have a large impact on a given setting—such as school. As Belsky wrote, "Consider the consequences of being a teacher in a kindergarten classroom in which many children have a lot of early, extensive, and continuous child-care experience versus being a teacher in a classroom in which many fewer children have extensive child-care experience." Given the aggression findings, to put his point rhetorically, in which room would you rather teach?

For daring to draw attention to these findings, Belsky has been excoriated by numerous colleagues as well as by many separationist writers—all the more so because the link between day care and aggression was only the latest in a series of negative effects turned up by his research. His personal story, a fascinating example of the professional perils of ideological heresy, is told in detail in several places, among them Brian C. Robertson's book, a chapter in Robert Karen's thorough 1998 work, *Becoming Attached*, and a recent essay by Belsky himself titled "The Politicized Science of Day Care."[12] Yet as Robertson also documents, Belsky's report on child aggression is only the latest to suggest that at least some children become more belligerent in day care than elsewhere. "As far as aggressive behavior goes,"

Robertson summarizes, "here too the recent studies simply underscore a long history of findings"—including those from a 1974 report in *Developmental Psychology* that found higher levels of verbal and physical abuse among day care children to numerous more recent studies which showed, as Belsky did, that at least some children institutionalized from infancy appear more likely to hit, kick, push, and otherwise behave badly than do children in noninstitutional care.[13]

This same idea—that institutionalized children might become more aggressive on account of their surroundings—also received strong independent support from a very different kind of study published in *Child Development* in 1998.[14] Here, researchers measured not behavior—which is intrinsically subjective—but, rather, levels of cortisol, a stress-related chemical, in day care children. And what they found was suggestive in the extreme—or, as the researchers put it, "remarkable and unexpected." While most humans apparently exhibit the same daily pattern in which cortisol is highest in the morning and falls in the afternoon, the day care children tested showed exactly the *opposite* pattern: Their cortisol levels were higher in the afternoon than in the morning. In other words, their internal stress, unlike that of other people, had apparently been mounting through their institutionalized day.

There is much more that one could relay in this social science vein about the connection between institutional care and aggression for at least some kids. Then again, just how many studies do we need to get the point? I have an independent, quite nonexpert source for the same connection, a mental picture worth a hundred research bulletins: biting. Yes, *biting*. Sitting next to me is a stack of advisory literature written for people who run day care centers or preschools, and apparently one of the most important things they must prepare for, to judge by the amount of attention it receives, is coping with the inevitable occasional outbreak of human biting. According to any number of authoritative sources, as one preschool publication puts it, the biting of one baby or toddler by another is "the earliest and most troublesome unacceptable behavior in the preschool," one that "can sweep through a preschool like the measles." Biting is one of the chief reasons that children are expelled from day care and preschool. An astonishing range of "strategies" have been devised for handling the problem, a range that of course also speaks to its ubiquity. To browse the literature is to learn that many babies and toddlers in institutional care bite and bite a lot. They bite themselves, one another, and, of course, teachers and adults, too.

Why is this fact so remarkable? Because it doesn't happen elsewhere the way it does in day care. On scholastic.com, for example, a resource for teachers, parents, and students, one parent invited to "ask the experts" about parental concerns put the point plaintively: "My two-year-old has been biting other kids at day care; however, she does not do this at home or at my friend's house. Why would she bite only at day care and play well everywhere else she goes?" Of course the "expert" answer is what one would expect—that the toddler may be lonely, in need of affection, frustrated, and so on. But the real point remains that day care, at least as ordinary experience suggests, makes biting and the feelings associated with it more likely.

This is something some readers will know not only from reading expert literature, but also from their own experience. Of course, as the experts stress, biting is a natural thing. A baby or toddler might do it in fun or because he is teething or simply because he is curious about what will happen. Many of us have seen that kind of biting (and felt it, too). But chronic biting? Contagious biting? No, that is something else altogether, and it is not the way children, even very small children, ordinarily behave. And why does this difference matter? Because if randomly assembled children of the same ages do not spontaneously start using their teeth as weapons, whereas the same kinds of children assembled in a day care situation do, this strongly suggests that the institutionalized ones are biting at least in part because something about their situation has them especially agitated. In other words, the attention given to biting in the literature on institutional care is itself a sign of what boosters deny—clear evidence that day care is causing aggressive behavior.

Our skeptical reader might say, "So what? Maybe biting isn't the best habit, but all of them will outgrow it. Besides, do any longitudinal studies show that recidivist biting of other children at the age of two predicts psychological or academic trouble down the road? No? Well, then, the problem is solved."

But of course the problem is not solved at all, because our skeptical reader has asked what for our purposes is the wrong question—the one about ends, not means. The right question, the one addressing the overlooked moral dimension of all this, is: *What, after all, is the mental state of a bunch of babies and toddlers who take up biting as a habit?* And we can all figure out the answer to that without reaching for the social science bookshelf: *Those kids aren't happy.* They are exhibiting a self-protective animal instinct, which suggests that they feel unprotected. It is something we would all understand readily enough if, say, zoo animals were to attack each other more frequently in their quarters than in the wild. (And if they did, we would, of course, deplore it and blame the zoo.) Doesn't that apparent internal turmoil say something undesirable about how institutional care is experienced by at least some small children?

"SICK" PLUS "BAD" EQUALS "GOOD"?

For parents who do not have options apart from institutional care, the increased likelihood that day care children will be sick and unhappy are facts of life. They are necessary evils, regrettable but far better than the alternative, which is no care at all. And yet the most curious fact in all our day care debate, one that brings us to a third and very interesting sort of harm being caused in all this, is that these problems are not seen that way by certain other adults—namely, the separationists dominant in the day care debate.

These advocates do not see institutional care as a "necessary evil." They do not write of mother-baby separation with the ambivalence most mothers feel. They refuse to acknowledge that day care might cause damage of any kind to any child—unlike the many parents who must use it and who worry about just that. The least analyzed and perhaps also the weirdest dimension of our day care wars so far is the insistence by such advocates that what most people think is bad news—more sick kids and worse-behaved ones—is actually good and maybe even great. And this brings us to a third kind of harm in our experiment in separation: *The ideological defense of separationism is further coarsening adult moral sensibility.*

For example, anyone actually charged with the care of little children knows that a sick baby or toddler is a uniquely pitiful thing, in part because such a child is too young to understand why. Yet such natural empathy is not the prism through which the sick child problem in day care is viewed by our advocates. Generally speaking, their response to the sick kids problem has run one of two ways: Either ignore it altogether or rewrite the script so that sicker is actually better.

Thus, in *A Mother's Place: Choosing Work and Family Without Guilt or Blame*, Susan Chira acknowledges "several studies have also shown that children in day care suffer from more ear infections and illnesses in general," and then brushes it off with "[but] they are hardier when they are older."[15] Susan Faludi in *Backlash* sounds the same note: "They soon build up immunities."[16] Similarly, when a well-publicized 2002 study showed that babies and toddlers in day care get sick more often than those at home—about twice as many colds, for example—the advocate cheer going up around the country was notably creepy. As one lead researcher explained, this finding "lifts a heavy stone off the backs of guilt-ridden parents who put their children in large day care centers. The benefit to having colds in the toddler years is that kids miss less school later when it counts."[17]

Now step back from this discussion for a moment and ask yourself: If we were talking about anything but day care here, would anyone be caught cheering for the idea that some little children get sick twice as often as others? I think we all know the answer to that one. And that dissonance raises the question of what exactly is going on with this sort of callousness about small children. It is very hard to spend even a day in charge of a sick baby or toddler and be able to accept the Nietzschean line that what does not kill him will make him stronger—in other words, that being sick is good for him. But what if you are not around it, if it has been made someone else's problem? Might you then be a little less tuned in to just how much a sick baby or toddler needs?

And just as some people have managed to find "good news" in the increase in sick kids, so, too, has there been no lack of advocates who give a thumbs-up to the documented increase in aggression and other behavioral trouble. Belsky antagonist Allison Clarke-Stewart, for example, rationalized the aggression problem in 1989 this way: "Children who have been in day care think for themselves and want their own way" and "are not willing to comply with adults' arbitrary rules." Others have gone further. A University of Chicago psychologist offered the particularly Orwellian response to the 2001 NICHD study that "aggression" was actually "self-assertion" and that day care babies and toddlers were simply "much more sturdy little interactors" than tots at home. A writer for *Salon* similarly opined that it is "better to be smart and cheeky than dim and placid." It was elsewhere suggested that the traits being measured by NICHD are the same alpha qualities of future corporate titans. As with the advocates who have no trouble finding a silver lining in sick kids, so has there been no shortage of those who have translated bad behavior into diapered rugged individualism.

And here again the moral sensibility of our separationists seems to be a different order from that of most people—including most parents, whether they use day care or not. Anyone who has ever done playground duty with small children knows exactly the difference between an "assertive" little boy playing loudly with a truck and another little boy who just used the same truck to hit another child over the head. Just about anyone who has spent time around small children knows the difference between real aggression and childish high spirits. But what about parents who *aren't* around to learn this much in the first place? Might they not have a dimmer understanding of that distinction than other people do?

And here is the point in the argument where we leave the narrow matter of institutional care and look more widely at what is said about babies and children more generally in the service of the separationist experiment. Here, too, interestingly enough, the same sort of callousness implicit and explicit in the day care literature makes routine appearances. Consider a recent example from the letters page of the *Atlantic*. Writer Caitlin Flanagan had recently penned a largely favorable review of a book by Laura Schlessinger, a review that angered some readers, including one named Nancy, who chided Flanagan for worrying overmuch about middle-class children of divorce. Flanagan aptly replied, "Since writing my review of Laura Schlessinger's new book, I have had countless people tell me that they can't stand her because she's 'mean.' But Laura says you'll hurt a child if you divorce; don't do it. Nancy says she can't work up much compassion for a nine-year-old from a broken home. So who's mean?"[18]

What Flanagan did not go on to say in her short space, but what anyone reading the cable traffic on separationism will know, is that this bitter letter writer to the *Atlantic* is not alone. She represents a robust tradition of advocates and ideologues who have spent decades doing just what she did: getting very worked up over what mothers ought to have freedom to do and, simultaneously, becoming very dismissive of the possible fallout for children.[19] And once again it seems fair to ask whether practicing what one preaches has had the effect of numbing our separationist advocates just a little as to what babies and children actually need.

Look, for example, at what counts as the moral limbo bar in the day care debate—the lowest one imaginable. Essentially, advocates have settled for this position: If it doesn't lead to Columbine, bring it on. But that is obviously a very low perch from which to judge day care or anything else. Commenting on the NICHD study linking time spent in day care to aggression, scholar Stanley Kurtz observed something important that ought also to have been obvious to other readers: that the adverse implications were hardly limited to the kids bullying and hitting and that things were likely quite a bit worse than the numbers on aggression alone might suggest. Rather, "Chances are, if a significant percentage of children in day care evidence clear behavioral problems, or show up as insecurely attached to their mothers, then there are plenty of other children in less obvious, but still significant trouble. If some kids are responding to chronic separation from their mothers with anger, surely others are feeling depressed. Low-level depression is a lot harder to find and verify observationally than obvious classroom bullying, but that doesn't mean it's not there."[20] *Less obvious, but still significant trouble.* For advocates hardened by the demands of separationism, this kind of moral nuance does not exist.

Similarly, the insistence on the equality of "good" institutional care simply erases from the equation something important and also subjective: how very young humans see the world. Routine and familiarity are everything for small children. Yes, everything. I am no absolutist about nonmaternal care—with four children that would be a physically and intellectually untenable position. Very often some warm body—an older sibling, a babysitter, my husband, assorted grandparents—stays with my youngest so that I can do any one of the many things that small children make difficult or impossible. But the separationist insistence that it doesn't matter whether a baby or toddler is in the house or not simply rings ignorant of what the first two or three years of life are all about. Just being at home carries with it all those nonparental things so comforting to little children—from a familiar bump in the wall to the presence of a pet or sibling to a ripped-up book that must be found this minute.

Even the recent boomlet of lifestyle pieces about mostly well-off career women who have decided to stay home with their small children exhibits an inadvertently revealing one-sidedness of feeling—again, one obviously connected to the influence of separationist thought. One of the more discussed *New York Times Magazine* articles in 2003, for example, was "The Opt-Out Revolution" by Lisa Belkin. It argued about the "glass ceiling" problem that more women aren't hitting because they just don't want to, and one reason they don't want to is that they want to enjoy the company of their children. Similarly, *Time* magazine's cover story in March 2004, "The Case for Staying Home," cited dropping out of the rat race and enjoying the children as two lures that are perhaps more powerful than yesterday's generation of mothers understood. Even mothers who are vigorously pro-separation speak of the same unbidden pull they feel toward their children. Joan K. Peters, as staunch a defender of day care as any, has herself related, "Once, when I was late [getting home from work], I arrived nearly hysterical with worry that I had passed some absolute point of emotional safety for my infant—that in divine retribution for my absence, something awful might have happened. I was so upset that I snatched my daughter from my babysitter's arms and sank with her on the couch, holding my coat around us both."[21]

What could be more natural than that? Of course women and men want to enjoy their children; children are enormously enjoyable. But in that one-sided focus on what women want, a hidden but very real insensitivity betrays itself once more. If mother-child separation is so hard on mothers that even pro-separation feminists see it feelingly, then how much worse is that separation for a baby or toddler who does not understand time or distance?[22] Once more, doesn't that added confusion and distress, all the harder for a being unable to grasp what is happening, carry moral weight of its own?

A third body of evidence that suggests how far our separationist experiment has dulled our thinkers to real babies and children is this: Virtually every sophisticated school of thought now ascendant has participated one way or another in the rationalization of hands-off parenting. In an important book published in 1999, Kay S. Hymowitz broke particularly crucial theoretical ground explaining just this. She examined the state of American childhood, not from the bottom up but from the top, at the level of the numerous contemporary theories that have served to justify parental disengagement. *Ready or Not: Why Treating Children as Small Adults Endangers Their Future—and Ours* outlined in field after field (law, education, and psychology both popular and academic) how the past thirty years have seen a transformation in the way children are perceived—one that de-emphasizes adult guidance and authority while ultra-emphasizing the intrinsic capacities of the child in the absence of such guidance.[23] Uniting all these apparently disparate theories, she demonstrated, is "the idea of children as capable, rational, and autonomous, as beings endowed with all the qualities necessary for their entrance into the adult world—qualities such as talents, interests, values, conscience and a conscious sense of themselves."

The same insistence that Hymowitz discerned in elite fields of thought is true also of popular child-rearing advice books, which take their direction from a medical establishment profoundly reluctant to roil the political waters over day care. Almost all leading cultural authorities, including the American Academy of Pediatrics, have now managed a good word for the putative benefits of "early socialization," which is to say nonparental child-rearing; and though some are careful about the issue of institutional care, almost all glow with the putative benefits of having mothers out of the house. The country's leading popular child care experts have all revised downward over the years their estimations of just how much young children need their mothers, with every single one concluding that children need less of their mother's time and presence than was previously thought.[24]

Then there is the telling literature of a different sort: the kind for children themselves. This literature emphasizes parental needs and resolutely draws a happy face over children's longings; pamphlets exhort those too young to tie their shoes to be "independent," and stories, articles, and self-help columns share the message that the happy and fulfilled (that is, less encumbered) parent is also the better parent.[25] Has anyone strolled the children's aisles of the bookstore lately? Have you seen a copy of *Carl Goes to Day Care* or any of the many other books for children who are years away from reading—who, indeed, don't even have all their baby teeth yet—but are targeted for the theme that separating from Mommy every morning isn't all that bad? Do we really think the new get-tough approach reflected in these texts for tots is in any way an improvement on the at-home adventures of Dick and Jane?

Those texts are also only one manifestation of the desensitization that proceeds apace. Not only ideologically but also practically, the signs of other envelope-pushing are out there—including round-the-clock day care, or night care, a trend already established in Scandinavia and now beginning to appear in the United States in response to parental demand.[26] Though only a dozen or so centers currently exist, every reporter mentioning the trend predicts robust growth; "some people have to be available [for work] at all hours," as one trend analyst puts it.[27] And what is it like for these children who are not even allowed the familiarity of their own beds? Not to worry. After all, "each child brings something special to his or her cot: a pillow, a well-worn blanket, a favorite toy."

Similarly, during 2003 alone, several stories sprang up around the country about parents using public libraries—yes, libraries—as emergency day care centers, including depositing children there for the day who are far too young to read.[28] In short, from real-life stories to expert literature of all sorts, there is one and only one prevailing cultural answer to the question of just how much babies and toddlers need, and it's this: *They need less than previously thought.*

SHRINKING THE NEED DOWN TO SIZE

Laura Schlessinger once asked members of an audience to stand up "if you could . . . come back as an infant . . . raised by a day care worker, a nanny, or a babysitter." No one did, and Schlessinger went on to ask why anyone who could choose otherwise would prefer this for their children. In effect, she was asking a question not about outcomes, but about the immediate moral content of the experiment. Of course she was excoriated in the usual places. But should she have been? How many readers thinking of their own childhoods would answer her question any other way?

In sum, the real trouble with day care is twofold: One, it increases the likelihood that kids will be unhappy, and two, the chronic rationalization of that unhappiness renders adults less sensitive to children's needs and demands in any form. Of course, as advocates often say, most children not in home care are likely to turn out fine (they *are* resilient). Of course, many adults have to work, and some absolutely have to use out-of-home care. Of course, no one can have his mother all the time, and likely no one should. Of course also, by extension, children are only one of several actors in any given drama, even if they are also the most vulnerable; in other words, their immediate emotional needs cannot and do not always trump.

But can they, should they, ever trump? That is the question advocates will not answer. Single parents, frantic parents, infants being packed off to hospital-style rows of cribs called "school," toddlers who go for institutionalized walks roped together like members of a miniature chain gang—this is what the experiment means day to day. But our separationists manage to worry instead about the *opposite*: an alleged excess of maternalism, of "overparenting" (Joan K. Peters), an oppressive "mommy myth" (Susan J. Douglas and Meredith W. Michaels), and all the other phantoms said to be haunting and impeding—who else?—the modern mother.

Their own rhetoric and that of the long-running day care wars proves overwhelmingly otherwise, and so do the plain facts. The 2000 census clinched the point that more and more mothers continue to opt out. Between 1975 and 1993 the percentage of children under age six with employed mothers rose from 33 to 55 percent. By 2000 it had climbed to 70 percent. Of course not all those women are working full-time and out of the house, but the trend away from home and toward the workplace is very clear. And so is what it represents: the near-total cultural about-face in the way society views working mothers. Once, as has been widely noted, staying home with one's children was judged the right thing to do, both intrinsically and for reasons of the greater good, by mothers, fathers, and most of the rest of society. Today, the social expectations are exactly reversed.

Before we start worrying ourselves about the alleged perils of too much mothering, we might first look at how much energy and sophisticated thought continues to go into rationalizing too little mothering and what exactly that says about us. We have collectively become one of Shakespeare's most unattractive characters—wicked daughter Regan who, when faced with an old father demanding his prerogatives of age, diminishes those wants of his over and over. However many horses and knights King Lear demands, she allows fewer; whatever he agrees to, she reduces further still. Just so, contrary to the bitter complaints of our separationists, has our social standard governing exactly what babies and children can demand of us veered in the direction of *less*.

Once upon a time, after all, parents and experts worried about whether five-year-olds needed a mother in the house; now, when kindergarten has become full days in many or even most districts, and before- and after-school programs abound, that worry has apparently gone the way of the buggy whip. Not so long ago, parents and experts wondered whether two- and three-year-olds could thrive if they were out of their homes and away from their families at preschools or day care all day, but when packing them off became routine rather than rare, and subjecting them to a rotating set of strangers became thought of as a head start, a good many adults with other things to do decided that that problem had been pretty much solved, too. Having so efficiently shrunk the pool of children we might need to worry about by quite a lot, we now reduce ourselves to scholastic nitpicking over the few who are left: infants and toddlers.

Well, how about it? What real need does a five-year-old have of his mother or home? What need does a three-year-old have? A babe in arms?

King Lear has a pretty famous answer to questions like those: Oh, *reason not the need*. What the ideological devotion to day care finally amounts to is just that—reasoning the need, ruthlessly trying to square what for the youngest children will always be a circle with many orbits but only one center.

2

The Furious Child Problem

IN MARCH 2001, WHEN THE MOST PROMINENT TEENAGE KILLER of that year opened fire in a high school near San Diego with the deadliest display of such violence since the murders at Columbine two years earlier, the usual public scramble for explanations of his behavior followed the "cultural script," as sociologists call it. The *New York Times* weighed in immediately with a stern editorial, "Guns in Young Hands," urging President George W. Bush to convene a White House conference on teen violence. Simultaneously, reporters from the news services fanned out across the country to interview as many acquaintances of the killer as they could— most of whom would earnestly testify that nothing about the boy ever seemed amiss. True to form, a disproportionate share of the "blame" for the young killer's actions was deposited not quite at his own feet ("an obviously troubled young teenager," as the *Washington Post* editorialized and just about all other sources agreed) or at those of the adults around him, but, rather, at those of his peers—the bullies who tormented him, the acquaintances who dismissed his threats to "bring the school down" as idle boasts, the fellow drinkers at a party the weekend before who had heard the killer say he had a gun he was taking to school and did nothing about it.

In what again appears to be cultural routine, just about every detail of the case was reported and analyzed at length, with the *New York Times* even waxing lyrical about a "Joan Didion world of dropouts and tough teenagers." Every detail, that is, but one. The *Washington Post* managed to relay that one detail deep in a story on the teenager's clueless friends: "[He] was known as a latch-key child who often ate dinner and slept over at friends' homes." Piecemeal, in various reports and in a handful of opinion columns, other details of the killer's deprived emotional life filled in the blanks. The child of a decade-old divorce, he had resided, loosely speaking, with his father in California. As a boy he was left largely to his own devices, slept elsewhere much of the time, and called his friends' mothers "Mom." He had spent the preceding summer with neither parent but, instead, in Knoxville, Maryland, with the family of former neighbors there. His mother, distraught and horrified by the events in San Diego, as any mother would be, was giving her anguished post-shooting interviews from behind a closed door where she herself lived—on the other side of the country, in South Carolina.

That San Diego killer was only the latest such celebrity verifiable as a home-alone child. The litany of sensational murder cases is replete with just such people—the teenage or adult version of feral, abandoned, uncivilized children. Another entrant in the category would be the late cannibal-murderer Jeffrey Dahmer, whose evil habits developed as a teenager when his parents divorced; he was left by his mother *and* father to live alone in the former family house for a year before being retrieved. Charles Manson, the most notorious mass murderer of the 1970s, was abandoned on and off by his mother, sometimes while she did jail time and sometimes just because he was in the way. Theodore "Ted" Bundy, one of the most infamous serial killers of the 1980s, exhibited perhaps the weirdest pattern of all: He was abandoned by his father and raised by his grandparents, but with his mother in the house all the while, pretending to be his sister.[1]

And so one headlined story after another continues the trend. In a striking coincidence unremarked upon at the time, the other mass murderer most in the news in 2001 (because of his ongoing trial) had a background almost identical to that of the San Diego teen killer: a parental divorce in middle childhood, after which the mother abandoned son and husband to move across the country when the boy was fifteen, leaving behind a teenager whose father worked nights and who spent most of his time either unsupervised or in other people's homes. That was Timothy McVeigh, who was executed in 2001 for murders committed during the Oklahoma City bombing of 1995, in which 168 people died.

The most sensational murder cases of 2003 also bore out the principle that parental absence, perhaps even more particularly mother absence, is practically prerequisite to a career as a killer. The two sniper-murderers who terrorized the Washington, D.C., area that fall, John Mohammed and John Lee Malvo, were both textbook cases of parental abandonment. Malvo, who never knew his father, had been left by his mother for most of his early years to be raised in Jamaica by other relatives. Less noticed but equally interesting was that the older John Mohammed's past was almost identical—abandoned by his father and raised by an aunt and grandmother. (His mother, also absent, died when he was an infant.)

And serving as the very template of the modern teen killer was the tragedy in 1999 known as Columbine. Though initially touted as the case that "proved" school violence could happen to anyone, this, too, turned out to affirm the principle that adolescent abandonment is the precondition of spectacular savagery. This was better-off and materially cushioned abandonment, to be sure, but abandonment nonetheless. Eric Harris and Dylan Klebold had been left on their own for a great many of their waking hours. They were boys who spent their lives in dark corners of the Internet, who acquired and assembled war weapons in their suburban garages and bedrooms, who threatened neighbors, tortured animals, read and wrote obsessively about suicide and murder, and who otherwise did all but broadcast from the rooftops what are technically known as "warning signals." These signals were evident *if*—and this appears to be a major qualification—anyone besides like-minded cronies had been around to notice them.

In his recent book, Brian C. Robertson observed in a particularly sharp roundup of the evidence:

> The specifics of the Columbine case affirmed the link between school violence and parental inattention. Dylan Klebold and Eric Harris came from relatively affluent homes in which both parents worked. The teenagers were allowed a great deal of autonomy. . . . In the face of abundant warning signs, it seems that the Klebolds and the Harrises paid remarkably little attention to what their sons

were up to in the months preceding their bloody attack. They were repeatedly made aware by school administrators, public authorities and other parents of the boys' indulgence in violent, rage-filled murderous fantasies and other threatening behavior. . . . They also managed to construct some ninety bombs without their parents' notice and store them in their homes. Eric Harris's bedroom in particular was a veritable arsenal of poorly concealed weapons.[2]

In short, far from demonstrating that mass-murdering teenagers could happen to anyone, Columbine turned out to confirm rather than break the rule that absent parents, however inadvertently or tragically, help establish the conditions in which feral intentions flourish and go on to bear violent fruit.

The purpose of this recitation is to establish an important point that usually does not get made in the aftermath of the latest killing spree: that when we look at the extreme end of feral humanity, the modern cold-blooded killer, the rest of us are really not surprised to see a connection between parental abandonment and savage behavior. We intuitively understand that while having two attentive parents does not guarantee success or happiness or even decent character, *not* having them can turn out to be disastrous. Of course, many people who are deprived of their parents or who are otherwise victims of extreme adversity can turn out just fine.[3] Of the ones who do not, however, the rest of us grasp elementally that absent or abusive parents probably had something to do with it. As Jonathan Kellerman put this collective understanding in a 1999 book that examines the patterns of cold-blooded child killers: "The most reasonable conclusion that can be drawn about environment and psychopathy is that some combination of environmental stressors—physical abuse, social chaos, parental drug use and alcoholism, and *overall rotten families, especially rotten and/or absent fathers* [emphasis added]—contributes to severe antisocial behavior in young boys."[4] Again, it is hard to imagine anyone arguing with that statement; there is simply too much empirical evidence of all kinds to affirm it.[5]

We are generally agreed, therefore, that extreme deprivation can make for extreme depravity. Why is that seemingly obvious proposition remarkable? It is remarkable because it contradicts something that a generation of certain social scientists and advocates has ferociously denied: the possibility of a causal connection between parental absence and undesirable child behavior. The reason that contradiction is meaningful is that it raises this important corollary: *If feral behavior at the extreme seems rooted in extreme parental absence, it may be possible that feral behavior of other kinds is also rooted in less extreme but nonetheless significant parental absence.*

This chapter lays out evidence for believing that corollary. Contemporary feral behaviors among children and teenagers—from suicide rates to the increase in elementary school violence—have increased in tandem with the vanishing of many adults from their lives. There is simply too much suggestive evidence to deny the connection.

That is not to say that all indices of savagery one might name are moving the same way. They aren't. There is good news when it comes to certain statistics about adolescents. Most notably, violent juvenile crime has dropped significantly (as has adult violent crime) in recent years. There is also an apparent dip in the teen suicide rate. In the specific sense that any teen murder or suicide averted is by definition a good and positive thing, there are indeed some developments on the adolescent scene worth a cheer.

At the same time, and as this chapter will argue, it is wrong to take those particular pieces of good news and use them as cultural proxies for the state of American children and teenagers—which is exactly how some commentators have wielded them. The distinction that needs to be added to the public ledger is this: Today's good news does not reflect on the connection between kids and parents, whereas today's bad news does. By expert accounts, the vectors moving in the right direction are moving that way for reasons independent of parental influence, and the vectors going in the wrong direction remain linked to exactly that. In short, the furious child problem is not limited to Columbine or crack dealers, and it does not disappear if high school shootings diminish and the crack epidemic abates. That is why it is a real and ongoing problem.

CRIME AND SUICIDE: A CLOSER LOOK

First, let us scrutinize the good news. The fall in the juvenile crime rate over the past decade or so is indeed one of the most unexpected and interesting social changes on the domestic scene. Between 1970 and 1993 the homicide rate for teenagers (fifteen to nineteen) more than doubled (7.7 to 20.5 per 100,000). Between 1993 and 2001 it fell sharply, to 9.4—still significantly higher than the 1970 level, but dramatically lower than that 1993 peak.[6] This is what people mean when they say that the news on crime is good. In relative terms, it is.

Of course, and as some experts have cautioned, things do look somewhat less dramatic if considered in a broader historical context. James Q. Wilson, the nation's preeminent crime expert, said in 2000, "Crime rates will not stay down forever. In Los Angeles, the murder rate has begun to rise sharply, largely because of heightened conflict between street gangs. I suspect serious crimes will go up in other cities as well for one simple reason: They always move up and down, and there is nothing in history to suggest that the present levels will persist. And in any event, *the rate of violent crime today is still three times higher than it was in 1960* [emphasis added]."[7] I have emphasized that last point because it shows us the sort of thing we miss if we look only at a one- or two-year change in rates. Wilson points to one problem with today's enthusiasm over falling crime rates: Measured by historical standards and societies elsewhere, juvenile crime in America is still unconscionably high.

The deeper problem with using crime rates as a bellwether for the well-being of today's kids is a logical one: It is an illegitimate polemical leap from "crime rates are down" to "this shows that today's kids are doing just fine." And the reason the second proposition does not follow from the first becomes clear if we pause for a moment to answer this question that optimists tend not to consider: Why did juvenile crime fall in the first place?

There is no consensus on the answer. Both liberals and conservatives seek credit for the juvenile crime reduction, and they will likely continue slugging that one out for a long time. Even so, the explanations so far are all highly suggestive of a different point. Some observers (mainly conservatives) cite tougher laws for juvenile offenders, which they say both deterred other potential criminals and depressed the juvenile crime rate still further by locking up the worst kids. Others (mainly liberals) point to the trend toward restricting personal firearms during those same years. Many on both sides also attribute some role in the crime drop to the decline in crack cocaine use and the gangsterism that accompanied it. Just why crack fell out of favor as much as it did is another much-debated point; some attribute its decline to more intense policing, others to the speculation that a generation of kids who grew up with the ravages of the drug declined to put their own teen selves in harm's way. In addition to theories such as those, another one stresses the growing economy of the late 1990s, arguing that once people could afford to buy their own $150 sneakers, they were less inclined to shoot someone else to obtain theirs.[8]

What is important in this brief review is what is *not* being postulated in any of these theories—that the crime rate fell because something about family life was getting better. Thus, though the experts might disagree on what the exact reason for the decline in crime may be, there is a tacit common denominator to their theories: Something external, or more likely a number of external factors, has caused that drop; however, those external factors do not tell us anything about the emotional state of most kids or about their families.

Just as the drop in the violent crime rate does not prove the optimistic view that the kids are therefore all right, neither does the other very recent trend from which overly large conclusions are similarly drawn: the dip in the teen suicide rate. In 1970 that rate was 5.9 per 100,000.[9] By 1994 it had risen to 11.1 per 100,000—nearly double. In 2001 it declined significantly to 9.4 per 100,000, which was still a third higher than it had been in 1970.

How to account for the drop between 1994 and 2001? Some experts say the wider use of antidepressants might account for it (though their argument faces the conceptual problem that the same antidepressants have simultaneously been argued to *contribute* to teen suicide, as is discussed in chapter 5). Some also believe that better awareness—more crisis hotlines and less stigmatization of mental illness—might also be responsible. Such may well be true, but even this is a communal, as opposed to a familial, factor. Thus, once again, as in the example of crime statistics, the good news about teen suicide does not suggest any improvement in mental or emotional well-being attributed to the family, but rather that there are other, external factors influencing behavior for those considering suicide.

Meanwhile, the crucial larger point remains this one: If we look only at the immediate decline in rates, we miss the real historical and moral point of the teen suicide phenomenon. Adolescent self-murder rates have been far higher in the United States and in other advanced countries over the past half century or so than they were before.[10] What makes this bleak development more baffling is that there is no corresponding rise in poverty over this period—quite the opposite—and little in the way of other external evidence to suggest why the materially well-off adolescents are killing themselves at such shocking rates. This is one of the sociological puzzles of our time, one that many—from the great sociologist Émile Durkheim on down—have tried to answer.

Some answers suggest a link between suicide and absent parents and family.[11] In *Bowling Alone*, for example, Robert D. Putnam uses figures from the U.S. Public Health Service and other sources to put the point in arresting historical terms—that "Americans born and raised in the 1970s and 1980s were three to four times more likely to commit suicide as people that age had been at mid-century."[12] He also advances one speculation of note: "social isolation." He cites *The Ambitious Generation*, a 1999 study of seven thousand adolescents by educational sociologists Barbara Schneider and David Stevenson.[13] They report that the average American teenager spends about three and a half hours alone every day, and, perhaps even more breathtaking, "adolescents spend more time alone than with family and friends."[14] One does not have to read Durkheim to see the isolation writ large in these numbers or to speculate about the effects of such endemic isolation on a chronically melancholic adolescent temperament.

What several decades of research into this puzzle has further established is this: Teen suicide also appears causally linked to parental absence in a variety of other ways. Writing in the *British Journal of Psychiatry* in

1998, Eric Fombonne examined more than six thousand subjects spanning twenty-one years and found strongly suggestive evidence of a link between "the increase over time of suicidal behaviors in adolescent boys and a contemporaneous increase in substance misuse."[15] Substance abuse, as studies mentioned on other pages in this book emphasize, is linked elsewhere and repeatedly to parental absence. Thus, a causal chain is suggested in which home-alone teenagers pick up alcohol and drug habits that, in turn, make it easier for them to imagine and act on feral behaviors, including suicide.

Suicide is also causally linked, of course, to parental divorce. I say "of course" because there is a small mountain of evidence linking divorce not only to higher rates of substance abuse in children and adolescents, but also to numerous other factors associated with suicide: depression and other psychiatric problems, conduct problems, low academic achievement, and low self-esteem.[16] According to David Lester, one of the leading suicidologists in the country who has looked closely at numerous data that correlate with teen suicide, "Only divorce rates were consistently associated with suicide and with homicide rates."[17] Nor is social science the only way of establishing that link. The chapter on teen music later in this book cites lyrical evidence suggesting that when teenagers think about suicide—or at least when their celebrity bards do—they commonly make exactly the causal link that Lester identifies, the one tying suicide and thoughts of suicide to broken homes, particularly absent fathers.

In sum, the reduction in juvenile crime and the fall in the suicide rate do not prove what advocates who use them in the service of family "diversity" want them to prove. The crime rate fell for reasons quite apart from the state of the family, and the suicide rate, still astonishingly high among adolescents, is repeatedly linked to absent parents in various forms. Welcome as they are in and of themselves, these recent changes in the crime and suicide vectors do not allow us to infer that the kids are all right. We should consider, however, what optimists do *not* discuss when they invoke the falling crime and suicide rates for ideological reasons— that is, the bad news about today's furious children.

SAVAGE SCHOOLKIDS

The ideological misreading of what is actually going on in the crime and suicide statistics has one other undesirable implication: It risks detracting attention from something that *is* new and troubling on the scene, which is the apparent rise in feral behavior among some of the youngest children.

In 2003, to begin with an intriguing example, *Time* magazine reported on a survey of thirty-nine child care centers, elementary schools, and pediatricians in the Fort Worth, Texas, area. According to the group conducting it, 93 percent of the schools responding said that today's kindergartners have "more emotional and behavioral problems than were seen five years ago." Moreover, over half the day care centers said that "incidents of rage and anger" had also increased over the last three years. *Time*'s reporter further quotes the survey leader as explaining, "We're talking about children— a 3-year-old in one instance—who will take a fork and stab another child in the forehead. We're talking about a wide range of explosive behaviors, and it's a growing problem."[18]

Numerous sources quoted elsewhere in the *Time* piece—"sources" meaning teachers, administrators, and other professionals who are actually around young children all day, unlike many parents—affirm the article's point. A director of the National School Safety Center in California, which tracks school violence nationwide, observes that violence across the country "is getting younger and younger," further observing that a growing number of school districts have lately created special elementary schools for disruptive youngsters. ("Who would have thought years ago that this would be happening?" he wonders aloud.) A director of psychological services involved with eighty thousand students in the Fort Worth area adds, "The incidents have occurred not only in low-income urban schools but in middle-class areas as well. . . . We're talking about serious talking back to teachers, profanity, even biting, kicking and hitting adults, and we're seeing it in 5-year-olds"—moreover, not the five-year-olds already officially labeled "emotionally disturbed" but the "normal" ones.

Several of the points made in the *Time* piece are reiterated in a 2003 article in *USA Today*, which similarly quotes educators and others from various parts of the country.[19] They voice the same apprehension that something very odd is going on with at least some young children. A school security coordinator in Indiana says, for example, that "kicking and biting and scratching and hitting" are all up among the elementary school set, adding: "If someone had asked me this ten years ago: 'Chuck, how many primary school students have you responded to?' I would have said, 'None.' Now it's an all-too-frequent occurrence." A chief of police in Palm Beach County, Florida, says that police officers entered elementary schools for the first time in the preceding few years—in part to deal with obstreperous parents "who become angry when their children are disciplined." The *USA Today* piece also makes the point that although juvenile violent crime lumped together has indeed dropped in the aggregate, what few statistics we have suggest that the opposite is going on among the youngest children. In California, for example, "crimes against persons" in elementary schools, meaning assaults, nearly doubled between 1995 and 2001, even as vandalism and other property-type crimes fell markedly.

And then there is anecdotal testimony from teachers themselves. Consider a recent account by Joshua Kaplowitz in *City Journal.* He asserts that his own experience as a fifth-grade public school teacher in Washington, D.C., of having to manage out-of-control children (and sometimes parents) "was hardly unique." Other teachers also "report the same outrageous discipline problems that turned them from educators into U.N. peacekeepers." His personal story is a striking one, for he was eventually hounded out of the system and sued for $20 million by parents of a particularly unruly child (apparently, suing school districts is increasing in popularity). Kaplowitz concludes:

> I've learned that an epidemic of violence is raging in elementary schools nationwide, not just in D.C. A recent *Philadelphia Inquirer* article details a familiar pattern—kindergartners punching pregnant teachers, third graders hitting their instructors with rulers. Pennsylvania and New Jersey have reported nearly 30 percent increases in elementary school violence since 1999, and many school

districts have established special disciplinary K–6 schools. In New York City, according to the *New York Post*, some 60 teachers recently demonstrated against out-of-control pupil mayhem, chanting, "Hey, hey, ho, ho; violent students must go." Kids who stab each other, use teachers as shields in fights, bang on doors to disrupt classes, and threaten to "kick out that baby" from a pregnant teacher have created a "climate of terror."[20]

What is going on in these classrooms, less *Rugrats* than *Lord of the Flies*? Interestingly, the sources cited in these various reports are not ambivalent at all about that question. They think they know. As in the upcoming chapter on specialty boarding schools, those close to the source in these institutions share the same sense: What is responsible for those feral children are the "stressed, single parent homes" that many of them come from (this from the chairman of disciplinary hearings in Lancaster, Pennsylvania) and, in the words of the *Time* summary, "more parents working longer hours than ever before," "kids spending more time in day care," and "everyone coming home too exhausted to engage in the kind of relationships that build social skills."[21] What is creating those furious children is an unbalanced world in which, as one elementary school administrator in Miami put it, "kids aren't getting enough lap time."

Some sources also make another commonsensical point: Some of these children are not only more tired and deprived than they ought to be, but they also have not learned the barest minimum of rule-following required to get through the school day because no one has taught them the little things that used to be common skills of children everywhere. The director of psychological services for Fort Worth schools told CBS News, "As I talk with parents, I often find scenarios such as, 'I really don't have time to sit at the table with my child; the food is there, and he can eat as he chooses.' So there isn't the interaction that gives the child the discipline."[22] His insight is exactly right. How is any child supposed to learn how to sit still and pay attention to what his teacher is saying when he is not even required to spend five minutes a night at the table doing just that with his mother or father or other family members?

WORK VERSUS HOMEWORK

This outbreak of bad behavior in school suggests one other connection between furious schoolchildren and a too-weak network of supportive parents, one that does not appear in the literature but that demands being weighed in its own right. Maybe some of those children are furious and acting up in school *because they are frustrated about not being able to do the schoolwork.* And maybe one reason they cannot is that there is no one to help them with it at home.

This is one possible answer to the question of why American lower-school education remains stagnant despite experiment after educational experiment. In the words of a recent emblematic *New York Times* headline, "Students in U.S. Do Not Keep Up in Global Tests." In this particular study, as in numerous others over the years, some nine thousand tested eighth graders demonstrated again what critics have long complained about: American students lag behind their peers in advanced countries by significant margins, and the gap in science and math grows wider as the student ages. Over the years many different explanations—demographic, sociological, pedagogical, and economic—have been offered for this gap, and many reforms, from charter schools to vouchers and the rest, have been devised to address it.

Yet one possible explanation that has not enjoyed wide circulation is the most obvious one of all: that many children need help and supervision with their homework, that in many homes nobody is there to provide that kind of support after school, that some children are physically ready for sleep, not study, by the time their parents return home, and that preoccupied adults who do find themselves supervising homework after a long and busy day themselves may hate every minute of it (and understandably so). All of these are facts so plainly related to school achievement that educators themselves are beginning to acknowledge the connections—if only because it is they who are frequently blamed for the consequences.

Not long ago, for example, the *New York Times* published an interesting short article by Richard Rothstein tellingly entitled "Add Social Changes to the Factors Affecting Declining Test Scores."[23] In it, Ted Stillwell, the director of the Iowa Department of Education "speculates that even greater social change may be a factor. . . . With parents less available, children may get less support at home for learning, Mr. Stillwell surmises." The same report also mentioned a problem familiar to many teachers, namely, the shrinking number of parents available for school events— from field trips to class parties to volunteer work to sudden developments requiring parental attention. A teacher with eighteen years of experience in Iowa observed that "this year, in her class of 23, there are only three mothers she can phone at home if a problem arises during school."

This same point—that many of today's parents simply are not as available for school and school activities as educational success may require— suggests itself even more emphatically if certain comparative facts are taken into account. Much has been made, for example, of Asian students' overall superiority on standardized tests and other academic endeavors, and much has been written about the factors, cultural, economic, and even (witness *The Bell Curve*) psychometric, that are argued to account for this difference. But little has been said publicly about a factor requiring no theory whatsoever—which is that, as Francis Fukuyama has noted and as readers familiar with Japan and Korea already know, "part of the reason that children in both societies do so well on international tests has to do with the investments their mothers make in their educations."[24] ("Investments" does not mean money, incidentally, but time.) Even for the most educated and accomplished mothers, staying home when children are of school age and helping with the studying and scholarly discipline is the norm.[25]

Another piece of suggestive evidence linking parental absence to school outcomes appears in *The Widening Gap*, a recent work of research on contemporary family life cited in the previous chapter on day care. Noting a variety of evidence linking poor performance on standardized tests to parental work hours, researcher Jody Heymann concludes: "Not having parents available to help in the evenings and nights also appears to have led to children having greater troubles in the first place." She then addresses the absent-parent connection head-on: "Can the relationship between parental working conditions and children's poor school performance be explained by other factors? Even when statistical methods are used to control for differences in family income and in parental education, marital status, and total hours worked, *the more hours parents are away from home after school and in the evening, the more likely their children are to test in the bottom quartile on achievement tests* [emphasis added]."[26]

Surely some of those kids end up hating school for reasons having nothing to do with ability but on account of this fact: Their lack of familial support puts them even further behind the children who do enjoy the attention of an adult or other older family member at home, thus increasing again the academic distance they have yet to travel. Who would *not* find that disadvantage overwhelming and a possible prompt to angry behavior?

HOW LOW CAN WE GO?

Statistically speaking, of course, few latchkey children grow up to be murderers. Yet beneath the public anxiety provoked by every such savage, beneath even the ritual media cycle that follows the recorded-for-television atrocities, lies an element of unspoken truth about the link between these adolescent outcasts and the rest of society. The fear shared by much of the adult world is that perhaps the kids aren't all right after all, that perhaps the decades-long experiment in leaving more and more of them to fend for themselves, whether for the sake of material betterment, career fulfillment, marital satisfaction, or other deep adult desires, has finally run amok. What troubles the public mind about the killers is not that they seem anomalous, but that they might be emblematic.

That is why, in the end, those falling crime and suicide rates do not hold up as a proxy for determining that the kids are all right. The optimism derived from them is wrong for the same reason that cheerleading for day care is wrong: It sets the moral bar for schools and children entirely too low. It is all to the good, of course, that there are fewer teenage crack dealers shooting one another up with Uzis. But since when did we say, in effect, "As long as you're not a crack dealer, everything will be just fine"? It is similarly heartening that fewer teenagers killed themselves in 2001 than in 1994, but since when does that make the ones who did kill themselves (still at historically high rates) become somehow less of a problem?

The answer is, since we collectively decided to avoid the ultimate furious child problem—the increase in bad and sometimes uncontrollable behavior in a great many schools and by a great many American kids—by emphasizing only the most spectacular and tragic variations on the theme. In the end that problem comes down to this: When Columbine is your moral yardstick, there is a lot you won't be getting to measure.

3

Why Dick and Jane Are Fat

A FRIEND OF MINE RECENTLY MOVED BACK TO THE UNITED STATES after living for several years in Hong Kong with her husband and four children. One day I asked what stood out most to her on returning to the American scene—expecting to hear her thoughts on education, popular culture, or some other obvious subject. Instead she answered immediately and unexpectedly, "That's easy. Fit parents, fat kids."

Fit parents, fat kids. Though some people might bristle at that blunt formulation, they really shouldn't. Juvenile obesity is believed by most medical experts to be a serious new health problem, and my friend's summary happens to be both striking and astute. It further captured something that I, too, had observed without really thinking about it. Our neighborhood abounds with schools and students spanning the widest social swath; several public and private schools, both coed and single sex and covering all ages, are within walking distance. Having watched the kids of those schools for a dozen or so years, and also the comings and goings of their parents, I know that, anecdotally at least, my friend hit something right on the head: A good many of those adults are markedly smaller in girth than their children. Among the better-off parents especially it is not rare at all to see, say, a sleek forty- or fifty- or even sixty-year-old of either sex traveling to or from the schools alongside a chubby or more seriously overweight child or teenager. And even among other parents—especially the immigrants, of whom there are also many in the neighborhood—it is not at all unusual to see children who are much bigger and wider than their mothers and fathers must have been at the same age.

That sight—children and teenagers who are considerably larger than their biological parents, whether or not their parents are actually "fit"—is not one that would have been common in the childhood of most current readers. It is indeed quite new, and in tandem with a burgeoning and concerned expert literature, it drives home just how novel and ubiquitous today's juvenile fat problem really is. It is a curious fact that at the same time Atkins-mad American adults are becoming fitter and more health conscious—or at least feeling they ought to be—American children and teenagers, far from enjoying the healthiest years of their lives, are becoming fatter and more sedentary.

We are familiar enough with the "hows" of all this—fast food, lack of exercise, cheap eats, herculean restaurant portions, and the rest of the depressing creed mentioned in recent news stories. Even so, the one aspect of this new phenomenon of child obesity that no one has raced to discuss is arguably the most important part of all: not *how* children get fat but, rather, *why*.

Historically, after all, parents or extended family or both have controlled most of what and when children ate. This responsibility has been exercised virtually everywhere in human history, from the savannah to the igloo to the Raj and back again. And it has been exercised by rich as well as poor, or else the history of better-off social classes would be replete with the oversized children and adults we see today (as it markedly is not). The "why" underlying the child fat problem can be formulated something like this: *In what kind of social universe do adults cease to perform the essential task of policing children's eating habits?*

The answer is that our own social universe has become one in which adults, particularly parents, are not around to do the policing in the first place. In other words, there is a relationship between absent mothers and fathers—particularly, as we will see, the former—and overstuffed children.

———————————

Compared to the deadly serious problems of terrorism and war and the rest—for that matter, compared to some of the other juvenile problems described in this book—the fact that a great many American children are carrying around a few pounds too many might seem to be the least of anyone's worries. That is, it might have seemed that way before 2003, during which a series of blue-chip studies on child obesity forced the juvenile fat problem into the very center of public awareness—a sea change further confirmed in March 2004, when yet another team of researchers confirmed that obesity may overtake smoking as the leading cause of preventable death.[1]

The statistics are dramatic—dramatically bad. One major 2002 study related in the *Journal of the American Medical Association* found that the percentage of overweight children and teenagers tripled between the 1960s and the late 1990s.[2] A report published in *Pediatrics* magazine in 2002 by researchers for the Centers for Disease Control (CDC) found that the costs of child obesity–related hospital admissions had also roughly tripled during the same interval.[3] Numerous other specialized reports have elaborated what anyone who has been to a mall lately will know: American kids are indeed fat, and they are getting fatter all the time. Witness the explosion of "husky" sizes in children's clothes. Witness the popularity of "hip-hop" styles among adolescents of all races—a form of bodily tent more akin to, say, the burka or the muumuu than to traditional Western dress.

Although a handful of contrarians have suggested otherwise, the child fat problem is uniquely troubling, both as a public health issue and as a social fact. It is one thing to see shirtless obese children paraded like circus freaks on the *Maury Povich Show* and to think the problem a sleazy artifact of trash TV. It is quite another to read accounts written by doctors of their actual suffering: the growing incidence of early heart trouble and fat-linked cancers in children only years removed from babyhood; the experiments, some of them parlous, with drugs and surgeries of all kinds; the doubling of diabetes diagnoses, the fivefold rise in sleep apnea cases, and the tripling of gallbladder disease, all during the past two decades. Perhaps most frightening of all is the increase in type 2 diabetes among children and adolescents, a long-term killer that might make their lives shorter than the spans enjoyed by their parents. Whatever else may be said about them, the public health issues raised by child fat are no media inventions.

One explanation for the child fat problem—and related lawsuits are making their way through the courts—targets the fast-food industry. "Big Food," as the critics call it, is also the culprit in a recent book by Greg Critser called *Fat Land: How Americans Became the Fattest People in the World.*[4] Some of what the critics claim is true—for example, that portions are considerably larger than they were thirty years ago. But it is also true that an abundance of supply does not guarantee an outpouring of vice— in other words, alcoholics aren't made by walking into liquor stores. For that reason it does seem reasonable to suppose that fast-food franchises and the like are responding to demand rather than creating it. Maybe Americans are *not* waddling zombielike to the trough just because Colonel Sanders tells them to. Maybe fast-food and other companies are merely engaged in business as usual, trying to keep customers fat and happy. The fact that McDonald's has recently reduced its french fry portions in re- sponse to concerns about obesity would seem to demonstrate as much.

A second and even more popular explanation for the child fat problem is that kids gain weight because they are genetically programmed to be that way. This speculation appears to have two main virtues. One, it reflects what everyone can see and what studies have documented: Heavy kids tend to have heavy mothers. Two, it is nonjudgmental. Child fat is an uncom- fortable and embarrassing issue to many people. If children cannot help be- ing fat, there is little for them or their parents to regret or work on.

And yet the heredity argument, like the fast-food argument, is also se- riously limited—this time by historical fact. Genetic programming alone cannot explain the great leap into heaviness and obesity of these past two or three decades. If people were truly "blueprinted" to gain weight, the obesity problem should have developed generations earlier, as soon as they had access to extra food. Most Americans (and other moderns) have been prosperous for a very long time. They could have eaten themselves to today's weights many years ago, but for some reason they did not. As Kathleen M. McTigue, lead author of a recent obesity study in the *Annals of Internal Medicine,* has put the point, "People born in 1964 who be- came obese did so about 25 to 27 percent faster than those born in 1957."[5] Heredity cannot explain facts like these.

Moreover, both the fast-food and heredity arguments are confounded by this critical fact: Misconceptions and undeserved reputations to the contrary, most other advanced countries share in the child fat and obesity problem, for the most part differing from us in degree rather than kind. The *Guardian* reported that in England in 2002, "Adult obesity rates have tripled and those in children have doubled since 1982."[6] In Canada, the *Globe and Mail* said in 2002, "More than a third of Canadian children aged 2 to 11 are overweight, and half that number are obese, according to newly published Statistics Canada data."[7] Moreover, "Canada now has more fat children than fat adults." As for Australia, a 2000 study there found that children of either sex were twice as likely to be defined as overweight in 2000 as in 1985.

Nor is the Anglo-speaking world alone. Continental Europe and its children are ballooning as well. In Italy, report researchers for the *Bollettino Epidemiologico Nazionale*, "Neapolitan children were more at risk of obesity than were children from France, Holland, the United States, and also than children living in Milan in northern Italy," while in the province of Benevento, "the prevalence of overweight and obesity was greater . . . than in England, Scotland, and the United States."[8] In Germany, according to researchers for the *International Journal of Obesity*, a "large study on all children entering school in Bavaria in 1997 shows patterns of overweight and obesity which are comparable with other European data" (though still "lower than U.S. and Australian data").[9] Even vaunted France, according to French researchers, has seen the prevalence of child obesity more than double in the last couple of decades.[10] If either fast food or heredity was the real culprit behind the fat problem, then the international statistics across varying cultures and diets would not look so much like our own.

Obviously, something else is going on in all these places—something that might have to do with who, if anyone, is supervising what goes into children's mouths. After all, the interval of 1980 to 1990, in which the threefold rise in obesity-related health problems mentioned earlier first occurred is exactly the same interval that saw *this* dramatic social change: Between 1980 and 1985 the percentage of mothers with children under six who were in the labor force first "crossed" the magic line into being the majority.[11] By 1990 that percentage had become higher still—58.2.

By 2000 it had climbed further, to 64.6 percent. In other words, the years in which the obesity epidemic appears to have accelerated are *the same years that the number of mothers of small children entering the labor force became the statistical norm.*

That is a striking and highly suggestive coincidence. Yet in all the volumes and bulletins and articles dedicated to the fat problem, there has apparently been only one serious American effort to examine the question of child fat and absent mothers head-on. This was a paper published in 2002 by Patricia M. Anderson, Kristin F. Butcher, and Phillip B. Levine of the Joint Center for Poverty Research (funded by the U.S. Department of Health and Human Services).[12] Titled "Maternal Employment and Overweight Children," their study uses data from ten thousand children participating in the National Longitudinal Survey of Youth (NLSY), among other sources. Its authors set themselves the goal of helping to determine "whether a causal relationship exists between maternal employment and childhood overweight." Obviously anticipating the ideological fusillade likely to come their way, the authors explain that they focus on maternal rather than paternal employment for three reasons: "It is mothers' labor supply that has changed dramatically over recent decades"; whether working outside the home or not, women "still bear the bulk of responsibility for child rearing"; and "data limitations in the analysis . . . only enable us to link the employment histories of mothers and children."

Do out-of-the-house working mothers increase the risk of their children becoming fat? The answer, according to the authors, is yes. In its arresting formulation, this study, "among the first to grapple with issues of causality," "presents robust evidence of a positive and significant impact of maternal work on the probability that a child is overweight." And while the percentages derived are not overwhelming—the authors show at one point how increased maternal employment could "explain" 6 to 11 percent of the growth in childhood overweight—there is no underestimating that this study uncovered an important link. As the authors emphasized, their work showed not only a correlation but a clear causal connection: "the mechanism through which this [child weight gain] takes place is constraints on the mother's time; it is hours per week, not the number of

weeks worked, that affects children's probability of being overweight."
Nor did the authors shy away from reporting a perhaps unexpected class
twist here: "This effect is particularly evident for the children of white
mothers, of mothers with more education, and of mothers of a high income level." In other words, the children of better-off career mothers, who
otherwise are advantaged compared to their peers, are actually *disadvan-
taged* in the child fat department.

This study by Anderson, Butcher, and Levine on maternal employment is unique, but they note that other efforts to gauge the connection
have been undertaken. In particular, a 1999 study of obese Japanese
three-year-olds outlined a similar causal chain, identifying "the mother's
job" as the environmental factor contributing the most to child obesity.[13]
That study aside—and it seems to be little known in the United States
outside expert circles—not much attention has been paid to the maternal
absence question, which is hardly surprising. Drawing attention to the
connection between childhood fat and absent parents, especially absent
mothers, is about as close to a thankless task as social science can get and
maybe even professionally suicidal. Yet while "Maternal Employment and
Overweight Children" may be among the first efforts to examine the link
directly, it is not the only evidence for a connection between absent mothers and fat kids. There are at least four other ways to establish that same
link, each pointing to an even stronger causal connection.

SITTING, WATCHING, EATING

To take our first example, nothing is as firmly established in the fat literature as the fact that television watching and overweight children go
hand in hand. This phenomenon, which has been studied many times
over, is pretty easily grasped: The more television a child watches, the
more likely he or she is to get fat. As to the mechanism at work here, this,
too, appears clear. People generally eat more when sitting in front of the
television than they do when sitting at a table, and if they have no one to
talk to, they also eat faster. Moreover, because metabolism slows to almost sleeplike levels after enough time in front of the tube, the food

taken in is metabolized more slowly—hence, in a more fat-friendly way—than it would be otherwise.

Thus the amount of television watched is an excellent yardstick of sorts for child (and adult) fat. Are children in the absent-parent household likely to watch more television or play more video games? Common sense fairly shouts "yes." Yet, surprisingly—or perhaps not, given the socially loaded nature of the inquiry—there has been little direct research on the specific question of whether children whose mothers are out when they come home watch more television or play more video games than those with a parent on the premises.

Nonetheless, intriguing pieces of other research suggest that the answer here, too, is an unequivocal "yes." While little may have been written about the viewing habits of middle- and upper-middle-class American children (some of whose working parents might take ideological exception to this sort of inquiry), some expert thought has gone into the question of what can be expected when lower-class parents are absent from the home. The evidence comes from an unexpected source: welfare reform.

One might think that a couch potato is a couch potato is a couch potato. In other words, given the strength of the link between low income and television watching, it might appear that watching TV is a kind of constant immune to other ongoing activity—particularly whether the mother of the house was working or at home. But this view turns out to be wrong, or so suggests a major four-year post–welfare reform study in California whose results were reported by the *San Francisco Chronicle* as follows: that "welfare reform's biggest effect on children is that they spend less time with their mothers and watch 22 more minutes of television [a day] on average."[14] What makes this evidence even more credible is that the researchers from Stanford, University of California at Berkeley, Columbia, and Yale were not looking for such a result but uncovered it incidentally in the course of their survey of seven hundred women. That increase effectively puts to rest any notion that television viewing is some class-based constant unaffected by other domestic variables.[15]

How much social science do we need to tell us that when parents are away, kids will play? And they will particularly play at electronics. Again, to whose surprise? Of course children are more likely to turn off the tube or the screen or the video game if there is an adult around to remind them to do so, just as of course they will eat two cookies rather than twelve if anyone with an opinion about what they eat is around to enforce it.

LESS MOTHER'S MILK, MORE FAT

A second, rather different way in which absent parents—meaning, in this case, absent mothers—are connected to child obesity has to do with a practice that lowers the risk of child fat but is at odds with the paid marketplace: breast-feeding. One does not have to be a member of the La Leche League to understand why doctors everywhere urge that babies drink human milk whenever possible; indeed, the American Academy of Pediatrics now officially recommends breast-feeding for at least the first year of life. A substantial body of evidence has developed over the years that suggests not only that mother's milk in the first year of life confers immunity and other protections for a variety of baby problems, but that it also reduces the likelihood of obesity later in life.

This was argued in an essay in the *Lancet* in June 2001 that was based on a study of 32,200 Scottish children.[16] The researchers' conclusion was that "breast-feeding is associated with a modest reduction in childhood obesity risk." As to just *how* human milk reduces fat, the answer appears to be simple: It is lower in calories than formula, and babies must work harder to extract it—meaning that the amount of mother's milk ingested in, say, ten minutes is both less in volume and less caloric than formula. Formula, by contrast, puts calories into baby much faster and thereby runs the risk of overfeeding. Put simply, there is practically no such thing as an obese breast-fed baby—something that cannot be said of babies who are fed formula.

Here again is an example of how maternal absence—this time during the first year of life—raises the risk of childhood and adolescent obesity. As medical experts and experienced mothers agree, breast-feeding works best when baby and mother are in constant proximity to each other. The typical breast-fed baby eats every two to four hours, often around the clock and sometimes for months on end. In fact, *nothing* could be more inimical to full-time, out-of-the-house employment. It is true that some working mothers diligently pump milk at work, thereby attempting to square nature's feeding circle. Unless they are able to do so at a pace resembling nature's own—and most offices would surely notice a twenty-minute absence three, four, or five times a day—they are not able to provide such protection to anywhere near the degree that the far more available at-home mother can. Moreover (and feminist-minded cheerleaders for the practice seem invincibly unaware of this), the physical strain of such a regimen, with its added fluid and caloric requirements and the hormonal changes induced by it (lactation releases oxytocin, which causes drowsiness), can be prodigious.

However laudable such mothers may be in sacrificing themselves in this way, it is hard to believe that most do not find it easier to throw in the breast-feeding towel sooner rather than later. Such is the stress and inconvenience of shoehorning into minutes here and there a practice designed by nature to be very nearly a full-time job. In this way, too, mothers who are substantially absent during the first year of life contribute inadvertently to the risk of child heaviness and obesity.

(DON'T) RUN OUTSIDE AND PLAY

A third way in which absent parents contribute to the child fat problem involves every expert's favored solution to it all: exercise. Generally speaking, children left unattended after school fall into two categories: those in after-hours care institutions and those who care for themselves, that is, latchkey children. Does nonparental care during those hours make exercise more likely during those hours or less? The answer is less.

While the children of the better-off might have nannies ferrying them to sports and workouts and playgrounds during those hours, thus easing what might be called the "exercise penalty" of absent parents, most children cannot similarly command a parent substitute to be sure that they, too, get the requisite run-around time. For many, those before- and after-school care programs are a barely supervised free-for-all in which tired and cranky children do more or less as they please within the limits of school or other grounds. This is certainly true of the many I have seen in our school-intensive neighborhood, and they are representative of the highs and lows of programs elsewhere. Some children will play a game of pickup ball; those who shun such things are unlikely to be forced into them. In addition there is the related problem that ought to be underlined in any discussion of child fat: Nonparental supervisory adults charged with managing legions of children use snack after snack during the school day itself—an issue that is separate from the commercial questions of vending machines and fast food and the rest.

One cannot blame the caregivers for failing to put exercise first or for exacerbating the problem by further overfeeding the kids. Once more the clash between parental and nonparental supervision makes itself felt. While parents retain a long-term interest in physical health, other supervising adults respond instead to a short-term problem—namely, having to manage large numbers of tired, cranky, and rambunctious children until their parents arrive to take over. The extra food that is bad for their long-term interests is nonetheless good from the point of view of the short-term management problem, at least for those charged with the managing.

What about the children who are not in programs at all, those who care for themselves after school (the current euphemism for latchkey kids)? For most, exercise is completely out. The reason is obvious: They are supposed to go home and stay there. "If you're parenting a latchkey kid," as Parenting.org puts the typical exhortation, "you need to teach him or her self-care skills, set rules and limits, and talk about basic safety information." Among the tips, according to the National Crime Prevention Council's typical checklist, are: "Check in with you [that is, the parent] or a neighbor immediately after arriving home." "Operate doors and window locks." "Answer the doorbell and phone safely." "Avoid walking or playing alone." All of these are based on the assumption that children are going home to stay put.

This is as it must be: If a child has to return to an empty home, it is better that he be locked up inside than be unsupervised out in the world. Once more, however, the paramount short-term concern of absent

parents—physical safety and security—is inimical to the long-term benefits of outdoor exercise, which often requires an adult nearby, at least in
many urban and suburban settings.

Here again, today's children and adolescents are inarguably disadvan-
taged in at least this area of life compared to what their own parents enjoyed
during their youth. Many of today's parents look back with fondness on
those after-school hours as the most leisurely time of day, filled with ball
playing, yard hopping, rope skipping, and other outdoor fun. Many express
nostalgia for the fact that their own children will never know such a world,
and some also wonder why. The answer is as plain as day: What made those
hours of play possible was the one thing many children and teenagers can
no longer command: a parent, typically a mother, at home at the end of the
school day. It was that adult presence that made "safety" and "outdoor" exercise compatible terms for yesterday's kids, rather than contradictory as
they are today. Moreover, that presence not only made their own children
safer, but other people's, too.

Scholarship backs this commonsensical point. As observers from Jane
Jacobs to the contemporary examples of Robert D. Putnam and Alan
Ehrenhalt have long argued, there is a strong connection between absent
adults and a lack of safety in the streets. Ehrenhalt writes of a southwest
Chicago neighborhood in *The Lost City* that what it and others like it now
lack is exactly what made such places real communities: "the sociability
of the front stoop on summer evenings, the camaraderie of the back alley
as an athletic field, the network of at-home moms who provided an instant neighborhood bulletin board seven days a week."[17] By contrast, "On
weekdays now, for long stretches of time, no one walks down the quiet
residential streets. That is in part because the older people worry about
crime and fear the streets almost as much as they took sustenance from
them in the old days." Of the development of a suburb called Elmhurst
ten miles away, he observes similarly, "There is the same sense of physical
continuity and social upheaval. . . . If the streets are pretty, they are also
empty just about all the time. Emery Manor, like nearly all the suburban
subdivisions in America, is now a neighborhood of two-job families, so
you don't see mothers with strollers on their way to and from the park the

way you would have in the 1950s. Nor, for that matter, do you see many older children playing outside by themselves in the late afternoon." He concludes, "The social consequences of the two-job family *extend far beyond the empty streets in the daytime* [emphasis added]."

In sum, the adult exodus from home during much of the day has reduced the "eyes on the street," which is shorthand for what makes neighborhoods good rather than bad, safe rather than unsafe. That reduction encourages crime itself (as a policeman in Washington, D.C., told me, break-ins in affluent neighborhoods often occur between 11 A.M. and 1 P.M. when by the criminal calculus people are least likely to be at home). But it has also contributed to a vicious cycle that has ever fatter children at its vortex: The more parents are out of the house, the more reluctant they are to have their kids play outside—because with so many other adults also out of the house, there is no informal network of like-minded adults to be alert to them. The fewer children who are allowed out to play, the less likely that other children will be allowed out. Thus, at a time when exercise and outdoor time are being curtailed in many schools, these last two facts that further constrict their after-school movements are sealing the fates of many a future fat child.

In the end, one enduring image of even our affluent neighborhoods is that of a child, or perhaps two, huddled indoors for hours on end in front of one screen or another with a cell or portable phone nearby, the burglar alarm system on, and no related adult in sight before dinner time—if there is a dinner time. To ask a larger question raised elsewhere in this book: Is this really an emotional or social improvement on what most adults their parents' age did with those same hours? At least this much about our snapshot is incontestable: It is not making American children any slimmer.

TREATS: THE GUILT DIVIDEND

One last way in which absent parents are obviously linked to the child fat problems concerns a phenomenon I have never seen described in social science, though all mothers and fathers know it intimately. Every one of us can repeat the commandment that generations of pediatricians and child care books have drilled into us: Never, never, never bribe a child with food. And just about every one of us breaks that commandment at times, even chronically. The simple fact is that when it comes to bribes, nothing else works quite like food—as I know very well, being a hardened violator myself on hundreds, if not thousands, of occasions that include everything from dangling a lollipop to get a screaming toddler into a car seat to laying in a weekend's supply of junk food before leaving town to visit an ailing parent.

The unwritten monologue of these transactions is also one that parents know by heart. *Mom won't be there for dinner, so why don't you treat yourself to pizza and those horrible cinammon things you like.* Or: *Kathy, the babysitter, is coming tonight, and, yes, we'll make sure she fixes cookies for you.* And: *Sorry I missed your game/play/assembly this morning. How about an ice cream to celebrate?* As these examples suggest, parents—or at least the mortals among us—use food bribes routinely, in particular to cushion the blow to children of being apart. We do it quite without thinking about it. In short, parental feelings of guilt are themselves an independent source of overfeeding. If we multiply that phenomenon by today's large-scale parental absences due to work and divorce and the rest, then we can really see how the calories add up.

After all, the fundamental fact about vending machines and access to fast food remains this: Someone is giving the kids money for all that stuff. And a great many someones are engaged in other unwritten dialogues such as these every day: *Mom can't be there when you get home from school, but your favorite doughnuts are on the shelf.* Or: *I don't want you going off to the park after school when I'm not around, but here's a few dollars you can spend at McDonald's on the way home.* And: *I know you don't like the snacks in after-care, so I put something special in your lunchbox today.* And many mothers in shared custody arrangements know this one by heart: *On HIS time last weekend, the kids ate nothing but hot dogs and McDonald's and brownie sundaes and all the candy he could shove into them.*

These are the subterranean themes, repeated by the millions, that echo across the adult-empty kitchens of America. They amount to a perhaps unquantifiable but very real force behind the fat problem—that extra treats are a kind of "guilt dividend" that absent parents especially use to placate the children separated from them. Moreover, it is a dividend increased by the fact that even when parents are in the house, sitting down together over food is something they are less likely to do. This decline in the number of meals that families take together, which has been observed and frequently decried in the expert and popular literature, is one more proof of the relationship between child fat and adult supervision or lack thereof. Statistically, people eat less and more slowly when sitting at a table talking with one another than they do when stuffing their faces in front of a screen.

Even so, for a great many people mealtime has increasingly been replaced by "eating like squatters." That phrase is taken from an uncommonly candid discussion in the *Washington Post* recently called "Family Dinner, Minus Family," in which a mother whose only child has been pestering them to eat as a family explains how it was that they have come to eat separate meals in separate places in front of different screens: "Like much of the nation, everyone in the family is so busy that we long ago became used to eating in shifts. . . . It is often a staggered affair, where people wander in on their own schedules, gaze into the refrigerator as if it were a 1950s automat, and make a selection."[18] In short, "Dinner at our house has become a time to consume food, not a time reserved for conversation."

We have come to the final snapshot of the child fat problem, which indicates that in one more respect today's children are not better off than their parents were. The kind of food ingestion described in the article in the *Post*—serial human grazing as opposed to a dinner hour—is virtually guaranteed to make everyone fatter, save those with serious internal discipline. But it is also surely less pleasant for many youngsters than an actual few minutes with parents would be, as is highly suggested by the *Post* piece, which opens with the teenager demanding (and not getting) just that.

ABSENT PARENTS, RAVENOUS CHILDREN

In the end, the idea that nonparental care plays a role in the child fat problem is not only defensible, given the evidence, but also obvious for the several reasons expounded. Not that this obviousness makes the news any more wanted. At least one commentator's response to the Anderson, Butcher, and Levine study was to blast it for the guilt it might induce in working mothers. "Guilt" is similarly the term of opprobrium hurled at anyone who makes the obvious connection here. Moreover, not only separationist ideology but also real life has a great deal to do with such resistance. At a time when many mothers work because they cannot do otherwise and many others are out of the house for reasons of overriding importance to them—everything from bills to pay to personal fulfillment to the extra goods that money can buy, including such child-oriented goods as tuition and travel—the news that absent mothers may be contributing to the fattening of their kids can hardly expect a soft landing.

The real-life health consequences to a good many children morally trump those adult feelings, or ought to. Those children—who are again, in this sense, *worse off than their parents were*—deserve something of an honest nod toward the evidence. And what the evidence strongly suggests is this: *Today's child fat problem is largely the result of adults not being there to supervise what the kids eat.* Common sense says these two trends are related: Children are eating more because they are less likely to be around anyone who tells them it is a bad idea. Who is more likely to get fat, the child who comes home to a mother who tells him to wait for dinner or the child in an after-school program or empty house who has access for several hours to snack trays, fast food, and bulging cupboards and refrigerators?

Pointing a finger at absent parents as the real source of the child fat problem has one added advantage: It illuminates at least some important aspects of the phenomenon that have so far eluded explanation. One is the fact that, as mentioned earlier and as is contrary to popular misconceptions, child fat and obesity are rising among most developed countries where mothers are also typically out of the house, regardless of differences in diet, culture, and the rest. Another is the fact that this link would also help explain why immigrant families—in which mothers also often work outside the home—are at a particularly high risk of becoming overweight.

By now some readers may be thinking that more ought to be said about fathers in all this and that mothers who are already busy to the point of exhaustion are being unfairly singled out. On this subject, unfortunately, and unlike many others in this book, mothers and fathers are not interchangeable units. It is the mother more than any other adult in a child's life who experiences the need to police what her children eat and to cajole and order them to eat as she believes they should. It is the mother, not others, who generally has the strongest opinions about such things, whether she is home with her children or not. Moreover, even the best-paid help is unlikely to be as attentive to what children eat as a mother would. The long-term health of the child is not the caregiver's chief concern (usually it is the short-term goal of keeping the child supervised and happy). For reasons that remain as mysterious as they are intuitively obvious, it is typically the mother, more than any other figure in a child's life, who is willing to risk the short-term gluttonous dissatisfaction of the child for the long-term benefits of a better diet.

Unwanted or not, the link between fat kids and the parent-empty home stands as a Janus-faced signpost: the sunny side showing our material wonderland in which everyone is free to leave home for the paid marketplace, and the darker side showing what that social exodus is leaving behind. It may yet turn out that the link is even deeper than we know. Perhaps what some children of the better-off countries are doing with their mouths and stomachs is filling gaps made elsewhere in their lives. Maybe the void being filled by overeating, to invoke the intriguing terms of Overeaters Anonymous and other dietary theorists, is even more acute in young human beings than in others. Maybe a little more contact and companionship, with real rather than virtual parents and other family, might make them a little less ravenous.[19]

Domestic life has its trials and traumas, without question, for children and adults alike, but it also has its pleasures and consolations. Unable to enjoy these traditional comforts in anything like the doses to which humanity has become accustomed, perhaps the Western child uses food to try to compensate for other things that are being missed. Maybe the worlds of home and work are out of joint. Maybe that is what the consolation of calories is at least partly about.

4

The Mental Health Catastrophe

WHEN PROGRESSIVE-MINDED PEOPLE ARGUE THAT KIDS TODAY are better off than ever before, or at least not worse off, there is one subject they never—to my knowledge—take on: The number of children and teenagers diagnosed with mental disorders has not just risen in the last decade and a half, it has exploded. Today's juveniles, among the most materially prosperous ever to walk the earth, are either suffering or thought to be suffering from unprecedented levels of mental affliction.

This mental health catastrophe, untouchable though it may be in the political circles friendly to separationism, is very familiar to the doctors, psychologists, and counselors who cope with these children and teenagers. In January 2001, the Surgeon General issued a report declaring that the United States is facing nothing less than "a public crisis in mental care for children and adolescents."[1] The report further predicted that childhood neuropsychiatric disorders will become one of the five most common causes of morbidity, mortality, and disability by the year 2020. Similarly, the National Mental Health Association now estimates that one in five American children has a diagnosable mental, emotional, or behavioral disorder and that up to one in ten may suffer from a serious emotional disturbance.[2] Clinical sources say much the same; the child psychiatric department of Massachusetts General Hospital reported in one article, "[C]hildhood psychosocial dysfunction, considered a 'new morbidity' twenty-five years ago, has become widely acknowledged as the most common chronic condition of children and adolescents."[3]

What has been going on elsewhere during the same twenty-five years? In

1980, the percentage of all children living in single-parent families was 19.7; in 2000, it was 26.7.[4] In 1980, 18.4 percent of all births were out of wedlock; in 2000, that number was 33 percent, or a full third of all children.[5] In short, many more children (proportionately) are now growing up without both parents. Partly as a consequence of more divorce and single-parent homes, mothers during those same years have also become more frequently absent from home. You may recall that the maternal employment rate for those with children under the age of six rose from 46.8 percent in 1980 to 64.6 percent in 2000, an increase of 28 percent in just twenty years.

Any particular statistic might be challenged, of course, and an isolated fact may prove only so much. The skeptical reader may already be objecting that this doesn't mean absent parents and children's mental problems are connected (a point to which we will return). Yet the point made by the Massachusetts General Hospital report, among others, stands firm: Many more children and teenagers are now believed by medical professionals to require psychiatric help than was the case even a couple of decades ago.

That explosion of problem children is also something readers may already know from their personal experience. Attention deficit disorder (ADD, or ADHD when it includes hyperactivity), oppositional defiance disorder (ODD), obsessive-compulsive disorder (OCD), conduct disorder, bipolar disorder, autism, depression—all these and other psychiatric labels are now kitchen talk and a daily reality around the country. Just about every school district and college campus in America has been altered to take account of the growing problem, from special equipment to separate accommodations to ongoing controversies over who gets what (and who pays for it). Likewise, mind-altering drugs—a subject so significant as to require a separate chapter in this book—have become a daily reality of childhood for millions.

Any way one looks at it, the fact that so many children and teenagers are considered mentally or behaviorally deficient appears to raise a social question of the very first order.[6] Perhaps the most fundamental way to phrase the question is this: *What exactly is going on that practically every index of juvenile mental and emotional problems is rising so dramatically?* There appear to be three distinct parts to that answer; and each one is a subset of a world in which children and teenagers are more separated from their families—particularly, of course, from their parents—than ever before.

SADDER AND MORE ANXIOUS THAN BEFORE

The first answer to the question of why so many children and teenagers look to be in such miserable mental shape is the simplest one: They have more to be anxious, depressed, and upset about. In other words, the reason for the rise in childhood problems is at least partly real.

Many doctors, for example, believe that the rise is too significant to be merely a diagnostic artifact. Some believe that depression in particular has been rising among the child population for decades. One frequently cited 1991 study in the *Archives of General Psychiatry* argues that depression rates in children and adolescents have risen tenfold since the end of World War II.[7] A 2000 article in *Postgraduate Medicine*, the peer-reviewed journal for primary care physicians, noted similarly that "evidence indicates that full-blown depression in children and adolescents is increasing in incidence and often is overlooked as a cause of behavioral and other problems."[8] Another 2000 article in another expert journal looked at 269 different studies from the 1950s to the 1990s and concluded that self-reported anxiety and depression increased dramatically over those years.[9]

Some medical professionals also believe that the particularly astounding increase in the number of children registering as autistic is reflecting something real, that it is not just a function of more finely tuned diagnoses. As Mitzi Waltz, an expert on the history of autism and author of *Autistic Spectrum Disorders*, has put the point: "Doctors are doing a better job of diagnosing, and they deserve credit for that . . . [yet] better diagnosis doesn't seem to tell the whole story. If you talk to doctors who began working in this field 20 or 30 years ago, they will tell you that there's been a large and noticeable increase. So will teachers and social workers."[10] In February 2004, responding to yet another round of front-page stories in the *New York Times* about the rise in autism, several letter writers echoed

Waltz's point. As one put it, "Many long-term educators and tutors will tell you that there are many more kids on the autism spectrum today—not just numbers being reclassified. If you spend time at play groups, schools and so on you will notice firsthand how many of these kids there are."[11]

There is also an abundance of what might be called indirect evidence, some of it presented elsewhere in this book, to suggest that some overall deterioration of child psychological well-being is now in progress. The unexplained overall rise in teenage suicide in virtually every Western country over the past few decades is one telling, albeit especially horrifying, piece of evidence, as is the equally unexplained fact that infanticide by teenagers is higher now than ever before.[12] There is also the fact that child sex abuse appears to have risen these last few decades (driven by the exodus of biological parents from the home, as discussed in chapter 7), and by extension the many psychological problems with which it is associated. To judge by behavioral criteria alone, therefore, it seems that something like a widespread breakdown appears ongoing. In addition to numbers and trends, there are also the observations of seasoned professionals such as teachers and professors, some of whom discern in today's students a truly novel anomie.[13]

A final reason for thinking that the mental health breakdown is partly real is that certain phenomena empirically associated with childhood mental problems are also on the rise throughout society. Consider, for example, certain factors linked to depression. The article cited earlier from *Postgraduate Medicine* summarized some of that evidence as follows: "Environmental factors that increase the risk of depression in children include death of a parent in childhood and a history of abuse or neglect. Developmental disabilities, including learning disorders, and physical impairments or chronic illnesses, such as diabetes, likewise increase the risk. *A chaotic home environment with parents who are physically or emotionally absent because of mental illness, substance abuse, behavioral or economic difficulties, or other problems is also a risk factor* [emphasis added]."[14]

One can quibble with that last sentence and ask exactly what is meant by "chaotic" and "physically or emotionally absent." One can imagine that what this formulation reflects is, say, a bullet-sprayed apartment in a ghetto or a trailer presided over by a drunken single mother. It is not at all obvious, however, that the social reality summarized by all the foregoing statistics is limited to cases as blatant as those. The notion that today's homes, in general, are more chaotic than before is a staple of public conversation; stories abound, as does experience, of family members who barely see one another, rarely take meals together, and use the home as a kind of rest-and-refueling stop between the events outside. Here again, without entering into wide arguments about causality, one can surely observe this much: What appear to be at least some of the concomitants of childhood depression and related mental problems show no sign of diminishing and every sign of increasing. From this we might infer that depression and the rest have increased in real terms, and will likely continue to do so.

One final reason to believe that the rise in childhood misery is real is the vast literature on another common trend linked to emotional, mental, and behavioral problems: divorce and illegitimacy, dubbed elsewhere in this book the absent-father problem. Consider just a few statistics chosen from the 182 depressing pages of the fourth edition of *Father Facts*, a compendium of abstracts and other summaries of studies from the professional mental health scene. From the *American Journal of Orthopsychiatry*: "In a survey of 272 high school students, family cohesion and marital status were the strongest protective factors against suicidal behavior. . . . Thirty-eight percent of teens in stepfamilies reported suicidal behavior, compared to 20 percent among teens from single parent homes and just 9 percent among teens from intact families."[15] From the Department of Health and Human Services: "Children in single-parent families are two to three times as likely as children in two-parent families to have emotional and behavioral problems."[16] The *Journal of Pediatric Psychology*: "A study of 352 families indicated that children who lived with their mother and her boyfriend were more poorly adjusted psychologically and had more behavior problems than children who lived with both biological parents."[17] Again, the point here is that while the phenomena of divorce and fatherlessness continue apace and also continue to be linked with an increase in child mental problems, there is evidence that the rise in those problems is real and that we can expect it to continue.[18]

DIAGNOSTIC CHANGES AND WHAT THEY TELL US

The second answer to the question of why the mental state of children and teenagers looks so parlous is what might be called the diagnostic or definitional explanation. Beginning about a decade ago, the conditions established by medical professionals for what constitutes a legitimate childhood mental problem—in particular the criteria of the *Diagnostic and Statistical Manual IV*—have changed considerably. Not only have new disorders been added, but existing disorders have been redefined with a notably broader set of criteria. The result of both changes has been the same: to expand the definition of juvenile mental illness in such a way that it encompasses many more children and adolescents.

Consider the example of ADD and ADHD, the most familiar and the most frequently diagnosed of juvenile mental problems. They were so designated by the American Psychiatric Association in 1980 after having undergone some twenty-five different name changes in the preceding hundred years.[19] To the medical establishment, as represented by the American Academy of Pediatrics, the American Psychiatric Association, and other distinguished groups, ADD is a neurobiological, neurological, or neurochemical disorder, a fault of the "wiring," in the mechanistic image commonly used. It is hoped that these tangled cords will eventually be identified by some form of hard science. Yet because psychology has yet to deliver the genetic, chemical, or biological goods, the diagnosis of ADD/ADHD—like those of other leading juvenile mental disorders—depends exclusively on behavioral criteria.

And therein lies at least part of the continuing controversy over just what ADD/ADHD is or isn't. As the 2003 report of the President's Council on Bioethics—the Kass Report, named after Chairman Leon Kass—puts the conceptual problem, "In florid cases, a symptom-based diagnosis is easy to make. But the symptoms themselves shade over along a continuum into normal levels of childish distractibility or impulsiveness. . . . As a result, the purely symptomatic diagnosis of ADHD, even when made by experienced experts after the requisite thoroughgoing examinations in home and school settings, is always at risk of scooping up children who lack the disorder but who are nonetheless comparably handicapped. Where the symptoms are less clear-cut and less severe, diagnosis is fraught with difficulty."[20]

Just how fraught the task of diagnosing might be becomes plain upon reading the required symptom list for ADD. The diagnostic criteria for children, according to *DSM-IV*, include six or more months' worth of some fourteen activities: fidgeting, squirming, distraction by extraneous stimuli, difficulty waiting turns, blurting out answers, losing things, interrupting, ignoring adults, and so on.[21] All are behaviors that anyone with hands-on experience of children, especially young children, will recognize as ubiquitous. As physician Lawrence Diller has similarly put it, "What often strikes one encountering DSM criteria for the first time is how common these symptoms are among children generally."[22]

Even apart from the question of how closely the ADD symptomatic list overlaps with normal childhood behavior, there is a separate problem that also pushes outward the number of children diagnosed: the troubling question of observer bias. What exactly is "hyperactivity" in the first place? No doubt some extremely active children pass the "know-it-when-I-see-it" test; I personally spent years around one such textbook child, and many readers can probably think of a similar example from their own lives.[23] Even so, there is no getting around the problem that any judgment of "hyperactivity" lies in the eye of the beholder. All kinds of things about that observer—age, intrinsic patience, and, above all, experience with real children—might affect his perception of whether a child is "too active."[24] At a time when many parents and children spend a lot of time apart and in nonintersecting worlds, it seems safe to say that the adult observer bias problem may well be magnified accordingly. Any three-year-old on a playground will seem "hyperactive" if what the attending adult wants to do there is, say, read a book or take a nap. Similarly, adults only itinerantly involved with children might consider any two-year-old wildly energetic— and they would be right. But where exactly does that exceedingly non-adultlike physical behavior cross the line into pathology?

To say that an ADD/ADHD diagnosis may be fraught with ambiguity is not to deny the sad reality of children who suffer genuine mental abnormality. Nor does it minimize the stress experienced by others in those children's families. The literature on ADD includes many stories of children who sleep remarkably little, who truly cannot sit still, who remain in perpetual motion; and it similarly abounds with testimonies by parents who speak eloquently and sadly to the point that such a child can impose unique burdens on family life. There is no discounting the passionately felt expressions of that reality, any more than one can discount the faith of many doctors in the independent, a priori existence of ADD/ADHD and related disorders.

Even so, to keep our eyes on the brain-and-behavior problem at large is to recognize immediately that such hard and obvious cases alone cannot explain the millions of children diagnosed as having ADD/ADHD today. What can explain it is that current criteria for the disorder are now casting as pathological a great many other children who have what could be called the now-you-see-it, now-you-don't variety.

The key features of the ADD diagnosis—intrinsic elasticity and profound subjectivity—are also constants of other childhood and adolescent mental disorders. Here, too, what was once judged normal (if bad) is now thought abnormal and diseased. Consider the example of "conduct disorder," only recently added to the psychiatric lexicon and defined as "behavior that shows a persistent disregard for the norms and rules of society." According to the American Psychiatric Association, this is "one of the most frequently seen disorders in adolescents," affecting up to 16 percent of boys and 9 percent of girls under eighteen. Some of the diagnostic criteria for "conduct disorder" are refreshingly straightforward. Whatever else might be said about them, there is not much ambiguity about setting fires, breaking into homes, stealing, and forcing sex on others. Even so, and as with ADD/ADHD, not all of what makes one eligible for a "conduct disorder" diagnosis is anywhere near as behaviorally clear-cut. "Often starting fights," for example, would seem to depend in part on who is doing the reporting—a policeman or an irritated stepfather. "Skipping school" is another criterion now judged pathological by *DSM-IV* that might raise an eyebrow, at least by the less-than-perfectly-rule-abiding among us.

en-I-see-it ones—but, rather, on the wide swath of other, more
ones. And what he observes is both obvious and important:
deal of what was yesterday judged normal behavior is now
ed and stigmatized in unprecedented degree. In sum, he won-
y colleagues and I were in school now, would we be considered
"

s a way of turning that subjective point on its head that almost
ars in the professional literature, though it should. It is the obser-
t yesterday's children—which is to say today's adults—enjoyed
of being considered "normal" in ways that today's children in-
do not. In a famous essay published in 1993, Daniel Patrick
coined the phrase "defining deviancy down" to explain how be-
ce seen as bad or pathological had come to be redefined as normal
cial pressures he outlined in detail.[30] In the case of the juvenile
oblem explosion, as a review of the diagnostic criteria makes clear,
pposite is going on: We are defining deviancy *up* so that children
d have been considered normal a quarter century ago are now
have intrinsic "brain problems" and are treated accordingly.
ere is where the *DSM-IV* revisions join a long list of other inno-
at have been influenced by our ongoing social experiment in
t and child-family separation. The new diagnostic criteria do in-
ct something real, albeit inadvertently, about the differences be-
previous generations of experts, parents, and children and the
hich we now find ourselves. What the innovations of *DSM-IV*
is a medical restatement of what is acceptable juvenile behavior,
*innovation erring in the direction of less tolerance on the part of
more*. In that sense they faithfully reflect one psychological fact
me-alone world: Adults who are not often around children and
ts find their behavior more problematic and in need of alteration.

NG DISABLED OR PARENT DISABLED?

fact feeding the mental disorder numbers is quite different from
he new diagnostic latitude, though it, too, reflects the reality of

Consider also the related and recently named "oppositional defiance disorder," or (as the unfortunate acronym has it) ODD, where the same elasticity also prevails. Characterized by "a pattern of disobedient, hostile, and defiant behavior towards authority figures," in the words of a National Institutes of Health fact sheet, it is thought to afflict as much as 20 percent of the child population.[25] In the case of ODD, too, what is now thought evidence of disease overlaps uncomfortably with what people with actual experience of children and teenagers might regard as "normal" (if intensely annoying and questionable) juvenile behavior, such as "arguing with adults," "spiteful or vindictive behavior," and being "touchy or easily annoyed." As the criteria for both ODD and conduct disorder further make clear, there can be no doubt that much of what used to be called "juvenile delinquency" or simply "bad behavior" is considered under the revisions of *DSM-IV* to be evidence of mental illness.

There is also the cluster of disorders known as anxieties, where the line between normal and abnormal child behavior appears to be similarly hard to draw. Most common among these, according to the professional literature, is something called "separation anxiety disorder," or (another unfortunate acronym) SAD. Defined as "developmentally inappropriate and excessive anxiety concerning separation from home or from those to whom the individual is attached," this syndrome is believed to affect about 10 percent of the nation's children.[26] Like conduct disorder, one of its symptoms is "refusal to attend classes or difficulty remaining in school for an entire day"—in other words, what used to be called truancy.

As for OCD, or obsessive-compulsive disorder, the National Institute of Mental Health's screening test is strikingly broad when applied to adults: "Have you worried a lot about terrible things happening" such as fires, burglary, losing something valuable, harm coming to a loved one? "Have you felt driven to repeat certain acts all over again"—checking the iron, collecting useless objects, rereading or rewriting unnecessarily, constantly seeking reassurances that what you have done is right? But to apply the more particular criteria to children is virtually to guarantee an explosion of diagnoses. Again, this is not to say that the "hard cases" of what OCD describes do not exist; they do, which is why this particular disorder, unlike some others, has counterparts across cultures and times (the French, for example, call it "the doubting disease"). But to read current American criteria is inevitably to wonder: What child does *not* have bouts of choosing lucky and unlucky colors, having nightmares or nightmarish thoughts, engaging in "meaningless" repetitive activities with toys, dinosaurs, or stamp collections?

As with ADD, ADHD, ODD, and OCD, the diagnostic criteria for bipolar disorder, or what used to be called manic depression, have similarly been redesigned. Here, too, the criteria now bear a close resemblance to a list of the more troublesome aspects of children themselves. Bipolar babies, the Juvenile Bipolar Research Foundation reports, may be hard to settle down, overly responsive to sensory stimulation, and suffer from "separation anxiety." As children they may be "hyperactive, inattentive, fidgety, easily frustrated," and prone to tantrums and nightmares. Some may be bossy, others silly; some have "social phobia," while others are "charismatic and risk-taking." Getting up in the morning is hard for these children; their energy seems to increase as the day goes on. As before, the suffering of the children and families who are dealt the inexplicable hand of real mental disorder is not to be minimized. Also as before, however, there is a great deal more to the story of OCD's apparent ascendancy. Merely to read the symptom list is to wonder what child might not qualify for a diagnosis at one time or another.

Then there is the conundrum known as autism. Not so long ago this would have been the preeminent "know-it-when-I-see-it" disorder for its classic and long-identified tragic symptoms: isolation, lack of eye contact, inability to play with others, and the rest. They are terribly and obviously distinct. Today, however, these symptoms are seen as just one extreme of what is called more broadly PDD (pervasive developmental disorders)—an umbrella term for several disorders and syndromes including autistic disorder, Asperger's, and more. At the other end of the spectrum lie a number of behaviors that some people (including many writers and academics, for instance) might find uncomfortably close to home: "lack of desire to interact with peers," "clumsiness," "formality," exhibiting a "pedantic" manner, and more.

It is little wonder, given the scope of symptoms so generalized, that

autism, too, has apparently galloped at a[s] child population. In the course of the 1[9] example of the many statistics one can [be docu]mented by California's developmental se[rvices] percent.[27] Federal education officials repo[rt] cial education" children in 1992–93, onl[y] tic, and ten years later that number had [United States alone in the autism epide[mic] 15,500 children in central England likew[ise] the rates of autism and PDD among its [had suggested.[28] Like American research[ers] whether this rise is actually or diagnosticall[y] report, "Whether the higher prevalence rat[es] a secular increase in the incidence of th[e] broadening of the concept of PDD toge[ther] and recognition cannot be assessed from th[

In a literary reflection on the new dia[gnosis] Harvard Medical School authority and [Groopman offered some interesting insight[s are being diagnosed and medicated ever[y younger ages." In reflecting on this trend w[ith dinner, one of whose sons had recently bee[n likely candidate for behavior disorder, Groo[pman teresting: "This anecdote provoked a star[around the table: Most of us, it turned out, [son." The "symptoms" that had triggered [Groopman and his colleagues recognized, we[re iors that make scientists in particular excel: p[time than one is "supposed" to on a task, a[nd and rechecking work that ought to be finishe[d

Unlike some critics, Groopman does not [OCD and assorted other disorders have so[me dent of social forces. But his point, like tha[t not on the hard and obvious cases of juve[nile

know-it-w[
ambiguou[
that a gre[
pathologi[
ders: "If [
abnormal[

There [
never app[
vation th[
the luxur[
creasingly[
Moyniha[n
haviors o[
due to s[
mental p[
just the o[
who wo[
judged t[

And [
vations t[
child-ad[
deed ref[
tween th[
one in w[
amount [
with eve[
adults, [
of the h[
adolesce[

LEARN[

Another[
that of [

absent adults in many children's lives. This is what might be called the "unintended incentive" problem: Some people stand to benefit significantly from a mental or learning-disordered diagnosis, and this incentive has placed upward pressure on the numbers of those tagged with a mental problem label.

This change did not come about nefariously, of course. Over the years the law has increasingly insisted that disabled people of all kinds should be able to enjoy a level playing field with those of normal abilities, and therefore the millions of newly diagnosed mentally ill have become actually and potentially eligible for hitherto unavailable benefits.

The growing list of special accommodations is especially dramatic in the case of education. Most crucial is the landmark 1990 Individuals with Disabilities Education Act (IDEA), which "mandates that eligible children receive access to special education and/or related services, and that this education be designed to meet each child's unique educational needs" through an individualized education program (or IEP). As a result, children deemed to be mentally afflicted or handicapped are now entitled by law to a long list of services, including separate special education classrooms, learning specialists, special equipment, tailored homework assignments, and more. The IDEA has also proved beneficial in another way: Public school districts unable to accommodate such children may be forced to pick up the tab for private schools.

Of all the benefits that a diagnosis of mental deficiency can secure, however, probably none is as sought after or significant as the extra time requirement on standardized tests. The reason is obvious: Extra time can translate into extra grade points. In the course of the 1990s, not surprisingly, learning and mentally disabled requests proliferated for extra time on the SATs, LSATs, MCATs, and other gatekeeping tests, and the exam rules were adjusted to accommodate these requests.[31]

So attractive have such benefits now become that some parents and students actively seek an adverse diagnosis in order to secure them. This is not to say, however, that such accommodations are *always* abused. The testimony of parents who are grateful to have a professional put a name to their child's problems and to have the schools making special arrangements for their academically troubled children is palpable in the mental problem literature.[32] Even so, human nature and parental competitiveness perhaps being what they are, the mere existence of financially and academically attractive benefits have lured many toward a diagnosis that seems ambiguous at best. Thus, though inarguably invented in order to give children with problems an educational break, the extra time benefit has come to be abused.

At least one suggestive measure of how far things have run amok is this: It is the country's most exclusive and competitive schools that register the highest rates of learning disability. "The clue lies in the percentages," as Michael Scott Moore put it in a 2000 essay for *Salon*. "While the nationwide fraction of nonstandard tests [i.e., those taken under a "special accommodation" arrangement] is only 1.9 percent, the number jumps to nearly 10 percent in some New England prep schools and wealthy districts in California."[33] Similarly, Arthur Levine, president of Teachers College at Columbia University, reported in 2000 that 36 percent of the kindergartners at New York's prestigious Dalton School had learning problems, a claim that will ring counterintuitive at best and more likely preposterous to the legions of parents perpetually trying to elbow their way in.[34]

In fact, so obvious has the extra time abuse become in some quarters that in 2000 a group of University of California regents called for an extensive review of such accommodations. They were responding to an article in the *Los Angeles Times* that reported a number of perversely impressive statistics: Claims of learning disability had jumped 50 percent since 1994, and a *Times* computer analysis showed that "students receiving special treatments are concentrated in the wealthiest communities and that students enrolled in private prep schools are two to five times as likely to get extended time."[35]

One might object to this way of describing things—that of course such problems are identified in the better-off schools; after all, it is the students in elite institutions who have financial access to the best and cutting-edge mental health care. Yet this objection, though earnestly intended, is no match for the cynical facts. At elite high schools and colleges around the country, "learning disabled" is broadly understood to be synonymous with "educational scam."

As one high school student summarized particularly well in an op-ed piece criticizing the extra time policies at his own private school, "While some students, especially those with dyslexia, genuinely need extra time due to medical handicaps, the majority of students receiving extra time simply obtained it to help their grades. . . . I have heard students who clearly have no learning disabilities decide to get extra time after receiving a poor grade on a test." He concluded, "Extra time gives an unfair advantage to a select group of students, especially those of higher economic status, who can afford to go to doctors as many times as it takes to be recommended for extra time."[36] Similarly, in a short essay published in 2001 called "Crippling Thoughts: The ADA's Powerful Psychological Hold," Peter Wood, associate provost of Boston University, outlined several problems with what he called the "immense folly" of persuading "healthy people that they are subtly disabled and entitled to various special considerations"; they range from perfectly able and privileged students who have learned to think of themselves as "math cripples" to the anecdotal case of a "fine student" now "traversing the college curriculum with her I-need-extra-time passport in hand."[37]

Just how much of the juvenile mental problem explosion can be attributed to the unintended incentive problem is hard to judge. Its impact is obviously limited to those students and parents who care deeply enough and who can spend freely enough to secure a diagnosis—in other words, a relatively select group. Even so, there is something uniquely emblematic and sad about the scramble by better-off children to join the ranks of the genuinely disabled. True, it diverts attention from the truly deficient and handicapped, and for that reason alone might seem wrong to some people. Yet the trouble with the scramble goes further still. What drives this perverse pursuit in the first place is a time-honored desire by parents to see their children excel, a desire formerly exercised through more traditional means such as poring over homework, reading aloud, volunteering in the classroom, and otherwise extending a helping educational hand. For that reason it is hard not to see the extra time racket—i.e., the diagnoses deliberately sought in order to extract individual concessions from the school system at the expense of other students—as a kind of educational "outsourcing" in itself. All genuine exceptions dutifully and respectfully acknowledged, the abuse of the disabled benefit system is in part the busy parent's answer to what used to be called helping with homework.

BLAMING THE BRAIN

Are today's children and teenagers really mentally worse off than ever, or are external factors just making them appear that way? On the strength of the variety of evidence reviewed, the answer would appear to be *both*. The mental problem numbers are inflated because changes external to children, *and* childhood and teenage unhappiness—or what professionals insist on calling disease and disorder—are on the rise as well.

To ask just how much of the brain-and-behavior problem is real is to run headlong into one final way in which the mental crisis reflects absent-adult reality. That is the profound bias in current psychiatry against what might be called the e-word, *environment*. To immerse oneself in the professional literature on child mental problems is to enter a conceptual one-way street. As John Richters and Dante Cicchetti, two of the few professional challengers to current thinking, put it in an exceptionally clear essay (provocatively titled "Mark Twain Meets *DSM-III-R*: Conduct Disorder, Development, and the Concept of Harmful Dysfunction"), *DSM-IV* now "resists all contextual information about a child's developmental history, capacities, strengths and circumstances, and assumes that the antisocial behavior necessarily stems from an underlying disorder."[38]

The Real Problem, almost all of the established expert literature insists, lies somewhere inside the child himself. The Real Problem can only be his neurochemistry, his biology, his genes, his serotonin, his dopamine, his overall "wiring"—anything but the world he inhabits or the other people who may or may not be keeping him company there.

Thus, most research on ADD, according to a characteristically mechanistic formulation by the support group Children and Adults with

Attention-Deficit/Hyperactivity Disorder (CHADD) and mirrored all over the professional literature, "suggests a neurobiological basis," and "inheritance appears to be an important factor." (The fiercest guardians of ADD orthodoxy go further still, with some insisting that people with the "brain disorder" ADD need medication in the same way that nearsighted people need eyeglasses.) New York Presbyterian Hospital's fact sheet on oppositional defiance disorder is similarly mechanistic. Though mentioning that ODD "may be related to the child's temperament and the family's response to that temperament," it immediately qualifies this nod to environment with three statements that point instead to some sort of mechanical disturbance of the human machine—that "a predisposition to ODD is inherited in some families," that "there may be problems in the brain that cause ODD," and that "it may be caused by a chemical imbalance in the brain."

The Child & Adolescent Bipolar Foundation similarly describes bipolar disorder first as a "neurobiological brain disorder," and though apparently conceding that "the onset of illness can be triggered by trauma," it also tempers that environmental note with the claim that a predisposition to the disorder is often inherited and that it "often appears with no identifiable cause." And so echoes the literature on OCD, with the Obsessive Compulsive Disorder Foundation noting that "research suggests that genes do play a role in the development of the disorder in some cases" and that OCD "tends to run in families."[39] Authoritative sources agree: The child with problems, and more specifically the mechanical inner workings of the child with problems, *is* the problem itself.

Such antienvironmental bias is even more vehement in the literature about autism, where the frantic search for causality is especially blindered.[40] To established thinkers, such as those in the Autism Society of America, autism is "the result of a neurological disorder that affects the functioning of the brain." The Center for the Study of Autism simply dismisses environmental influences outright: "Children with autism are born with their special needs. Parts in their brains work a little bit differently than other people's brains and because of this, we see these behaviors." The American Academy of Pediatrics advises likewise: "Although the cause of autism is unknown in most instances, the theory favored by many experts is that it is a genetically based disorder that occurs before birth."[41] Even critics of established thinking about autism are similarly searching for mechanistic "solutions" to the causal conundrum. They, too, believe that the ultimate answer will be found in things rather than in people— vaccines, mercury, other environmental poisons, and the rest. Thus does the antienvironmental bias of modern psychiatry exhibit profound and intricately entwined roots.

Plainly, this antienvironmental bias exists for deep reasons and serves deep purposes. One is that the widespread discrediting of Sigmund Freud has left a cloud hanging over any remaining branches of modern psychology that dare ask questions about any given child's environment. Another, very different important purpose served by today's antienvironmentalism is surely the human need of professionals themselves. Who wants to tell the single mother of a miserable and undisciplined boy that maybe, just maybe, his problem is the father he never sees? Surely a prescription and review of the criteria for ODD look more like progress—perhaps even to the boy himself and his mother and his teachers.

And even if counselors or therapists were willing to go so far as to identify familial rather than chemical imbalances as the basis of a given child's pain, what would they then be able to do to help? It is not as if experts can produce a mother instead of a Nintendo cube or a loving extended family instead of a pill. Moreover, child therapists in particular have a deep interest in not alienating the parents of their patients—as many surely would if they drew attention to some of the nonneurological facts of their small clients' lives. From the point of view of what dedicated professionals would like to accomplish, therefore, the wonder is not that labels and drugs have almost completely obliterated attention to environmental phenomena, but that the mechanistic turn was not taken earlier.

This current professional agnosticism about environment has its costs, however. It is not that today's research into brain events is one big detour; as the latest neurobiological studies confirm, brain events and outside influences are intimately connected. Brain changes might well show up not because of inborn defects, but because the organism has been shaped or misshaped by adverse environmental events. As Leon Kass has put it in a summary of current research, "The plasticity of the nervous system, and its sensitivity to all sorts of physical and psychological influences, means that, for example, environmentally induced stress and angst and frustration can write themselves into genuine physical changes in the brain."[42] That very dynamic, however, points up the severe limitations of today's brain-only emphasis. Even as research continues, Holy Grail–like, for something, *anything* that might qualify as a biological, chemical, neurological, or other hardwired marker of the various disorders, the question of environment, banished though it might be from the front door of modern psychiatry, creeps in through the back door routinely in the case studies—ever present and ever problematic.

It is striking, for example, how often the words *day care* are mentioned nonchalantly in connection with autism. Of course it would be presumptuous, not to say simpleminded, to assert that day care *causes* autism. It is nevertheless remarkable to see how this one radical change in the traditional infant/child environment—institutional out-of-home care—is taken for granted in the literature. Typical is a recent quote in the *New York Times* about a doctor who treats autistic spectrum disorder children: "He now sees children as young as 12 months, gets referrals from day-care centers and has a two-year waiting list." The unstated assumption seems to be that all babies and toddlers should be able to endure the long hours and psychological stresses of out-of-home institutional care and that those who can't hack it are thereby "proving" they have a brain disorder.

And here is where the official professional agnosticism about environment runs the risk of real unintended harm. Any number of facts about infants and toddlers and autistic spectrum disorder do point to environmental influences. First, among curious features of autistic spectrum disorder is an unexplained history of digestive and allergic disorders. Second, such digestive and allergic disorders, however mysterious their ultimate cause, have been shown by scores of studies to be lower in breast-fed children than in bottle-fed ones. Third, an intriguing Japanese study comparing infants who were breast-fed for short periods of time to infants breast-fed longer showed that the longer the nursing, the less likely the infants were diagnosed as autistic.[43] This suggests even stronger grounds for a causal link between autism and breast-feeding, with the latter apparently offering protection against the former. Fourth, under at least one dominant contemporary theory of causality, autism may be triggered in infancy or early childhood by exposure to viruses—another risk that human milk tends to *lower* but that is *raised* by hours in institutional care.

There is therefore ample evidence from disparate sources to suggest that at least one environmental practice—breast-feeding—is protective in some measure against at least some of the symptoms and/or suspected causes of autism.[44] Nevertheless, one can read the current literature on autistic spectrum disorder for many hours without finding any mention of this potentially prophylactic effect. The reason is crystal clear and undeniably ideological: Full-time breast-feeding, the kind associated with the aforementioned benefits, requires mother and baby to be in proximity to each other pretty much around the clock. In other words, what is required to get the medical benefits of breast-feeding is inimical to the common practice of day care specifically and to the even more widespread practice of mother-baby separation more generally. It would appear to be a case in which the professional, antienvironmental, pro-adult, pro-day-care biases of current psychiatry trump medical knowledge of a different sort—knowledge that might actually help the children now being diagnosed with autistic spectrum disorder.

And what if the connection between autism and institutional care is even stronger than that? What if some babies and toddlers just aren't cut out for spending most of their tiny lives in a room filled with unrelated children and unrelated adults, any more than other children can get straight A's in the hardest schools and still others qualify for the Olympic team? What if what we should be doing, instead of chasing down every genetic avenue in sight, is developing tests to identify such particularly vulnerable children early and to keep them from suffering more? Again, these are the kinds of questions that a psychiatric or medical establishment biased against environmental causes necessarily avoids.

Environment also rumbles right below the surface of the now widely diagnosed bipolar disorder. Recent research on the question of nature, nurture, and the "bipolar brain" suggests what some researchers have called a "surprisingly discordant finding." This quote is from a 2002 book called *The Bipolar Child* by F. Demitri and M. D. Papolos, and it refers to landmark genetic research among the Amish for origins of bipolar disorder in adults.[45] What researchers hunting for biological explanations found to their surprise was something quite different. The authors report that few Amish children "who go on to develop bipolar disorder are reported to have the same early co-morbid conditions [as other children being diagnosed]. For example, separation anxiety, symptoms of attention-deficit disorder with hyperactivity, and oppositional defiant behaviors are uncommon."

In other words, while some Amish adults do go on to exhibit some recognizable form of bipolar disorder, strongly suggesting that the syndrome found in adults does have a biological component or origin, Amish children *do not* exhibit the symptoms of bipolarity. That is to say, bipolarity in children, a disorder marked by nightmares, separation anxiety, and the rest, hardly even exists in certain environments. And that strongly suggests there is nothing biologically determined about it.

The authors also spell out exactly what they see as the environment that apparently spares Amish children this fate, which is worth emphasizing because of its uncharacteristic reference to wider family trends in the usually agnostic therapeutic literature: "The regularity and simplicity of the Amish lifestyle," the authors speculate, "characterized by consistent social values, a philosophy of nonviolence, strong family and community kinship stakes . . . *may modify many behaviors that could reach their extreme pitch in families that do not have such defined social and religious values and cannot provide such consistent boundaries* [emphasis added]."

HOW SICK IS SAD?

Such environmentally sensitive acknowledgments are relatively rare because to allow any link between behavior and environment is to admit something antithetical to the brain disease model. All those symptomatic children and adolescents might not be just neurological pinballs in some randomly selected universe of psychological suffering; they might actually have authentic *reasons* for doing what they do. In other words, they might be responding rationally to arrangements that look irrational, wrong, or stressful from their point of view.

It is a tantalizing, if obviously transgressive, line of thought. What if at least some of what is being diagnosed in the child and adolescent population is not mental defect, neurochemical short circuits, and the rest, but, rather, the normal reactions of youngsters to the arguably inhuman rhythms of their days? What if some ODD children have good reason to be sensitive, angry, or disputatious—because their parents are divorced or never married in the first place, say, or because they never see their fathers and their mothers are away working all day? What if the typical American child's day, in which he is underexercised, overstimulated by electronics, and overinstitutionalized with peers, partly contributes to the symptoms of what is called ADD? To turn the diagnostic tables, what if the preschooler exhibiting separation anxiety disorder—which the reader might recall is now said by professionals to be the most common childhood anxiety—is in fact behaving more normally than her no-problem mother, from whom she is parted for most of the day? *What if, in sum, some significant degree of the surliness and disaffection now being medicalized is a legitimate emotional response to the disappearance from children's lives of protecting related adults?*

These are not merely rhetorical questions. How they are answered draws the line between sad and sick, normal and diseased. But a world in which absentee adults must be accommodated as a fact of life—the world in which psychology and psychiatry are subsets—is unlikely to ask those questions in a spirit of genuine free inquiry.

As final proof of the current bias toward absent adults in the helping professions, consider also that the behavior-only diagnostic criteria according to which children are now judged "diseased" mark a one-way psychological street. There is no mental disorder listed in the *DSM* called, say, preoccupied parent disorder, to pathologize a mother or father too distracted to read *Winnie the Pooh* for the fourth time or to stay up on Saturday night waiting for a teenager to come home from the movies. Nor will one find divorced second-family father disorder, even though the latter might explain what we could call the "developmentally inappropriate" behaviors of certain fathers, such as failure to pay child support or to show up for certain important events. There is also nothing in *DSM-IV* like separation *non*-anxiety disorder to pathologize parents who can separate for long stretches from their children without a pang.

What the range of available evidence confirms is that both possibilities with which we began are true. There is simultaneously a real redefinition of what it is to be a normal child and a real concomitant outbreak of mental suffering among children and adolescents. Physician Lawrence Diller, author of the countercultural *Running on Ritalin*, puts the second of these points simply in his book: "Something is seriously out of balance in the lives of many families, and the impact on certain kinds of children is profound."

Of course some children have terrible mental problems. Some, by medical consensus, are tragically born that way. Others are created by awful circumstance—as has been recently confirmed by Romanian and other orphans adopted from a crippling system of deprivation, whose long-term behavioral problems are now only beginning to appear. If the example of those orphans proves anything, it is that extreme deprivation produces extreme psychological and behavioral damage. And if that widely accepted notion is true, then why isn't the more politically incorrect thesis also true—that deprivation and damage exist along a continuum rather than in a remote corner unconnected to the rest of us and that at least some of what is showing up in the mental health numbers is exactly the fallout of the *relative* parental and familial deprivation experienced by many of today's kids?

To review the evidence is to see that what is driving the mental health problem numbers upward is not the hard cases, the ones always with us. It is instead a dynamic in which adults who are not often around children find their behavior problematic and, simultaneously, children who are not often around parents and other family members feel and behave worse and worse. In short, without the absent adult-problem on today's scale, America's juvenile mental health problem on today's scale would not exist.

5

Wonder Drugs and Double Standards

IF YOU ARE WHITE, COLLEGE EDUCATED, AND FORTUNATE enough to have your children in a good public or private school, then you probably will already have formed an opinion about kids and drugs such as Ritalin. The reason is that if you happen to be all those things, then you are part of the American demographic in which psychiatric drug-taking among kids has become something like cognitive orthodontics—in other words, routine. Just how routine the drugs have become in some places can be seen in the following anecdote told to me by a friend in 2003.

This friend had a teenage daughter who was struggling in a particularly challenging school, and because she was unhappy about her academic performance, a doctor was consulted. That professional did not believe she had any real disorder but did prescribe a trial run of Concerta (a stimulant closely related to Ritalin) to see if it improved matters. Sure enough, the daughter perked up; she felt better about her schoolwork and did better at it. The experiment seemed to work.

Was this success? Apparently, yes. And yet my friend felt uneasy about it for this reason: One night, after treating his daughter and several of her classmates to dinner out, he realized that all the other kids at the table were taking some kind of psychotropic medicine, too. All had been prescribed similar "enhancements." Despite his own brief and positive experience with such drugs, this outcome quite unexpectedly disturbed him. After all, one case in such a group might make sense, or maybe two, but were so many otherwise socially and financially advantaged students really in need of mind-altering drugs just to get through the day? What, he wondered, did that say about us and about our world?

This chapter is an effort to answer that question, which goes straight to the heart of our unprecedented—and it is indeed unprecedented—national experiment with these drugs.[1] Consider just a few dramatic numbers from a front-page 2003 *Washington Post* story entitled "More Kids Receiving Psychiatric Drugs: Question of 'Why' Still Unanswered."[2] It relayed the conclusions of a groundbreaking study published in the January 2003 *Archives of Pediatrics and Adolescent Medicine*.[3] Based on a research sample of 900,000 children from around the country, that study verified what some observers had been claiming for years: that American children and teenagers are imbibing behavior-modifying drugs in record numbers and at a dramatically increased rate. The *Post*'s summary of the findings stated: "The number of American children being treated with psychiatric drugs has grown sharply in the past 15 years, tripling from 1987 to 1996 and showing no sign of slowing. . . . A newly published study, the most comprehensive to date, found that by 1996, more than 6 percent of children were taking drugs such as Prozac, Ritalin and Risperdal, and the researchers said the trajectory continued to rise through 2000."[4]

And that is only the beginning of statistics about kids and wonder drugs. Did you know, for example, that prescription drug use is growing faster among children than among the elderly and baby boomers?[5] That Ritalin production increased more than 700 percent between 1990 and 2000?[6] That prescriptions for selective serotonin reuptake inhibitors (SSRIs) among children under five increased tenfold between 1993 and 1997?[7] That as of 1996, according to Mark Olfson of Columbia University's College of Physicians and Surgeons, fully 1 percent of children under eighteen were using an antidepressant—more than 700,000, to extrapolate from the latest census figures?[8] This list is nowhere near exhaustive, of course, nor does it capture the fact that where one such drug is prescribed, others often follow. In that sense, the statistics on prescriptions alone, stunning though they may appear, actually understate the multifaceted reality of medication for many youthful clients.[9]

To enthusiasts that rise in prescriptions is a cause for celebration; it is proof that "children who suffer from a crippling mental disorder are now getting the medication they need," as medication advocate and science writer Michael Fumento has put it.[10] Many other observers, professional and lay alike, appear to agree. Much of established medical opinion— including the American Academy of Pediatrics, among other distinguished organizations—professes similar faith in the efficacy of today's wonder drugs. As advocates see it, ADD/ADHD, like most of the other mental disorders reviewed in the last chapter, are a priori neurological defects whose origins will someday be discerned by science, and the best treatment for such defects is mind- and behavior-altering medication. As science writer Malcolm Gladwell has enthused in the pages of *The New Yorker*, "We are now extending to the young cognitive aids of a kind that used to be reserved exclusively for the old."[11]

Can all those experts, parents, and other advocates really be wrong? The answer depends on what you think the risks of these drugs are when weighed against the benefits. The argument of this chapter is an unorthodox if eminently defensible one: that those risks are high—higher than most people seem prepared to admit—and that such drugs, administered on today's unprecedented scale, are creating more problems for children and society than they are solving.[12] A good deal of new evidence, much of which emerged in the last two years alone, bears out the thesis of this chapter: that today's rate of juvenile psychotropic drug-taking is incurring serious social, psychological, and moral costs, and the toll goes widely unacknowledged by a world increasingly invested in the drugs.

The real question before us, given this evidence about the multiple damages of today's high rates of prescription writing, is why wonder drugs for children continue to enjoy a medical and moral dispensation that is unique among other widely prescribed pharmaceutical substances. That is the "double standard" of this chapter's title. What purpose do these drugs serve so that a host of problems that would make other drugs off limits are instead routinely rationalized, minimized, or simply denied? What is the Prime Mover still pushing the psychotropic universe outward?

These questions will be addressed in the conclusion. But first there follows a detailed summary of four separate and distinct problems with

wonder drugs that would not exist if psychotropic prescription writing
for children and teenagers had not become routine.

SIDE EFFECTS: THE PROBLEM THAT WON'T GO AWAY

One problem is a familiar one: side effects. Although medical professionals
make a point of emphasizing how relatively safe and much studied these
medications are (research psychologist and stimulant advocate Dr. Russell
Barkley, for example, has called Ritalin "safer than aspirin"), every one of
the wonder drugs carries physical and other risks, as both the manufactur-
ers' literature and the widely used *Physicians' Desk Reference* acknowledge.
To observe as much is not to indulge in alarmism, of course, but it bears re-
peating that certain *known* risks of the drugs remain constant, underem-
phasized though they have come to be.

Events of the last several years, however, have called attention to a far
more troubling question: whether the lesser-known risks of numerous
drugs are worse than was previously thought, at least for children and
teenagers. One prominent example is the debate now raging in medical and
other circles over whether SSRIs or antidepressants might be further endan-
gering the juveniles they are supposed to help. On October 27, 2003, following years of adverse reports, the Food and Drug Administration (FDA)
issued a public health advisory on eight popular antidepressants, warning
doctors to take extra care in prescribing them for children. One of these
drugs, Paxil, has been associated by British researchers with a heightened
risk for suicide (and British doctors have been ordered not to prescribe it for
that reason). Another, Wyeth Pharmaceutical's Effexor XR, was reported by
the company itself to be associated with an increased incidence of "hostility
and suicide-related adverse events, such as suicidal ideation and self-harm."[13]
Perhaps the most remarkable fact about this advisory is that it illuminated
what many people may not know: Only one of these drugs—Prozac—had
been approved for use by adolescents and children in the United States in
the first place; the others are commonly distributed without it.

This practice, known as "off-label" prescribing, is increasingly common among American doctors and patients for drugs of all kinds. In

essence, the patient (or guardian) agrees to the prescription of a drug not thoroughly tested according to FDA rules by personally assuming liability for anything that might go wrong. In the specific case of antidepressants, however, the eagerness to assume liability is especially pronounced. In contemporary veterinary literature, to offer a counterexample where the question of psychotropic drugs for pets is also debated, conventional opinion frowns on the practice; after all, some vets emphasize, these drugs have not been adequately tested yet. Thus one way of underlining our apparent national eagerness for *pediatric* wonder drugs is this contrast: Many doctors are comfortable with prescribing substances for children that their own vets would not give to the family dog.

A second recent phenomenon raising questions about wonder drug side effects is the record of rampaging teenage murderers since the end of the 1990s. As was reported by many news sources in the wake of those killings, many or perhaps even most of our recent adolescent mass murderers were taking psychotropic drugs when they committed their crimes. (The qualifier "perhaps" is necessary only because some juvenile medical records remain sealed under law, meaning that even more shooters than those listed may have been taking prescription drugs without those facts having become public.)

At first glance this conjunction between the drugs and the violence might seem insignificant. After all, it is troubled kids who presumably are most likely to elicit psychiatric attention in the first place; thus, one would expect them to be overrepresented in any group of juveniles taking psychotropic medication—including whatever behavioral pool teenage mass murderers are drawn from. So a skeptic might reasonably object. But the facts could make even the most determined skeptic uneasy. Springfield, Oregon, killer Kip Kinkel, for example, who shot his parents to death and killed four and wounded three at his high school in May 1998, had been on Ritalin as a child and was taking Prozac at the time of the killings. In 1999 two other teenage shooters—T. J. Solomon, who wounded six in Conyers, Georgia, and Shawn Cooper, who wounded one in Notus, Idaho—were reported to be taking prescription drugs (in Solomon's case, Ritalin; in Cooper's, unspecified). Also in 1999 came the murders at

Columbine High School. Eric Harris, alleged mastermind of the killer duo, had Luvox in his bloodstream at the time of the attack. In 2000, the record continues, a girl named Elizabeth Bush wounded one in a school shooting in Williamsport, Pennsylvania; she was taking Prozac. And in 2001, Jason Hoffman of El Cajon, California, was reportedly taking two antidepressants, Effexor and Celexa, when he opened fire and wounded five at his high school.

The skeptical reader might respond: So what? Perhaps all the record really reflects is how widely prescribed psychiatric medicines have become among minors. After all, what if all the shooters had been taking other widely prescribed substances—antibiotics, acne medicine, muscle relaxants, drugs to control cholesterol or blood pressure? Surely no causal inference about the violence would be drawn from them.

But here our skeptical reader faces an obstacle that does not exist in the case of other widely prescribed substances. Every one of the psychotropic drugs ingested by those teenage shooters is said by its manufacturer to carry at least some risk of exactly what those teenagers exhibited: psychotic behavior. Adderall's manufacturer, for example, acknowledges that psychotic reactions are one rare side effect of the drug. As for Ritalin, the *Physicians' Desk Reference* says, "Toxic psychosis has been reported." Luvox's manufacturer says that manic reaction and psychotic reaction are frequent adverse effects. Effexor, as noted earlier, has been linked by its manufacturer to increased suicide in children, and its side effects include "severe changes in mood or mental state" and "seizures in those predisposed to them."

To acknowledge this shadow on the wonder drug record is not necessarily to argue that medication *caused* the teenage shooting violence. It is rather to make the point that the record of these incidents alone would seem to weigh against the promiscuous prescribing of such substances, at least until the causal question has been settled to everyone's satisfaction. Yet the report of teenage shooters taking psychotropic medication has not produced any such cautionary effect on wonder drug prescription writing.

Equally important is this related point about risks: Although both drug company representatives and medical professionals dismiss the occasional casualties as exceedingly rare, that particular numbers game only illustrates how sacrosanct these substances have become. Even when the physical risks of using psychotropic drugs are not as dramatic as a psychotic episode, suicide ideation, or a stroke, other problems are visited on at least some children so medicated—problems that are surely not as negligible from the child's point of view as from the adult's.

One needn't go so far as to spray a school with bullets to be considered as having an adverse reaction to the drugs. One side effect of Risperdal, for example, is dizziness upon standing up or sitting down quickly. Anyone aware of the frequency and speed of children's physical movements can only imagine how unnerving and constant this side effect can be. Similarly, methylphenidate and other stimulants have numerous well-documented physical consequences that adults discuss in dry clinical terms: weight loss, dizziness, insomnia, higher risk for tics. (It is precisely because of such side effects, in fact, that many physicians recommend drug holidays, meaning periods when the child is temporarily off the substance in order to be temporarily spared its unpleasant consequences.) Paxil, to take an example from the field of SSRIs, has as common side effects a long list of discomforts including diarrhea, fatigue, and dizziness. There is also the related fact that taking a child off a psychotropic drug typically creates a whole new set of side effects in the form of withdrawal—in Paxil's case, as the manufacturer describes on its Web page, "dizziness, sensory disturbances (including electric shock sensations), abnormal dreams, agitation, anxiety, nausea and sweating."

To repeat, those families and children who experience the drugs as actual lifesavers—what might again be called the "know-it-when-I-see-it" cases—will naturally regard such side effects as risks worth taking. But what about the other cases in which psychotropics are prescribed, those for whom the wonder drugs serve the more nuanced purpose of child "enhancement"? Do the benefits really outweigh the risks for all those children and teenagers, too? Isn't there something a little callous in the willingness of adults to discount the uneasiness, discomfort, and other adverse physical effects that the drugs produce in some significant fraction of their subjects? Similarly, many children also consider the experience intensely embarrassing, which many adults are challenged to understand.

A question mark about adult empathy also hangs over another subset of the psychotropic drug debate: the question of whether ADD/ADHD is overdiagnosed, which is to say misdiagnosed. There is very little controversy about the diagnostic point; just about every expert commentator, including some of the drugs' most prominent supporters, believes that prescription writing has gone further than it should in certain populations. Wade Horn, a former executive director of the vociferous advocacy group called CHADD, has been quoted in *Teacher* magazine saying that he believes Ritalin is drastically overprescribed.[14] Psychiatrist Sally Satel, author of *PC, M.D.: How Political Correctness Is Corrupting Medicine*, believes like many other medical observers that ADD/ADHD is *under*diagnosed in certain communities (which usually means, black and minority), but Satel, too, has asserted her belief that the disorder is overdiagnosed in other places.[15] Dr. Mark Stein, director of the Hyperactivity, Attention, and Learning Problems Clinic at the University of Chicago, who also believes in the utility of the drugs for certain children, told *Teacher* magazine in 1996 that "it's so overdiagnosed that I see normal 3- and 4-year-olds diagnosed with it."[16]

It is in this very consensus about misdiagnosis that the double standard for wonder drugs again makes itself felt. Though many professionals are remarkably, indeed singularly, matter-of-fact about erring on the side of assigning a label and a prescription even when in doubt, this common practice is not without risk (as we have seen) or without discomfort and perhaps even some suffering on the part of at least some children, however low-level or tolerable the presiding adults might judge that downside to be. Yet if ADD/ADHD is indeed being overdiagnosed, as numerous authorities agree, and if Ritalin, Adderall, and the rest are thereby wrongly prescribed, then some untold number of children are taking mind- and behavior-altering drugs who should not be. Why isn't *that* risk-taking more of an issue? The double standard becomes even clearer when one considers that the overprescribing of another drug, antibiotics, has resulted in changes in daily medical practices, with doctors and pediatricians much more reluctant now to dispense them routinely. Again, why is psychotropic medication different?

One answer is that parents who rely on the substances would rather have too many drugs in circulation than run the risk of having access to too few. As CHADD's spokesman put it in a revealing public letter of complaint to Montel Williams, host of a television show that featured parents testifying about adverse side effects: "No one will dispute that unnecessarily placing a child on medication is deplorable. But *the greater travesty* is delaying proper diagnosis and effective treatment for those who truly need it [emphasis added]."[17] There is no mistaking the parental anguish voiced here, but neither is there any mistaking what it has helped to cause: The phenomenon of widespread prescribing, which has greatly reduced the risks of any wonder drug shortage for the families who rely on them, has also simultaneously *raised* the risks of damage to other children who do not need the drug and who have been swept up in the phenomenon of better medicate than not.

To summarize the argument so far, the past few years have provided several new reasons to wonder whether the adverse effects of psychotropic medicine are worse than previously thought. Obviously—and this is a point to which we will return—the risks and discomforts of wonder drugs are measured by less rigid and lower standards than are other substances commonly prescribed for children.

STOCKPILING AND SNORTING: RITALIN ABUSE

A second problem with the wonder drugs that has also grown over time and that also would not exist apart from psychiatric medicating on today's scale concerns the subset of psychotropics known as stimulants. Like other experiments with stimulants in American history—particularly the promiscuous prescribing of amphetamines to "pep up" housewives of the 1960s and 1970s—today's is riddled with abuse but has a major difference: Most abusers are kids rather than housewives, so they are not on the collective adult radar screen. Acknowledged or not, the fact is that methylphenidate—also known as "rids," "pineapple," "uppers," "vitamin R," "jif," and "Rball" outside doctors' offices—is a recreational drug of choice across the campuses of America.[18]

Again, how could it be otherwise? After all, it was precisely on account of abuse that yesteryear's experiment with uppers (and downers such as Valium and Seconal) came ultimately to be abandoned and discredited. So why should kids be different? Writing about Ritalin abuse a few years back, I emphasized the rather simple point that "methylphenidate looks like an amphetamine, acts like an amphetamine, and is abused like an amphetamine." Yet this kind of fallout from wonder drugs, too, remains a problem about which doctors, parents, and support groups see no evil.

What the adults do not acknowledge is common knowledge on high school and college campuses. One February 2003 report for ABCNews. com, called "Wonder Drugs Misused: Teens Abusing and Selling Ritalin," made several points that many of those kids know already or at least would not be surprised by: that high school students with prescriptions command several dollars for every thirty milligrams of the drug; that most parents have no idea (in kid parlance, they are "clueless") about the fact that Ritalin especially is routinely sold, crushed, and snorted by students and other users seeking a speedlike high; and that, according to the Drug Abuse Warning Network, there has been a sixfold increase in emergency room visits associated with Ritalin abuse over the past decade—271 Ritalin-related visits in 1990 versus 1,478 in 2001.[19]

Then again, who really needs news reports to learn just how casual stimulant snorting has become? Special procedures for locking up the methylphenidate are now observed at virtually every high school, and Ritalin abuse is also singled out and proscribed in any number of prep school and college student handbooks. These two facts alone make one wonder how so many adults manage to stay clueless. There is also a variety of campus literature where the wink-nod of abuse acknowledgment is now commonplace. A particularly thorough essay entitled "The Ritalin Racket" on Student.com (an educational Web resource used by many high school and college students) quotes from students on campuses across the country and sounds many of the same themes mentioned earlier, only with better detail: that Ritalin abuse is ubiquitous (It "has become so common . . . that fraternities are stockpiling it with the same vigilance they take to ensure they never run out of beer"); that it is emphatically less benign when used in quantity than most adults understand (the "students interviewed for this article almost unanimously said they considered Ritalin highly addictive"); and that students, unlike their doctors, teachers, or parents, understand that abuse can be a serious problem (though "it's significantly less potent than its street forms, Crank and crystal, students say Ritalin has turned many a college geek into a drug freak").[20]

Other proof of the chop-and-snort problem has been issued repeatedly over the last ten years by the Drug Enforcement Agency (DEA)—to the ire of many parent advocates, it must be noted. According to congressional testimony in 2000 by Terrance Woodworth, DEA deputy director for diversion control, "A 1998 Indiana University survey of 44,232 students found that nearly 7 percent of high school students surveyed reported using Ritalin illicitly at least once and 2.5 percent reported using it monthly or more often."[21] He added that "anecdotal reports relating to the illicit use of methylphenidate among children continue to be reported to DEA on a daily basis." Other attempts to document abuse offer further anecdotal detail. Richard DeGrandpre's 1999 *Ritalin Nation* reprints scores of individual abuse stories from newspapers and other sources across the country. In his best-selling 1998 *Running on Ritalin*, Lawrence Diller cites several undercover narcotics agents' confirmation that "Ritalin is cheaper and easier to purchase at playgrounds than on the street." He further reports one particularly hazardous fact about Ritalin abuse: that teenagers especially do not consider the drug to be anywhere near as dangerous as heroin or cocaine. On the contrary, "they think that since their younger brother takes it under a doctor's prescription, it must be safe."

Despite this varied evidence, the question of how many pills are ending up in unprescribed noses is almost never addressed by either medical authorities or drug advocates. More interesting, what little acknowledgment the abuse problem does garner is remarkably unfeeling. Michael Fumento, for example, has dismissed one not-so-negligible consequence of Ritalin's ubiquity—the increase in emergency room visits mentioned earlier—with the observation that this "merely shows high percentage growth from a low baseline." Hey, those are live kids he is talking about—fourteen hundred of whom showed up in emergency rooms in 2001 because of a potentially dangerous drug they would not have had access to if prescriptions were harder to come by. Oughtn't that count for something in the cost-benefit anaylsis of psychotropics, "low baseline" or not?

A similarly dismissive reaction came from drug advocates in 2001 when the General Accounting Office (GAO) issued a report that attempted to gauge the prevalence of abuse in the schools. That document stated that 8 percent of 735 principals surveyed across the country could report "having seen instances of theft or abuse of stimulant drugs used to treat attention disorders." From any objective point of view, that report ought to have been cause for concern; after all, if 8 percent of the principals surveyed had actually witnessed the problem, it seems fair to suppose that the numbers underestimate the phenomenon by quite a bit. This was not the way advocates saw the matter, however. In a move that would have excited comment had the substance in question been anything but a wonder drug, CHADD and others actually hailed the report for demonstrating that abuse was not as widespread as feared. Try to imagine the American Lung Association reacting that way to a study about adolescent smoking ("Teen Smoking Rising Less Than Expected: Problem Solved, Say Authorities").

To the extent that abuse is acknowledged in the pro-drug literature, it is invoked to make the point that most child and adolescent users of prescribed stimulants do not go on to become drug addicts. But that man of straw is beside the point.[22] The real question for defenders of the psychotropic status quo is whether the staggering number of minors taking the drug daily is responsible for the widely documented rise in methylphenidate abuse. In an effort to give their own children a cognitive or behavioral leg up, are some well-meaning parents and doctors unwittingly putting other people's children at risk for illicit drug use? That is a question about wonder drugs and wonder drugs alone—to observe the double standard once again—whose existence is nowhere acknowledged by admirers of the psychotropic universe. Would other commonly prescribed substances survive medical scrutiny under conditions like these? If prescription acne medicine were chopped up and snorted for an amphetamine high and teenagers were using it that way, wouldn't it be yanked from drugstore shelves tomorrow whether or not that deprived teenagers of their "self-esteem"?

The ethical bottom line of the abuse phenomenon is this: Many kids who would not go out of their way to buy stimulants from a drug dealer are nevertheless experiencing them illicitly thanks to the promiscuous prescribing of methylphenidate. The well-meaning doctors, parents, and teachers responsible for putting that drug into common circulation have inadvertently jeopardized other children and adolescents. It is small wonder that advocates of stimulant drugs avoid addressing that problem. Nevertheless, the rationalization of abuse is one more example of how the pharmaceutical alleviation of problems for some people is creating another problem for others—including other people's children.

"RITALIN MAN": THE ETHICS QUESTION

If the questions of side effects and abuse potential weren't enough to raise a doubt or two about today's current pediatric prescription rates, there is another way in which psychotropics escape scrutiny: the commercial dimension of the child-drug regimen. One can argue that there is something uniquely vulnerable about the parents and children who find themselves in the market for psychiatric prescriptions. One can further posit that on account of this vulnerability, pharmaceutical companies ought to feel special pressure to avoid at least the appearance of exploiting child unhappiness. One might even assume that if the companies were to exceed ethical boundaries in that way, social outcry would check any such imbalance. Both of these last assumptions, however, would be wrong.

To be fair, the commercial creativity of some companies in purveying psychotropic medication for children is not new. One emblematic example dates to 1975 when Ciba-Geigy, the former maker of Ritalin (whose manufacturer is now Novartis), created a seven-inch Mr. Potato Head look-alike toy called "Ritalin Man" to "help make the medicine go down" (also usable as a pencil holder, according to one toy museum).[23] In 2003 Celltech, a company that makes the stimulant (and Ritalin competitor) Metadate CD, similarly created statues of a cartoon superhero who looks much like Spider-Man—a move that at least resulted in the FDA telling Celltech to cease and desist on the figurine front.[24] (The company, for its part, maintained that the superhero figure was aimed at getting the attention of doctors, not children.)

What is new as of 2003, however, is that thanks to certain regulatory changes, the commercial leash for companies in the psychotropic drug business is now less rigid. "In a major (and worrisome) change from previous practice," the Kass report observes, "drug companies have taken to marketing drugs directly to parents, with spot ads depicting miraculous transformations of anxious, lonely, or troublesome children into cheerful, confident, honor-roll students."[25] Though unable under the law to mention their products directly, companies instead create ads posing as "information bulletins" about a given disorder, with captioned come-ons such as "Thanks to new ways for effectively managing ADHD, homework may be a more relaxing time at the Wilkin house." Also part of the marketing, Lawrence Diller further relates in *Salon*, is the toll-free number that parents can call for "the latest treatment information," following which they receive a government report on attention deficit disorder and information from the company about a drug.[26]

All corporate claims to consciousness-raising aside, the fact that these news and information bulletins serve as ads is hard to miss. As Diller observes in his review of several such commercial devices, "Companies involved in advertising stimulants for kids by promoting 'awareness' of ADHD maintain that they are performing a public service. However, in the affluent suburban middle-class community where I work, you'd have to be living in a cave without children for the last 10 years to be unaware of ADHD."[27]

To say that some corporate commercial practices look ethically provocative is not to say that the companies actually created the market for wonder drugs, as certain conspiracy-minded observers believe. (This theory, incidentally, appears to be increasingly popular in England where psychotropic drugs for children are only beginning to catch on and where the phenomenon is being scrutinized for that reason.)[28] In an age when tobacco and fast-food companies have become legal targets for marketing harmful or potentially harmful products to youths, one comparative point is as plain as the smile on Ritalin Man's face: With the exception of newly expired "Metadate Man," the drug companies enjoy a different—that is, looser and freer—cultural standard of corporate responsibility.[29]

This review of the sometimes troubling commercial history of psychotropics raises one other point we will revisit. As many experts have repeatedly stressed, the fact that stimulant drugs effectively restrain restless, difficult, and otherwise problematic children has been known and remarked upon for decades. That is to say, the psychotropic drug revolution for children could have started much earlier than it did—in the 1960s or 1970s, say, instead of the 1990s. What stopped it? Conversely, what are the conditions of our own time that kicked it into gear?

YOU'RE IN THE ARMY, NOT

A fourth problem with wonder drugs on today's scale will probably come as a surprise to you since it is mentioned almost nowhere in either expert or popular literature. The fact remains, however, that Ritalin use, particularly after age twelve, like other psychotropic drug use during the teenage years, *disqualifies one for military service*—including, of course, combat.[30] The Department of Defense Directive 6130.3 states: "Physical standards of appointment, enlistment and induction disqualify those with a chronic history of academic skills or perceptual defects secondary to organic or functional mental disorders that interfere with work or school after age 12."

This language has been interpreted to mean that individuals diagnosed with ADD/ADHD may or may not be allowed to serve in the military if they have been labeled with the disorder, but they will not be allowed to serve if they have taken medication "to improve or maintain academic skills" as teenagers. These guidelines are not always broadcast as clearly as they might be; in particular, as an American Academy of Pediatrics report notes, recruiters trying to keep their personal numbers up do not always give full information to potential recruits, who are instead typically confronted with disqualification further down the bureaucratic road.[31] (Eric

Harris, one of the two high school shooters in the Columbine case, had reportedly received just such a letter of disqualification on account of his Luvox prescription three days before committing the murders.) Whether emphasized for public consumption or not, current military guidelines concerning psychotropic medication are plain enough, and they are also enforced.

Just as plain are the reasons for that restriction. The directive quoted earlier, which names methylphenidate specifically as an example of a disqualifying drug, goes on to explain that "Ritalin is a controlled drug with considerable abuse potential." Not only methylphenidate but all other psychiatric medications have the same disqualifying effect. As a recruiter for the Navy put it in an interview for About.com titled "ADHD in the Military: Ritalin Is Not Welcome in the Armed Services": "Again, medication [for depression, bipolar disorder, and other behavioral disorder] seems to be the key. If an individual has a mental disorder and does not require any medication, the situation will be taken under review. . . . [But] if prescription medication is currently part of the treatment process and is needed to maintain stability, then most likely the individual would not be eligible to serve."[32] It is no wonder that, as one ROTC recruiter noted in a 2003 newspaper interview, taking Ritalin after age twelve is one of the "two greatest physical disqualifiers" to enlistment (the other being asthma).[33]

This outcome is something of a conceptual challenge to ADD/ADHD orthodoxy, which holds that stimulant medication for attention-deficit-disorder sufferers is no on-again, off-again option but, rather, a lifelong medical necessity. But even that problem pales beside the staggering social implications of the psychotropic universe as it collides with the intensely real post-9/11 world. The many middle- and upper-middle-class white teenagers now taking psychotropic drugs are disqualified from military service under existing rules, a socially lopsided fact that will likely strike many people as unfair.

The military ban on psychiatric drugs might also explain another interesting fact that has long gone unexplained: the traditional antagonism toward such substances in parts of the black community.[34] As a group—and to the continuing exasperation of many medical professionals who believe

ADD is "underdiagnosed" by race—black Americans have long viewed psychotropic medicine with skepticism and even hostility. Perhaps one reason for this opposition is that such drugs can be prohibitive to military life, a time-honored and critical socioeconomic ladder up for materially worse-off young black men and women. It is interesting to realize, if ethically problematic, that if the well-intentioned experts now urging more such drugs on poorer black communities have their way, they may be unwittingly closing for life one of the traditional doors to advancement for some of those young people. We have here another kind of potential harm caused by psychotropic drugs on today's scale.

It is in the matter of who will be eligible for the American military on account of these drugs that the psychotropic double standard makes a socially painful appearance. One recent literary illustration comes to mind. In *Vernon God Little*, a critically acclaimed, satirical, coming-of age novel set in Texas that won the 2003 Booker Prize in England, the teenage protagonist at one point thinks ruefully of how his PlayStation has been broken by a wild ten-year-old who won't admit to having done it. Vernon knows there will be no justice because, as he reflects, the other boy "has an authorized disorder that works like a Get Out of Jail Free card." In effect, the kind of psychotropic drug-taking increasingly common among better-off children and teenagers does something similar: It might be called a "Get Out of War Free" card.

If there were any other factor in the post-9/11 American world that would lead to a socially explosive result like this one—a great many otherwise able young men, most of them white and better-off, being disqualified for military service on account of the drugs used to treat their diagnosed "brain defects"—it would have become a public issue by now. Any other drug with such a potentially disastrous result would bear scrutiny for this reason alone. But once again, wonder drugs get a pass.

WONDER DRUGS: THE BACKLASH FROM KIDS

A final problem with America's pharmaceutical fix that may not be as immediately dire but is perhaps the most poignant and also the most neglected is the fact that the psychotropic universe can be hard on children and teenagers in many ways, but their disaffection has no moral standing in the vast establishment literature on the drugs. Several years ago, in an essay called "Why Ritalin Rules," I tried to get at this point by quoting children who had given voice to their sadness or discontent: "It takes over of me [sic]; it takes control." "It numbed me." "Taking it meant I was dumb." "I feel rotten about taking pills; why me?" "It makes me feel like a baby." "I don't know how to explain. I just don't want to take it anymore."

We don't need new case studies to update the point. Yesterday's children of the wonder drug regimen are already today's teenagers and young adults, and their popular culture increasingly reflects something interesting: Among the harshest critics of behavior pills are some graduates of that social program, including certain adolescent role models (or, as the case may be, antimodels).

For example, the late grunge-rock guru Kurt Cobain (an addict who died an apparent suicide by way of heroin) appears in retrospect as a kind of antiposter boy for child stimulants. Prescribed Ritalin at the age of seven, Cobain believed that his experiences with the drug led to his later abuse of related substances. One biographer, referring to Cobain and his wife, Courtney Love, put it this way: "Kurt's own opinion, as he later told her, was that the drug was significant. Courtney, who also was prescribed Ritalin as a child, said the two discussed this issue frequently. 'When you're a kid and you get this drug that makes you feel that feeling, where else are you going to turn when you're an adult? It was euphoric when you were a child—isn't that memory going to stick with you?' "[35]

Many parents loathed what Cobain and Love stood for (if they were aware of it), just as many today have particular loathing for Marshall Mathers, also known as rap superstar Eminem. Interestingly enough, Eminem is another prominent self-perceived victim of the label-and-medicate momentum. In a recent interview with Howard Stern reported in *Rolling Stone* magazine, Eminem said that his mother suffered from Munchausen syndrome by proxy, meaning in his case that "his mother misdiagnosed him with attention deficit disorder. 'My mother said I was a hyper kid and I wasn't,' he said. 'She put me on Ritalin.' "[36] It is a theme sounded elsewhere in a song called "Cleaning Out My Closet," which includes the line "My whole life I was made to believe I was sick when I wasn't." It is an odd point but perhaps worth pondering that Cobain's and Eminem's fans might get a stronger antistimulant message from their examples than they do from their parents, teachers, and doctors.

It is also interesting that the very generation supposedly reaping the benefits of psychotropic drugs is also satirizing them in just about every venue reflecting adolescent popular wisdom—from sites such as the Onion and McSweeney's to any number of shows catering to teenagers and young adults, including such perennial favorites as *MAD TV* and *Saturday Night Live*. In three particularly iconographic reflections of the adolescent imagination, the *Simpsons, South Park*, and *King of the Hill*, stimulants have been objects of either mockery or contempt.[37] In one *Simpsons* episode, Bart is put on a drug called Focusin after a prank runs amok. He becomes a model student for a time, and then in a paranoid fit steals a tank and is finally taken off the drug. (Bart Simpson's voice for the show, Nancy Cartwright, has said that one of her favorite episodes is "when they put Bart on Focusin" because it "was such a powerful comment on drugging children in our school system.")[38] A *King of the Hill* episode in which a character is misdiagnosed with ADD after eating too much sugared cereal likewise reflects the dictum that ADD is a label potentially slapped on anyone who defies what adults want. This same point is made even more cynically in the *South Park* episode satirizing the drug when a character whose real problem is mental retardation is automatically diagnosed with ADD and given Ritalin, leading to a me-too clamor from the other children and their parents. (This episode resolves when a protagonist convinces pharmacists to give him the fictitious antidote to Ritalin, called Ritalout.)

Criticism of the child-drug phenomenon is also the hallmark of certain writers who self-identify as members of "the Ritalin generation." One such is Elizabeth Wurtzel, author of the best-selling 1999 *Prozac Nation*. In 2002 she published another book, *More, Now, Again: A Memoir of Addiction*, detailing her harrowing descent into Ritalin addiction after a well-meaning doctor gave her the drug to help her focus on her writing. "[U]ntil now," as she wrote later in the *New York Times*, "little attention has focused on the harm Ritalin can cause anyone, at any age. My own anecdotal evidence from attending Narcotics Anonymous meetings includes mothers' accounts of stealing Ritalin pills meant for their children and stories of plenty of grown-up 'Ritalin kids' who got started on the stuff before they could even write in cursive.' "[39]

Another critic of the child-stimulant regimen is essayist and novelist Walter Kirn, whose 1999 coming-of-age novel, *Thumbsucker*, features an orally fixated teen who among other scams cons his dentist into a continuing Ritalin prescription ("He'd told me that Ritalin was just a bridge, that someday I'd come off it, but onto what?" the protagonist wonders). Like Wurtzel, Kirn has also testified to the nonfiction downside, at least in his own case, of the ADD/stimulant phenomenon. In a December 2000 article for *GQ*, he related his own lifelong problems in focusing on his work (which he called Frankenstein), his powerful attraction to stimulant drugs, his eventual realization that Ritalin was ruining his life, and his final decision to throw his prescription away.[40] "Frankenstein and I are working things out," he concludes, "but what about the estimated 2 million American kids who don't have the option of canceling their prescription . . . ?"

Well, what about them? To ask a question that seems obvious by now: Why is it that some intended beneficiaries of the child-stimulant regimen question it? What explains why the drugs are almost universally mocked in teen popular culture—a phenomenon that seems even more demanding of explanation given that some of these same teenagers are also snorting their friends' or little brother's pills on the sly?

Here's an educated guess: In the essay called "OCD" cited in the last chapter, Dr. Jerome Groopman quotes a dissenting clinical psychologist named Anthony Rao whose words elegantly formulate the point. "Rao believes," writes Groopman, "that the D.S.M. label resonates in the child's mind and among family members and friends in pejorative and embarrassing ways. 'Your brain is your soul,' Rao said fiercely. 'You're telling a kid that there is something wrong with who he fundamentally is.' "

Your brain is your soul. Maybe psychologist Rao is on to something about the adolescent psyche here that other authorities with the best of intentions have yet to figure out. And maybe, by extension, the dissent about wonder drugs that comes through loud and clear in adolescent popular culture amounts to that insight writ larger—that at least some teenagers profoundly resent having been judged defective a priori in the very place they all know counts most with the adult world: their heads.

WHAT'S IN IT FOR ADULTS?

When one weighs all the problems and questions created by the child psychotropic explosion—from physical side effects to abuse to the question of commercial manipulation, from its impact on the American military to questions about the morality of labeling juveniles defective and "fixing" them with chemicals—the amazing thing is not that there is criticism of the psychotropic drug regimen, but that the phenomenon itself not only endures but thrives.

Why that double standard persists is a question that current literature is not equipped to answer because most of it resolutely denies that all those pills have wider implication. One exception was Francis Fukuyama's 2002 work, *Our Posthuman Future*, which argued that such drugs are the tools by which our largely postphysical society moves everyone closer to androgyny. He writes, "There is a disconcerting symmetry between Prozac and Ritalin. The former is prescribed heavily for depressed women lacking in self-esteem; it gives them more of the alpha-male feeling that comes with high serotonin levels. Ritalin, on the other hand, is prescribed largely for young boys who do not want to sit still in class because nature never designed them to behave that way. Together, the two sexes are gently nudged toward that androgynous median personality, self satisfied and socially compliant, that is the current politically correct outcome in American society."[41]

Another exception to the general lack of philosophical reflection on the subject is the 2003 report by the President's Council on Bioethics. That document suggests that at least one force keeping the psychotropic universe in motion is the profound and honorable desire of nearly all parents for what the report calls "enhanced" children. "The wish of parents for 'better children,' " in the words of *Beyond Therapy*, "most often takes the form of a desire for children who are more well-adjusted, well-behaved, sociable, attentive, high-performing, and academically adept. Parents are moved not only by reasons of parental pride but also by the belief that children who possess these qualities are more likely to succeed and flourish later in life. These are perfectly fitting desires and proper motives, and we might well find fault with parents who did not share them, at least to some considerable degree." This argument casts the wonder drug explosion in perhaps its most benevolent light: the desire of parents to reconfigure children in such a way that those offspring will ultimately be rendered more successful, more productive, and thereby happier.[42]

No doubt both Fukuyama's and the Council's reflections capture some facet of the truth, and yet to review the drugs' manifold problems and question marks as we have here is to suspect that a darker reading is also in order. Perhaps the psychotropic revolution is in full swing today because something about our world has made the technological quick fix more necessary than before. And perhaps that "something" is the obvious thing: the profound change in everyday life according to which yesterday's norm of family-centered childhood has been replaced by today's parental and family absence in all their varieties. In other words, perhaps children and teenagers are increasingly treated with performance-enhancing drugs not only to help them compete, but also to relieve the stresses that their long, out-of-home, institutionalized days add to the adults around them, the teachers, parents, and other authorities.

Precisely because they spend more time in the care of others, today's children have less behavioral and emotional room for error. A late-afternoon tantrum on the kitchen floor by a tired five-year-old is just that. The same act committed by the same child in a barely supervised after-school-care program becomes something else: a disciplinary infraction demanding parental attention and perhaps even a medical "intervention." Isn't that part of the reason that drugs are so powerfully appealing, because they caulk the behavioral gap so that the infraction doesn't happen?

Similarly, those one, two, or three extra hours in day care or preschool required by full-time parental jobs might just be one, two, or three hours too many in which to behave as required without special (read: pharmaceutical) help. Does Justin's teacher recommend Ritalin? She does. But why do Justin's parents bend to her? In part because they may not be equipped to counter that judgment; after all, she sees more of him than they do. Through just such imagined but real scenarios does the absent-parent problem inadvertently ratchet up the pressure on children and teenagers. In essence, what might get written off as normal behavior in the more forgiving and supportive at-home context becomes a "syndrome" in more pressurized settings. Again, this increases the pressure for non-parental "fixes" of all sorts.

There is also the related if neglected fact that not only do kids see less of their parents, but the parents also see less of their kids. In other words, most have relatively little experience of children compared to the adults of preceding generations. Yesterday's parents had more *of* them, for one thing, and mothers spent more time in their proximity during the early years at a minimum.

Why does today's relative adult inexperience matter? Because it suggests a highly provocative answer to the question raised earlier in this chapter about why the psychotropic revolution for children did not happen earlier. Maybe on account of their wider experience with children and teenagers, yesterday's parents and experts had a more expansive idea of child normality and, correspondingly, a more conservative idea of what is a justifiable pharmaceutical intervention in a child's life—one that acted as a brake on the psychotropic universe until very recently.

And what about, say, teachers and other educators who do have immediate experience with children? A skeptic might note that some of them have been notoriously quick to point a diagnostic finger at children, so quick that some parents have lately sought legal recourse through legislation.[43] How does their enthusiasm square with the notion that inexperience is what drives prescriptions up? Recalling the evidence on behavior in chapter 2, the answer is that teachers become pill advocates because significant numbers of children are unable to behave in a classroom. Thus, for easily understandable reasons, experienced adults such as teachers, day care workers, and psychologists might lean toward pharmaceutical help for behavior management, just as less experienced adults do.

In the end, the wonder drug phenomenon cannot be detached from the larger social condition in which it flourishes despite the problems it simultaneously creates. To return to our metaphor, the most obvious prime mover pushing the psychotropic universe outward, the one signature feature of our time that satisfactorily explains why the double standard for wonder drugs exists, is the increasing separation and diminishing contact between parents and children. It is this separation that leads parents and other authorities to put a premium on the benefits of the drugs (behavior management) while simultaneously desensitizing today's adults to the phenomenon's manifold problems and risks (side effects, possible abuse, commercial manipulation, unfair social consequences, and psychological harm). Wonder drugs enjoy a double standard today because they accomplish something that was not considered important until today. They operate at least in part as the pharmaceutical outsourcing of childhood.

6

"Ozzie and Harriet, Come Back!": The Primal Scream of Teenage Music

"YOU KNOW, REALLY, IF I HAD AN OPPORTUNITY TO SHOOT Britney Spears, I think I would." These words, delivered off-the-cuff at a conference in October 2003, may have temporarily roiled the public waters for Kendel Ehrlich, the wife of Maryland's current governor.[1] But they also summoned a collective cheer from the many adults—especially mothers and fathers—who are sick to death of everything Britney and her music represent. If there is one subject on which the parents of America passionately agree, it is that contemporary adolescent popular music, especially the subgenres of heavy metal and hip-hop/rap, is uniquely degraded—and degrading—by the standards of previous generations.[2]

At first blush this seems slightly ironic. After all, most of today's baby-boom parents were themselves molded by rock and roll, bumping and grinding their way through adolescence and adulthood with legendary abandon. Even so, the parents are correct: Much of today's music *is* darker and coarser than yesterday's rock. Misogyny, violence, suicide, sexual exploitation, child abuse—these and other themes, formerly rare and illicit, are now as common as the surfboards, drive-ins, and sock hops of yesteryear. So it is little wonder that today's teenage music, more than others before it, is the music parents most love to hate—even parents for whom the likes of Jim Morrison, Janis Joplin, and Mick Jagger summon feelings of (relatively) wholesome nostalgia.[3]

So overwhelming is the adult consensus about the unique awfulness of this stuff that the c-word, *censorship,* has been raised among people on both sides of the political aisle.[4] And while such efforts have so far scored

only limited success, they do demonstrate what most adults feel in their
bones: that certain of today's music is egregious by any reasonable standard, as even some executives who profit from it will agree.[5] In yet another
expression of adult concern that is without precedent, contemporary rock
and rap have lately even caught the attention of several august medical
bodies who wonder aloud about its possible malign influence on impres-
sionable minds.[6]

In a nutshell, the ongoing adult preoccupation with current music
goes something like this: *What is the overall influence of this deafening,
foul, and often vicious-sounding stuff on children and teenagers?* This is a
genuinely important question, and recent serious studies and articles,
some concerned particularly with current music's possible link to violence, have lately been devoted to it. Nonetheless, this is not the focus of
this chapter. Instead, I would like to turn that logic about influence up-
side down and ask this question: *What is it about today's music, violent and
disgusting though it may be, that resonates with so many American kids?*

As the reader can see, this is a very different way of inquiring about
the relationship between today's teenagers and their music. The first question asks what the music *does* to adolescents; the second asks what it *tells*
us about them. To answer that second question is necessarily to enter the
roiling emotional waters in which that music is created and consumed—
in other words, actually to read and listen to some of it.

As it turns out, such an exercise yields a fascinating and little-
understood fact about today's adolescent scene. If yesterday's rock was
the music of abandon, today's is that of abandon*ment*. The odd truth
about contemporary teenage music—the characteristic that most separates
it from what has gone before—is its compulsive insistence on the damage
wrought by broken homes, family dysfunction, checked-out parents, and
(especially) absent fathers. Papa Roach, Everclear, Blink-182, Good
Charlotte, Eddie Vedder and Pearl Jam, Kurt Cobain and Nirvana, Tupac
Shakur, Snoop Doggy Dogg, Eminem—these and other singers and
bands, all of them award-winning top-40 performers who either are or
were among the most popular icons in America, have their own generational answer to what ails the modern teenager. Surprising though it may

be to some, that answer is: dysfunctional childhood. Moreover, and just as interesting, many bands and singers explicitly link the most deplored themes in music today—suicide, misogyny, and drugs—with that lack of a quasi-normal, intact-home personal past.

To put this perhaps unexpected point more broadly, during the same years in which progressive-minded and politically correct adults have been excoriating Ozzie and Harriet as an artifact of 1950s-style oppression, many millions of American teenagers have enshrined a new generation of music idols whose shared generational signature in song after song is to rage about what *not* having had a nuclear family has done to them. This is quite a fascinating puzzle of the times, among the most striking of all the unanticipated fallout in our home-alone world. The self-perceived emotional damage scrawled large across contemporary music may not be statistically quantifiable, but it is nonetheless pathetically, if rudely and sometimes violently, articulated—as many examples demonstrate neatly.

DEMIGODS OF DYSFUNCTION

To begin with music particularly popular among white teenage boys, one best-selling example of broken-home angst is that of the "nu-metal" band known as Papa Roach and led by singer/songwriter "Coby Dick" Shaddix (dubbed by one reviewer the "prince of dysfunction"). Three members of that group, Coby Dick included, are self-identified children of divorce. In 2000, as critics noted at the time, their album *Infest* explored the themes of broken homes and child and teenage rage. The result was stunning commercial success: *Infest* sold more than 3 million copies. MTV.com explained why: "The pained, confessional songs struck a nerve with disenfranchised listeners who were tired of the waves of directionless aggression spewing from the mouths of other rap-rockers. They found kinship in Papa Roach songs like 'Broken Home' and 'Last Resort.'"

In fact, even their songs about other subjects hark back to that same primal disruption. One particularly violent offering called "Revenge," about a girl hurting herself and being abused by her boyfriend, reflects on "destruction of the family design." Of all the songs on the album, however, it is the singularly direct "Broken Home" that hit its fans the hardest, which summarizes the sad domestic story it elaborates in a pair of lines: *"I know my mother loves me / But does my father even care."*

Another band that climbed to the top of the charts recently is Everclear, led by singer Art Alexakis (also a child of divorce, as he has explained to interviewers). Like Papa Roach, Everclear/Alexakis explores the fallout of parental breakup not from the perspective of newly liberated adults, but from that of the child left behind who feels abandoned and betrayed. Several of Everclear's songs map this emotional ground in detail—from not wanting to meet mother's "new friends," to wondering how the father who walked out can sleep at night, to dreaming of that father coming back. In the song "Father of Mine," the narrator implores, *"take me back to the day / when I was still your golden boy."* Another song, "Sick and Tired," explicitly links the anger-depression-suicide teen matrix to broken homes (as indeed do numerous other contemporary groups): *"I blame my family / their damage is living in me."*

Everclear's single best-known song, a top-40 hit in 2000 that ruled the airwaves for months, is a family breakup ballad ironically titled "Wonderful"—to some fans, the best rock song about divorce ever written. Though the catchy melody cannot be captured here, the childlike simplicity of the words brings the message home loudly enough. Among them: *"I want the things that I had before / Like a Star Wars poster on my bedroom door."*

Another group successfully working this tough emotional turf is chart-topping and multiple award-winning Blink-182, which grew out of the skateboard and snowboard scene to become one of the most popular bands in the country. As with Papa Roach and Everclear, the group's interest in the family breakdown theme is partly autobiographical: At least two members of the band say that their personal experiences as children of divorce have informed their lyrics. Blink-182's top-40 hit in 2001, "Stay Together for the Kids," is perhaps their best-known song (though not the only one) about broken homes. *"What stupid poem could fix this home,"* the narrator wonders, adding, *"I'd read it every day."*

Reflecting on the particular passion with which that song was embraced by fans, Blink-182's Tom DeLonge told an interviewer, "We get e-mails about 'Stay Together,' kid after kid after kid saying, 'I know exactly what you're talking about! That song is about my life!' And you know what? That s***s. You look at statistics that 50 percent of parents get divorced, and you're going to get a pretty large group of kids who are p***** off and who don't agree with what their parents have done."[7] Similarly, singer/bassist Mark Hoppus remarked to another interviewer curious about the band's emotional resonance, "Divorce is such a normal thing today and hardly anybody ever thinks how the kids feel about it or how they are taking it, but in the U.S. about half of all the kids go through it. They witness how their parents drift apart and all that."[8]

Then there is the phenomenon known as Pink, whose album *Missundaztood* was one of the top-10 albums of 2002, selling more than 3 million copies. Pink (dubbed by one writer the "anti-Britney") is extremely popular among young girls. Any teenager with a secular CD collection will likely own some of her songs. Pink mines the same troubled emotional territory as Blink-182 and numerous other bands, but even more exclusively: *Missundaztood* revolves entirely around the emotional wreckage and behavioral consequences of Pink's parents breaking up. A review of the album on ABCnews.com noted, "*Missundaztood* is full of painful tales of childhood—divorce, rebellion, disaffection and drugs. It's the stuff that may make parents shake their heads, but causes millions of alienated kids to nod in approval."[9] In Pink's especially mournful (and perhaps best-known) song, "Family Portrait," the narrator repeatedly begs her father not to leave, offering even the pitiful childish enticement, *"I won't spill the milk at dinner."*

Yet another popular group generating anthem after anthem about broken homes and their consequences is Washington, D.C.-area–based Good Charlotte, profiled on the cover of *Rolling Stone* in May 2003 as the "Polite Punks." Their first album went gold in 2002. Led by twins Benji and Joel Madden, whose father walked out one Christmas Eve and never returned, Good Charlotte is one band that would not even exist except for the broken homes in which three of its four members (guitarist Billy Martin being the third) grew up. The twins have repeatedly told interviewers it was that trauma that caused them to take up music in the first place, and family breakup figures repeatedly in Good Charlotte's songs and regularly shapes its stage appearances and publicity. (In a particular act of symbolic protest, the twins recently made the legal changeover to their mother's maiden name.)

For Good Charlotte, as for many other newly successful singers and groups, the commercial results of putting personal trauma to music have proved dramatic. Their first and eponymous album sailed up the charts partly on account of a teenage angst ballad ironically entitled "Little Things." The song opens with a dedication to every teenager wrestling with the issues of adolescence—all those "little things," including Mom's stint in a mental institution and Dad's abandonment of the kids (*"We checked his room his things were gone we didn't see him no more"*). Another song on the album is "Thank You Mom." Rather anomalously by the standards of yesterday's rock and punk, but not at all anomalously in the worlds of their descendants today, this song is devoted wholly, and without irony, to the mother who raises children after their father walks out (*"You were my mom, You were my dad / The only thing I ever had was you, It's true"*).

Rolling Stone groused about this band: "What the hell happened to punk?" Now that's a fair point. But whatever happened, the result has literally turned to gold; Good Charlotte's second album, called *The Young and the Hopeless*, sold more than a million copies. Two of its thirteen songs are apotheosized lyrics for an absent father. One is "My Old Man" (*"Last I heard he was at the bar / Doing himself in"*). Another song, "Emotionless," reads much like the related narrations of Everclear, Papa Roach, and many more. The narrator here reminds his missing father of his sons and little girl, wondering, *"How do you sleep at night?"*

Like numerous other groups, Good Charlotte weaves another prevailing theme—teenage suicide—in and out of the larger theme of parental abandonment. Perhaps the best known is the antisuicide clarion "Hold On," in which the singer implores a desperate teenager to remember that although your *"mother's gone and your father hits you . . . we all bleed the same way you do."*

Papa Roach, Everclear, Blink-182, Pink, Good Charlotte: These bands are only some of the top-40 groups now supplying the teenage demand for songs about dysfunctional and adult-abandoned homes. In a remarkable 2002 article published in the pop music magazine *Blender* (remarkable because it lays out in detail what is really happening in today's metal/grunge/punk/rock music), an award-winning music journalist named William Shaw listed several other bands, observing, "If there's a theme running through rock at the beginning of the twenty-first century, it's a pervasive sense of hurt. For the past few years, bands like Korn, Linkin Park, Slipknot, Papa Roach, and Disturbed have been thrusting forward their dark accounts of dysfunctional upbringings. . . . As the clichéd elder might mutter, what's wrong with kids today?" Shaw answers his own question this way: "[T]hese songs reflect the zeitgeist of an age group coping with the highest marital-breakdown rate ever recorded in America. If this era's music says anything, it's that this generation sees itself as uniquely fractured."

As he further observes, so powerful are the emotions roused in fans by these songs that stars and groups themselves are often surprised by it. Shaw relates the following about "Coby Dick" Shaddix of Papa Roach, who wrote the aforementioned song "Broken Home": "He's become used to [fans] coming up and telling him, over and over: 'You know that song "Broken Home?" That's my f****** life, right there.' 'It's a bit sad that that's true, you know?' [Shaddix] says." Similarly, singer Chad Kroeger of Nickelback reports of a hit song he wrote on his own abandonment by his father at age two: "You should see some people who I meet after shows. . . . They break down weeping, and they're like, 'I went through the exact same thing!' Sometimes it's terrifying how much they relate to it." That Nickelback hit song, titled "Too Bad," laments that calling *"from time to time / To make sure we're alive"* just isn't enough.

Shaw's ultimate conclusion is an interesting one: that this emphasis in current music on abandoned children represents an unusually loaded form of teenage rebellion. "This is the sound of one generation reproaching another—only this time, it's the scorned, world-weary children telling off their narcissistic, irresponsible parents," he writes. "[Divorce] could be rock's ideal subject matter. These are songs about the chasm in understanding between parents—who routinely don't comprehend the grief their children are feeling—and children who don't know why their parents have torn up their world."

That is a sharp observation. Also worth noting is this historical point: The same themes of adult absence and child abandonment have been infiltrating hard rock even longer than these current bands have been around—probably for as long as family breakup rates began accelerating.

Both musically and emotionally, many of today's groups owe much to the example of the late grunge-rock idol Kurt Cobain, who prefigured today's prominent themes both autobiographically and otherwise. A star whose personal life has legendary status for his fans, Cobain was a self-described happy child until his parents' divorce when he was seven. The years following were a miserable blur of being shuffled around to grandparents and other caretakers, including a spate of homelessness. The rage and frustration of that experience appear in some of Cobain's famously nihilistic lyrics, including the early song "Sliver," about a boy kicking and screaming upon being dropped off elsewhere by Mom and Dad yet again. The later, markedly cynical "Serve the Servants" reflects on how his traumatic childhood became exploited for personal gain. As with Cobain, so, too, with his friend Pearl Jam singer Eddie Vedder. For more than a decade Pearl Jam has reigned as one of the best-known bands in current rock, and Vedder as one of the most adulated singers; indeed, the band's distinctive sound commands instant recognition among almost every American under the age of thirty with working ears. And Pearl Jam, like the aforementioned groups, has achieved that success, according to Vedder, partly because of the group's frankness about the costs of fractured families and about related themes of alienation and suicide.

In a 1994 interview that focused on the death of Kurt Cobain, Vedder noted with particular insight:

> "We [that is, Vedder and Cobain] had similar backgrounds, yeah, things that happened with our families and s***. . . . I think that's something that comes out in what we wrote in our songs,

definitely. . . . But what makes it more similar is the way people re-sponded to what we wrote and sang about, the intense identifi-cation. . . .

"And I think it was maybe a shock to both of us that so many people were going through the same things. I mean, they under-stood so completely what we were talking about. . . . Then all of a sudden, there's all these other people who connect with them and you're suddenly the spokesman for a f****** generation. Can you imagine that! . . . when our first record came out, I was shocked how many people related to some of that stuff. . . . The kind of letters that got through to me about those songs, some of them were just frightening. . . .

"Think about it, man," he says. "Any generation that would pick Kurt or me as its spokesman—that must be a pretty f***** up generation, don't you think?"[10]

Well put. And as it turned out, Cobain and Vedder were only the beginning.

RAPPERS ASK: WHERE'S DADDY?

Even less recognized than the white music emphasis on broken homes and the rest of the dysfunctional themes is that the popular black-dominated genres, particularly hip-hop/rap, also reflect themes of abandonment, anger, and longing for parents. Interestingly enough, this is true of particu-lar figures whose work is among the most adult deplored.

Once again, when it comes to the deploring part, critics have a point. It is hard to imagine a more unwanted role model (from the parental point of view) than the late Tupac Shakur. A best-selling gangsta rapper who died in a shoot-out in 1996 at age twenty-five (and the object of a 2003 documentary called *Tupac: Resurrection*), Shakur was a kind of polymath of criminality. In the words of a *Denver Post* review of the movie, "In a perfect circle of life imitating art originally meant to imitate life, Shakur in 1991 began a string of crimes that he alternately denied and reveled in. He claimed Oakland police beat him up in a jaywalking arrest, later shot two off-duty cops, assaulted a limo driver and video directors, and was shot five times in a robbery." Further, "At the time of his drive-by murder in Law Vegas, he was out on bail pending appeal of his conviction for sexual abuse of a woman who charged him with sodomy in New York."

Perhaps not surprising, Shakur's songs are riddled with just about every unwholesome trend that a nervous parent can name; above all they contain incitements to crime and violence (particularly against the police) and a misogyny so pronounced that his own mother, executive producer of the movie, let stand in the film a statement of protesting C. DeLores Tucker that "African-American women are tired of being called ho's, bitches and sluts by our children."

Yet Shakur—who never knew his father and whose mother, a long-time drug addict, was arrested for possession of crack when he was a child—is provocative in another, quite overlooked way: He is the author of some of the saddest lyrics in the hip-hop/gangsta-rap pantheon, which is saying quite a lot. To sophisticated readers familiar with the observations about the breakup of black families recorded several decades ago in the Moynihan Report and elsewhere, the fact that so many young black men grow up without fathers may seem so well established as to defy further comment. But evidently some young black men—Shakur being one—see things differently. In fact, it is hard to find a rapper who does not sooner or later invoke a dead or otherwise long-absent father, typically followed by the hope that he will not become such a man himself. Or there is the flip side of that unintended bow to the nuclear family, which is the hagiography in some rappers' lyrics of their mothers.

In a song called "Papa'z Song Lyrics," Shakur opens with the narrator imagining his father showing up after a long absence, resulting in an expletive-laden tirade. The song then moves to a lacerating description of growing up fatherless that might help to explain why Shakur is an icon not only to many worse-off teenagers from the ghetto, but also to many better-off suburban ones. Here is a boy who *"had to play catch by myself,"* who prays: *"Please send me a pops before puberty."*

The themes woven together in this song—anger, bitterness, longing for family, misogyny as the consequence of a world without fathers—make regular appearances in some other rappers' lyrics, too. One is Snoop Doggy Dogg, perhaps the preeminent rapper of the 1990s. Like Shakur and numerous other rappers, his personal details cause many a parent to shudder; since his childhood he has been arrested for a variety of crimes, including cocaine possession (which resulted in three years of jail service), accomplice to murder (for which he was acquitted), and, most recently, marijuana possession. ("It's not my job to stop kids doing the wrong thing, it's their parents' job," he once explained to a reporter.) In a song called "Mama Raised Me," sung with Soulja Slim, Snoop Doggy Dogg offers this explanation of how troubled pasts come to be: *"It's probably pop's fault how I ended up / Gangbangin', crack slangin', not givin' a f***."*

Another black rapper who returned repeatedly to the theme of father abandonment is Jay-Z, also known as Shawn Carter, whose third and breakthrough album, *Hard Knock Life*, sold more than 500,000 copies. He also has a criminal history (he says he had been a cocaine dealer) and a troubled family history, which is reflected in his music. In an interview with MTV.com about his latest album, the reporter explained: "Jay and his father had been estranged until earlier this year. [His father] left the household and his family's life (Jay has an older brother and two sisters) when Shawn was just 12 years old. The separation had served as a major 'block' for Jay over the years. . . . His most vocal tongue-lashing toward his dad was on the *Dynasty: Roc la Familia* cut 'Where Have You Been,' where he rapped 'F*** you very much / You showed me the worst kind of pain.' "[11]

The fact that child abandonment is also a theme in hip-hop might help explain what otherwise appears as a commercial puzzle—namely, how this particular music moved from the fringes of black entertainment to the very center of the Everyteenager mainstream. There can be no doubt about the current social preeminence of these black- and ghetto-dominated genres in the lives of many better-off adolescents, black *and* white. As Donna Britt wrote in a *Washington Post* column noting hip-hop's ascendancy, "In modern America, where urban-based hip-hop culture dominates music, fashion, dance and, increasingly, movies and TV, these kids are trendsetters. What they feel, think and do could soon play out in a middle school—or a Pottery Barn–decorated bedroom—near you."[12]

EMINEM: IT'S THE PARENTS, STUPID

A final example of the rage in contemporary music against irresponsible adults—perhaps the most interesting—is that of genre-crossing bad-boy rap superstar Marshall Mathers, or Eminem (sometime stage persona "Slim Shady"). Of all the names guaranteed to send a shudder down the parental spine, his is probably the most effective. In fact, Eminem has single-handedly, if inadvertently, achieved the otherwise ideologically impossible: He is the object of a vehemently disapproving public consensus shared by the National Organization for Women, the Gay & Lesbian Alliance Against Defamation, William J. Bennett, Lynne Cheney, Bill O'Reilly, and a large number of other social conservatives as well as feminists and gay activists. In sum, this rapper—"as harmful to America as any al Qaeda fanatic," in O'Reilly's opinion—unites adult polar opposites as perhaps no other single popular entertainer has done.

There is small need to wonder why. Like other rappers, Eminem mines the shock value and gutter language of rage, casual sex, and violence. Unlike the rest, however, he appears to be a particularly attractive target of opprobrium for two distinct reasons. One, he is white and therefore politically easier to attack. (It is interesting to note that black rappers have not been targeted by name anything like Eminem has.) Perhaps even more important, Eminem is one of the largest commercially visible targets for parental wrath. Wildly popular among teenagers these last several years, he is also enormously successful in commercial terms. Winner of numerous Grammys and other music awards and a perpetual nominee for many more, he has also been critically (albeit reluctantly) acclaimed for his acting performance in the autobiographical 2003 movie *8 Mile*. For all these reasons, he is probably the preeminent rock/rap star of the last several years, one whose singles, albums, and videos routinely top every chart. His 2002 album, *The*

Eminem Show, for example, was easily the most successful of the year, selling more than 7.6 million copies.

This remarkable market success, combined with the intense public criticism that his songs have generated, makes the phenomenon of Eminem particularly intriguing. Perhaps more than any other current musical icon, he returns repeatedly to the same themes that fuel other success stories in contemporary music: parental loss, abandonment, abuse, and subsequent child and adolescent anger, dysfunction, and violence (including self-violence). Both in his raunchy lyrics as well as in *8 Mile,* Mathers's own personal story has been parlayed many times over: the absent father, the troubled mother living in a trailer park, the series of unwanted maternal boyfriends, the protective if impotent feelings toward a younger sibling (in the movie, a baby sister; in real life, a younger brother), and the fine line that a poor, ambitious, and unguided young man might walk between catastrophe and success. Mathers plumbs these and related themes with a verbal savagery that leaves most adults aghast.

Yet Eminem also repeatedly centers his songs on the crypto-traditional notion that children need parents and that *not* having them has made all hell break loose. In the song "8 Mile" from the movie soundtrack, for example, the narrator studies his little sister as she colors one picture after another of an imagined nuclear family, failing to understand that *"momma's got a new man." "Wish I could be the daddy that neither one of us had,"* he comments. Such wistful lyrics juxtapose oddly and regularly with Eminem's violent other lines. Even in one of his most infamous songs, "Cleaning Out My Closet (Mama, I'm Sorry)," what drives the vulgar narrative is the insistence on seeing abandonment from a child's point of view. *"My faggot father must had his panties up in a bunch / 'Cause he split. I wonder if he even kissed me good-bye."*

As with other rappers, the vicious narrative treatment of women in some of Eminem's songs is part of this self-conception as a child victim. Contrary to what critics have intimated, the misogyny in current music does not spring from nowhere; it is often linked to the larger theme of having been abandoned several times—left behind by father, not nurtured by mother, and betrayed again by faithless womankind. One of the most violent and sexually aggressive songs in the last few years is "Kill You" by the popular metal band known as Korn. Its violence is not directed toward just any woman or even toward the narrator's girlfriend; it is instead a song about an abusive stepmother whom the singer imagines going back to rape and murder.

Similarly, Eminem's most shocking lyrics about women are not randomly dispersed; they are largely reserved for his mother and ex-wife, and the narrative pose is one of despising them for not being better women— in particular, better mothers. The worst rap directed at his own mother is indeed gut-wrenching: *"But how dare you try to take what you didn't help me to get? / You selfish b****, I hope you f****** burn in hell for this s***!"* It is no defense of the gutter to observe the obvious: This is not the expression of random misogyny but, rather, of primal rage over alleged maternal abdication and abuse.

Another refrain constant in these songs runs like this: Today's teenagers are a mess, and the parents who made them that way refuse to get it. In one of Eminem's early hits, for example, a song called "Who Knew," the rapper pointedly takes on his many middle- and upper-middle-class critics to observe the contradiction between their reviling him and the parental inattention that feeds his commercial success. *"What about the make-up you allow your 12-year-old daughter to wear?"* he taunts.

This same theme of AWOL parenting is rapped at greater length in another award-nominated 2003 song called "Sing for the Moment," whose lyrics and video would be recognized in an instant by most teenagers in America. That song spells out Eminem's own idea of what connects him to his millions of fans—a connection that parents, in his view, just don't (or is that *won't?*) understand. It details the case of one more "problem child" created by *"His f****** dad walkin' out."* "Sing for the Moment," like many other songs of Eminem's, is also a popular video. The "visuals" shows clearly what the lyrics depict—hordes of disaffected kids, with flashbacks to bad home lives, screaming for the singer who feels their pain. It concludes by rhetorically turning away from the music itself and toward the emotionally desperate teenagers who turn out for this music by the millions. If the demand of all those empty kids wasn't out there, the narrator says pointedly, then rappers wouldn't be supplying it the way they do.

If some parents still don't get it—even as their teenagers elbow up for every new Eminem CD and memorize his lyrics with psalmist devotion—at least some critics observing the music scene *have* thought to comment on the ironies of all this. In discussing *The Marshall Mathers* LP in 2001 for *Music Box*, a daily online newsletter about music, reviewer John Metzger argued, "Instead of spewing the hate that he is so often criticized of doing, Eminem offers a cautionary tale that speaks to our civilization's growing depravity. Ironically, it's his teenage fans who understand this, and their all-knowing parents that miss the point." Metzger further specified "the utter lack of parenting due to the spendthrift necessity of the two-income family."[13]

That insight raises the overlooked fact that in one important sense Eminem and most of the other entertainers quoted in this chapter would agree with many of today's adults about one thing: The kids *aren't* all right out there after all. Recall, for just one example, Eddie Vedder's rueful observation about what kind of generation would make him or Kurt Cobain its leader. Where parents and entertainers disagree is over who exactly bears responsibility for this moral chaos. Many adults want to blame the people who create and market today's music and videos. Entertainers, Eminem most prominently, blame the absent, absentee, and generally inattentive adults whose deprived and furious children (as they see it) have catapulted today's singers to fame. (As he puts the point in one more in-your-face response to parents: *"Don't blame me when lil' Eric jumps off of the terrace / You shoulda been watchin him—apparently you ain't parents."*)

The spectacle of a foul-mouthed bad-example rock icon instructing the hardworking parents of America in the art of child-rearing is indeed a peculiar one, not to say ridiculous. The single mother who is working frantically because she must and worrying all the while about what her fourteen-year-old is listening to in the headphones is entitled to a certain fury over lyrics like those. In fact, to read through most rap lyrics is to wonder which adults or political constituencies *wouldn't* take offense. Even so, the music idols who point the finger away from themselves and toward the emptied-out homes of America are telling a truth that some adults would rather not hear. In this limited sense at least, Eminem is right.

SEX AND DRUGS, ROCK AND ROLL, AND BROKEN HOMES

To say that today's popular music is uniquely concerned with broken homes, abandoned children, and distracted or incapable parents is not to say that this is what all of it is about. Other themes remain a constant, too, although somewhat more brutally than in the alleged golden era recalled by some baby boomers.

Much of today's metal and hip-hop, like certain music of yesterday, romanticizes illicit drug use and alcohol abuse, and much of current hip-hop sounds certain radical political themes, such as racial separationism and violence against the police. And, of course, the most elementally appealing feature of all, the sexually suggestive beat itself, continues to lure teenagers and young adults in its own right—including those from happy homes. Today as yesterday, plenty of teenagers who don't know or care what the stars are raving about find enough satisfaction in swaying to the sexy music. As professor and intellectual Allan Bloom observed about rock in his 1987 bestseller, *The Closing of the American Mind*, the music "gives children, on a silver platter, with all the public authority of the entertaining industry, everything their parents always used to tell them they had to wait for until they grew up and would understand later."[14]

Even so, and putting aside such obvious continuities with previous generations, there is no escaping the fact that today's songs are musically and lyrically unlike any before. What distinguishes them most clearly is the fixation on having been abandoned personally by the adults supposedly in charge, with consequences ranging from bitterness to rage to bad, sick, and violent behavior.

And therein lies a painful truth about an advantage that many teenagers of yesterday enjoyed but their own children often do not. Baby boomers and their music rebelled against parents *because* they were parents—nurturing, attentive, and overly present (as those teenagers often saw it) authority figures. Today's teenagers and their music rebel against parents because they are *not* parents—not nurturing, not attentive, and often not even there. This difference in generational experience may not lend itself to statistical measure, but it is as real as the platinum and gold records that continue to capture it. What those records show compared to yesteryear's rock is emotional downward mobility. Surely if some of the current generation of teenagers and young adults had been better taken care of, then the likes of Kurt Cobain, Eminem, Tupac Shakur, and certain other parental nightmares would have been mere footnotes to recent music history rather than rulers of it.

To step back from the emotional immediacy of those lyrics and to juxtapose the ascendance of such music alongside the long-standing sophisticated assaults on what is sardonically called "family values" is to meditate on a larger irony. As today's music stars and their raving fans likely do not know, separationists and other adult-friendly liberationists have been rationalizing every aspect of the adult exodus from home—sometimes celebrating it full throttle, as in the example of working motherhood—longer than most of today's singers and bands have been alive.

Nor do they show much sign of second thoughts. Representative sociologist Stephanie Coontz greeted the year 2004 with one more op-ed piece aimed at burying poor metaphorical Ozzie and Harriet for good. She reminded America again that "changes in marriage and family life" are here to stay and aren't "necessarily a problem"; that what is euphemistically called "family diversity" is or ought to be cause for celebration. Many other scholars and observers—to say nothing of much of polite adult society—agree with Coontz. Throughout the contemporary nonfiction literature written of, by, and for educated adults, a thousand similar rationalizations about family "changes" bloom on.

Meanwhile, a small number of emotionally damaged former children, embraced and adored by millions of teenagers like them, rage on in every commercial medium available about the multiple damages of the disappearance of loving, protective, attentive adults—and they reap a fortune for it. If this spectacle alone doesn't tell us something about the ongoing emotional costs of parent-child separation on today's outsize scale, it's hard to see what could.

7

The Ravages of "Responsible" Teenage Sex

PROBABLY NO OTHER POP-CULTURAL LOW IN RECENT HISTORY—not Bono's expletive at the 2003 Golden Globe awards or even Madonna and Britney's openmouthed kiss at the 2003 MTV awards—proved quite as cathartic to the long-suffering parents of America as the Super Bowl 2004 halftime show. This time around, as the weeks following the Janet Jackson–Justin Timberlake sexual fumble made clear, no corporate or personal apologies would suffice. For once, real adult disgust over virtual sex on the airwaves exploded across the kitchens, papers, and Web pages of America. For once, too, something came of that disgust, including commercial penalties for the performers, an FCC investigation, and even the line jumping of a 2004 congressional bill aimed at stiffening penalties for broadcasters who violate the indecency provision.

With very few exceptions, opinion makers of all stripes pronounced Janet Jackson's maladroit "costume reveal" the final cultural straw. The *Wall Street Journal* slammed MTV owner Viacom hard for "simulated masturbation," "simulated sex," and "soft-core (albeit legal) kiddy porn," noting also that "the entire world has now got a taste of what passes for entertainment on MTV every day."[1] In the right-leaning *Washington Times*, columnist Suzanne Fields called Jackson "a heroine for our time" for confirming just how base popular culture had become, further urging "boycotts of raunchy shows and public protests against specific vulgar and obscene entertainers." In the left-leaning *Washington Post*, columnist Marjorie Williams took the feminist angle that "only the desecration of a sacred, adult-male-oriented rite can awaken Authority's outrage at the slime in

which our children are daily bathed." But she, too, spoke for parents everywhere when she went on to decry the "smarmy innuendo" of movies, the
sleazy marketing of video games, and all the rest of the "long list of hazards
parents are supposed to police." For a brief moment, as these and many
other reactions to Super Bowl 2004 made clear, the parents of America
united firmly around one proposition: We hate the sexual sewage that the
entertainment industry heaps on our kids.

Yet this very real sense of unity, this collective moment of parental
primal scream, brings us to a rather interesting contradiction. Elsewhere
in the United States during the past few years, certain other, generally
more enlightened-sounding observers have come to carry the banner for
the opposite point of view—that when it comes to sex, today's teenagers
are handling things just fine. According to this take on teen sexuality, the
real news is good news: Today's teenagers are actually more sexually responsible (read: less of a problem for adults to worry about) than those
before them. And the linchpin of this more relaxed way of looking at
things is one widely documented social fact: The number of babies born
to teenagers has declined for several years in a row, dropping by 30 percent between 1992 and 2002 for all teens, and 40 percent for black teens.
This is largely due to the increased use of implanted or injectable long-
acting female contraceptives, or so say the experts.

Because of that fact, in Katha Pollitt's words, we can "break out the
champagne," and, rhetorically speaking at least, there has been no shortage of people happy to do it. "Teens respond sensibly when adults reach
out and give them information and support to make responsible decisions," *Salon* enthuses.[2] "Teens in every state, across ethnic and racial
groups, are making more responsible life decisions," gushes no less an authority than Bill Clinton. This enlightened consensus rests on a technological premise: that contraceptives are cheap and within easy teenage
reach. About this point, too, the optimists are agreed and complacent.
Gregg Easterbrook summarized the benign consensus in *The Progress
Paradox*: "So long as birth control is used, sexual activity for teens is in
and of itself neither good nor bad—it depends on the person, and the
person's beliefs."[3]

And so it has come to pass that while a certain vocal fraction of American parents—call them our populist pessimists—have taken to screaming all over the airwaves for something, anything, that might reduce the amount of smut to which kids are now chronically exposed, certain other people—our enlightened optimists—conclude from the fact of teenage pregnancy decline that once again the kids are all right. This chapter argues something different: The optimists have the real story about teen sex dead wrong, and even the pessimists do not realize just how bad it is.

There is indeed something new in the adolescent sexual arena—actually, several scores of somethings—and they are singularly awful. Of reported cases of chlamydia in 2000, 74 percent occurred in persons aged fifteen to twenty-four, and that number is judged to be "a substantial underestimate of the true incidence of chlamydia among young people," in the words of the Alan Guttmacher Institute.[4] An estimated 11 percent of people aged fifteen to twenty-four are infected with genital herpes, and 33 percent of females in the same age group are thought to be infected with human papillomavirus (HPV), about which more later. This age group is also thought to account for 60 percent of gonorrhea cases, which are further thought to be underreported and underdiagnosed by about 50 percent. On and on the litany goes, perhaps best summarized by this statistic from a work published in 2004: Of 18.9 million new STD cases in the United States in 2000, about 9.1 million, or half, were found in people between the ages of fifteen and twenty-four.[5]

Thus, while the eyes of current pessimists remain glued to what is happening on the tube or screen, and while those of optimists are meanwhile tunnel-visioned to falling teen pregnancy rates, the more fundamental story about teen sex today is not being told in anything like the decibel strength it demands. That story is not about virtual sex or theoretical learning curves. It is about *real* sex and what it is doing to some of today's future adults. It is also partly the story of the disappearance from many adolescents' lives of parents and other authorities who might once have protected kids from this kind of harm. This story, which teenagers of the baby boom generation were largely spared, begins but does not end in a single acronym: STD, for sexually transmitted disease.

THE SEXISM OF STDS

In fairness, the enlightened optimism about falling teen pregnancy rates has already taken a scholarly drubbing on other grounds. As the Alan Guttmacher Institute has further observed, that good news is counterbalanced by certain other less happy facts, including that "the proportion of young people who have had sex at an early age has increased" and that rates of both pregnancy and childbearing "continue to be substantially higher among U.S. adolescents than among young people in comparable industrialized countries."[6] Moreover, out-of-wedlock births, though not accelerating at their previous rates, remain at a level unprecedented in American history; a third of all births in 2003, for example, were to unwed mothers. As one demographer has put the point, "The *best* anyone can say about the rate of illegitimacy is that it appears to be slowing—nothing more."[7]

All that is true enough, but it is also somewhat beside the point compared to this fact: Nothing, but nothing, is as potentially destructive of adult complacency over teen sex as the statistics on what today's teenagers are contracting because of it. The adolescent epidemic of STDs is one of the most underreported bad-news stories on the American scene.[8]

Just how underreported is perhaps best summarized by a two-part *New York Times* series in March 2004 dedicated to the putative new trend of adolescent restraint about sex. Like related efforts to make that point lately, this one infers from two real facts—falling pregnancy and birth rates—a conclusion that does not necessarily follow: that is, that there has been a similar decline in teen sexual activity. To the contrary: The most in-depth recent study of teen sexual behavior by the Centers for Disease Control (CDC), based on ten years' worth of surveys and six groups of teenagers whose sample sizes ranged from ten thousand to sixteen thousand each, concludes: *"During 1991–2001, the overall prevalence of current sexual activity did not change."*[9]

Even so, the deeper problem with the *Times* report is not that it rests on some pretty suspect numbers (though it does that; one of the studies the reporter cites to show "restraint," for example, says that oral sex rates have held steady among white teenagers and risen among black teenagers these last ten or so years—a point that matters because oral sex spreads the herpes virus). The deeper problem is the emblematic one: In the thousands of words explaining what's new in teen sex, part one of the series does not even mention STDs apart from HIV, and part two uses the term just twice, cursorily.

This is not to say that media neglect of the STD explosion is willful, but it is real and appears driven by two different forces. One, the feminist-inspired kids-are-all-right crowd needs to ignore the STD story out of sheer ideological necessity; after all, if teens are indeed handling the sexual revolution just fine, the fact that millions of them have simultaneously contracted incurable and sometimes dangerous diseases on account of it is a polemical bummer. Two, from the point of view of the people who think teen sex is a problem, the STD story appears less than attractive for other reasons. Some of them, including social conservatives, do not want to talk about teen sex, period. Others, those who are already supervising their children and teenagers intensely, do not see the problem of STDs as an immediate priority.

Whatever the sociology behind the story's relatively low profile, the teenage STD problem remains one of the worst health problems that adolescents face. As with the example of smoking several decades ago, the medical consensus to that effect is far ahead of other public opinion. STDs are also like smoking in this other way: They are unlikely to cause teenagers permanent damage right now (though they will to some) but very likely to cause serious problems later on—some irreversible and some even fatal, and especially to girls. Anyone who thinks either of these claims is overstated or who is still shaking the pom-poms for those falling teen pregnancy rates should read a scientific volume published in 1997 by the authoritative Institute of Medicine called *The Hidden Epidemic: Confronting Sexually Transmitted Diseases*.[10]

This tome, eighteen months in the making and involving the work of hundreds of medical professionals nationwide, is a thoroughgoing expert examination of sexually transmitted infections in the United States. While its findings are not the household knowledge they ought to be, they do reflect the rising alarm of the physicians who actually wrestle with the

STD epidemic day in and day out.[11] Dr. David Satcher, who later became Surgeon General, wrote this professional perspective for the book's jacket: "This report on sexually transmitted diseases will go down in history as one of the outstanding contributions of this organization to the health of people in this country and the world."

So how bad *is* the problem? "Of the top ten most frequently reported diseases in 1995 in the United States," according to the Institute of Medicine, "five are STDs," a blanket term for more than twenty-five infectious organisms transmitted through sexual activity. "The spectrum of health consequences," the report goes on to document, "ranges from mild acute illness to serious long-term complications such as cervical, liver, and other cancers and reproductive health problems." Moreover, "STDs predominantly affect healthy youth and young adults," and "the consequences can be lifelong. *This impact is largely unrecognized by the public and even some health care professionals* [emphasis added]."[12] In sum, STDs "represent a growing threat to the nation's health, and national action is urgently needed."

The Hidden Epidemic also draws attention to another critical fact that most people do not understand: The STD epidemic is sexually biased in its damages; it is generally far more serious for girls than boys. (The exception is males who engage in unprotected homosexual sex, which puts them at the highest risk for certain life-threatening STDs—HIV infection, hepatitis B virus infection, and anal cancer, as well as unique risks of anal syphilis, urethritis, and "a range of oral and gastrointestinal infections."[13]) The reasons for this epidemiological bias are numerous.

One, the infections are often "silent" or without symptoms in females. To take one of numerous examples, "30 to 80 percent of women with gonorrhea are asymptomatic, while fewer than 5 percent of men have no symptoms."[14] This means that many infected females do not seek treatment early on but instead become aware of the infection only after it has had years to wreak its havoc.

Two, by dint of their more complex physiology, females are more likely to have complications of all sorts. Human papillomavirus, or HPV, in particular, increases risks of cancer of the cervix and cancers of the vagina, vulva, and anus. This currently incurable sexually transmitted virus is now thought to be the most prevalent STD of all, though it was barely even recorded twenty years ago. (By contrast, heterosexual men infected with these virus types face only the risk of cancer of the penis, which is relatively rare.) Moreover, this virus not only increases those risks down the road but also now. One of the most frightening sentences in the book reads, "Cervical cancer rates and cohort mortality from cervical cancer . . . are increasing among young women, *undoubtedly a reflection of increased exposure to STDs such as human papillomavirus* [emphasis added]."[15]

Three, adolescent females are not only more likely than grown women to get these infections, but certain things about their bodies, including the sorts of cells in and around their cervixes, mean that some infections will afflict them disproportionately and at times almost exclusively, including gonorrhea and chlamydial infection (both curable but often undetected, and both have the potential to complicate giving birth).[16] *The Hidden Epidemic* further reports that up to 30 or 40 percent of sexually active adolescent females had already been infected with chlamydia according to studies over a dozen years old.[17]

Four, there is the subject that has been fodder for scores of stories in the last couple of years: the increase in oral sex among teenagers, specifically of the girl-on-boy variety.[18] Many girls apparently think this kind of contact is safe and that they are unlikely to contract diseases from it, but they are wrong. While it is a less efficient transmitter of some infections than other kinds of sex, oral sex does increase the risk of herpes, another incurable disease that causes mouth ulcers and other problems ranging from the uncomfortable to the more serious. Some professionals now believe that most of these problems are spread by oral sex.

Finally, females also complicate the STD epidemic by passing along at least some infections to babies. These include chlamydial infection, gonorrhea, syphilis, cytomegalovirus infection, genital herpes, and HIV. Some of these lead to serious problems in pregnancy such as preterm delivery, premature rupture of membranes, sepsis, and postpartum infection. Others cause neurological and other problems in babies, including stillbirth, low birth weight, conjunctivitis, pneumonia, and sepsis.

Now we come to a hurdle that even the most determined optimist cannot leap. People with an enlightened view might ask, "What about condoms? Don't they solve the problem of STDs?" No, they emphatically do not. Yes, they do form an effective barricade against many viruses and bacteria, subject to user competence and motivation (both chronic issues), but they do not stop the STD that has health professionals particularly alarmed: HPV. The Centers for Disease Control estimated in 2004 that 2 million women a year become infected with HPV. In fact, as of March 2004, the FDA has been weighing the possibility of placing a warning label on condoms for just that reason. The use of condoms will not stop HPV from causing its signature problems: recurring genital warts (removable by being burned off with acid, injected with chemicals, and occasionally by surgery) and cervical cancer.

There are many more profoundly unsettling statistics to be found in *The Hidden Epidemic*, but the bottom line for adolescent girls is especially clear: Millions of them acquire these diseases each year, and "*many of them will have long-term health problems as a result* [emphasis added]."[19] Those numbers are also only the statistical beginning. STDs are very much a work in progress since eight new pathogens were identified between 1980 and 1995 alone. More recent scientific studies suggest that the scope of the problem may be even worse than was understood in 1997. In their work published in 2004, researchers at the CDC and elsewhere used a variety of data—national STD case reports, surveys, and statistics from the World Health Organization (WHO)—to make estimates of incidence and prevalence for the year 2000. In addition to the prevalence estimates cited earlier in this chapter, these researchers further found that 88 percent of the increase in young people's STDs had to do with three particular infections: human papillomavirus, trichomoniasis, and chlamydia. Each one of these is associated with real problems, at least for some girls, including cancer risks, complications of pregnancy and delivery, or infertility.

For readers interested in putting a human face on some of those dry medical statistics, there is also a book that was published in 2002 called *Epidemic: How Teen Sex Is Killing Our Kids*.[20] Author and doctor Meg Meeker reports from what she calls "the front lines" of the war on

STDs: her pediatric office. In the course of twenty years she has shifted increasingly to handling problems seldom seen before in teenage patients—abnormal Pap smears, herpes, pelvic inflammatory disease, HPV, and the rest. That experience has changed her thinking about how advisable it is to enable teen sex. What Meeker describes are examples from her own caseload, and some of her stories are enough to stop any crypto-optimist cold. They include "precancerous conditions in girls as young as 14, infertility in girls barely old enough to get pregnant, babies infected with STDs their mothers didn't know they had."[21] At one point she has to tell a boy who is still wearing braces that he has HIV. She is particularly chilling on the subject of HPV for the same reason that the hundreds of doctors represented by the Institute of Medicine also zeroed in on it: "It has the dubious distinction of being one of the few causes of cancer we know about, and is directly responsible for 99.7 percent of cervical cancer cases and the deaths of nearly 5,000 women per year."

Is anyone still looking to "break out the champagne" over teen sex after reading that sentence? If so, one other point emphasized by Meeker might stay their hands. She spells out acutely the dark side of what teen-sex optimists proudly proclaim: *The very contraceptives that have made the teenage birth rate go down have also made casual sex easier than ever, thus making the STD rate simultaneously rocket up.*

Therein lies a question mark not only for parents but also for a medical profession that has effectively subsidized the infections now colonizing millions of teens via the easy provision of contraceptives. Meeker writes: "Twenty years ago, I wouldn't have hesitated to prescribe oral contraceptives to teenage girls. In fact, any form of birth control was fine with me, as long as the patient used it consistently. As a young doctor swept away by the message of 'safe' sex, I didn't know any better. To me, 'safe' meant not getting pregnant. . . . But today, I think long and hard about prescribing birth control pills or Depo-Provera to kids because this puts them in such grave danger of contracting an STD. In giving a girl birth control that I know will protect her from pregnancy, am I inadvertently encouraging her to pick up a sexually transmitted disease?"[22]

In short, both anecdotally and statistically, the story on teenage STDs contained in these books and in doctors' offices around the country offers powerful evidence that today's sexually active teenagers face serious problems that their parents did not. The STD epidemic has caused real harm to millions of teenagers and young adults, most of them females, whose bodies are being silently impaired by viruses and bacteria that may cause long-term trouble—from infertility to complications of pregnancy to increased risks of various cancers.

PARENTS: THE ULTIMATE PROPHYLACTIC

Well enough, our stalwart skeptical reader might say: The prevalence of sexually transmitted diseases among teenagers does look to be higher than most people realize, but what evidence connects the acquiring of those diseases to absent parents? What facts show that the one-parent or dual-career household is more likely to produce kids experimenting with sex? Where exactly is the social science smoking gun in this?

Some readers, I sincerely hope, will be snorting up their decaf skim lattes at that last question. Not all of us need the social sciences to guess which way the "causal vectors" between absent parents and sexually active teenagers might run. It does take a heart of stone not to laugh at the earnest efforts to "prove" the connection, as when the *Atlanta Journal-Constitution* discovered that "Unsupervised Teens Have More Sex." On the other hand, to ward off the inevitable chorus of "correlations don't prove causality," it should be noted that research does confirm what some students of human nature might already suspect: Teenagers whose parents are not around have more sex (and drugs and alcohol and cigarettes) than teenagers whose parents are around.[23]

To my knowledge, the most suggestive study is the one whose authors thought to ask this rather fundamental question: Where are kids *having* sex? This was the inquiry behind a study published by several researchers in the December 2002 issue of *Pediatrics*.[24] Their answer, based on a sample of over a thousand boys from six different public schools, was very simple: "Among the respondents who had had intercourse, 91% said that the last time had been in a home setting, including their own home (37%), their partner's home (43%), and a friend's home (12%), usually after school." Moreover, not only did empty homes invite more sex, but the longer they were empty, the more sex was had. "Youths who were unsupervised for 30 or more hours per week were more likely to be sexually active compared with those who were unsupervised for 5 hours a week or less." In conclusion: "As youths come of age, parents probably believe that it is appropriate to leave them increasingly on their own, and, accordingly, prevention approaches have concentrated on providing information and motivation for abstinence or safer sex. However, given the independent association between the amount of unsupervised time and sexual behaviors (with STD rates suggestive of particularly risky sexual behaviors) and substance use behaviors, it is worth considering increasing youth supervision, if not by parents, then by programs organized at school or other community settings."

Looking again at that breakdown of where kids have sex, you may be wondering: Whatever happened to the proverbial backseat? Well, who needs a cramped plastic bench when your family's (or girlfriend's) adult-empty home is so much more comfortable and convenient?

Any teenager hell-bent on having sex will find a way, and a great many things in adolescents' lives are really or effectively out of parental reach—parties, friends' homes, sleepaway camps, and more. But to sound an obvious note, this does seem to make it all the more crucial to supervise them whenever one can. Teenagers potentially face obstacles, sexually and otherwise, that adults do not—from lacking the car keys to having curfews to being cut off from the pocket money that finances their social lives. Teenagers have home computers that can be history-checked. Teenagers remain vulnerable to an adult saying no to all kinds of things. And so, with sex as with any other aspect of child-rearing, arranging incentives either for or against an activity depends at least in part on whether an adult is around to do it.

ABSENT FATHERS, EARLIER SEX?

The fact of the STD epidemic alone should demolish any lingering complacency about those falling pregnancy rates. But as it turns out, that epidemic is only one way of making the connection between lack of parental supervision and teen sex. There are at least two other ways in which absent parents have contributed to the sexual jump-starting of some of today's children and adolescents. These two ways are unlikely to be talked about in celebrations of family diversity or enlightened discussions of sexual learning curves, though they really ought to be.

One way in which absent parents—specifically, absent fathers—may inadvertently increase the likelihood of their teenagers having sex has yet to be proven as fact, though the theory is an interesting one. It concerns the question of a possible relationship between earlier menstruation and absent fathers. A girl's age at her first period correlates strongly with the age at which she engages in sex. That is to say, and as studies confirm, the earlier Western girls start menstruating, the earlier they are likely to engage in sexual relations. As a 2003 report from the Alan Guttmacher Institute puts it, "Age and age at menarche strongly affect the likelihood of sexual initiation and teenage pregnancy."[25] Throughout the Western world, the age at which girls first begin menstruating has been falling for the last hundred years— from roughly 14.8 years in 1890 to 12.5 in 1988, according to figures widely accepted in the medical community.

It is all the more intriguing, then, that recent research suggests that one factor lowering the age of menarche may be the absence of biological fathers from many homes. This hypothesis, thought unusual only a few years ago, has lately been gaining new respect as one possible answer to the puzzle of what is going on with earlier menstrual periods. One 1999 study in the *Journal of Personality and Social Psychology* summarizes, and other studies have also suggested, that "the quality of fathers' investment in the family emerged as the most important feature of the proximal family environment relative to daughters' pubertal timing."[26]

How can this be? Some researchers believe the answer is pheromones. These secreted substances, which humans pick up via their noses without being conscious of it, trigger certain chemical responses. Although the process may sound mysterious, it really may not be; it is pheromones, for example, that are thought to explain a phenomenon common to women living in a house or dorm together: the synchronization of menstrual periods. For that very reason, the notion that pheromones play a role in setting the point of menarche for young girls makes a certain intuitive sense.

According to this theory, just as the father's presence in the house seems to delay menarche because his pheromones signal to the daughter that her sexual maturation is in no hurry, so, too, conversely, the presence in the household of nonbiological males is thought to biologically accelerate certain young girls. Maternal boyfriends, stepfathers, stepbrothers, and other unrelated males, researchers theorize, give off a chemical signal that is different from the biological father, one that speeds up the process of maturation instead. That is one reading of another study on the subject, a 2000 publication in *Child Development*.[27] In this study three factors apparently associated with the onset of puberty were isolated: absence of the biological father, depression in the mother, and the presence in the home of a nonbiologically related male. According to the study, the younger the girl at the time the unrelated male is introduced, the earlier her period will begin.

If the theory about pheromones turns out to be true, it will connect absent parents to other dimensions of the teen-sex matrix. The earlier sexual activity starts, the more partners a girl is likely to have; the more partners, the more risk of STDs. A 2003 study of more than ten thousand women was summarized as follows in "Father Absence, Parental Care, and Female Reproductive Development" in *Evolution and Human Biology*: "Divorce/separation between birth and 5 years predicted early menarche, first sexual intercourse, first pregnancy, and shorter duration of first marriage."[28] In other words, it predicted more teenage sex.

The pheromone theory remains speculative, but a third and final connection between absent parents and the sexualization of kids is not a hypothesis at all but proven fact: The absence of protective adults from children's lives has increased child sexual abuse. Family breakdown and related parental absence have put a great many children in harm's way, particularly where sexual predators are concerned. This structural problem will not go away anytime soon, which is why child sexual abuse won't, either. In essence, *the fastest way to raise a child's risk of sexual abuse is to take one or both biological parents out of the home.*

Certainly the upward trend since divorce and unwed motherhood became commonplace is highly suggestive. The most comprehensive ongoing study of child sexual abuse in the United States is that of the National Clearinghouse on Child Abuse and Neglect (NCCAN), which has reported in detail on data gathered from three periods: 1979–80 (NIS-1), 1986–87 (NIS-2), and 1993–94 (NIS-3), the latest year for which the data have been analyzed.[29] These congressionally mandated reports show a clear spike upward in child sexual abuse for the years represented. In particular, NIC-3 reports that "there have been substantial and significant increases in the incidence of child abuse and neglect since the last national incidence study was conducted in 1986," and that "sexual abuse more than doubled" between 1986 and 1993—by their numbers, from 133,600 incidents to 300,200.

Now let us connect some social dots. What was happening elsewhere in the country when those numbers on sexual abuse started to rise? By 1985 more than half of American mothers with young children were in the paid marketplace. That was also the year that the last hold-out state, South Dakota, adopted no-fault divorce laws, a new legal arrangement that made divorce much easier to get. In other words, the rise in sexual abuse cases coincides remarkably with the two engines of the empty-parent home kicking into higher gear.

Moreover, although acknowledging that at least some of that dramatic rise might stem from better reporting, the NCCAN also emphasizes that there are reasons for believing the rise to be real. How could it not be? In the case of sexual abuse, unlike that of other kinds of harm to children catalogued by the abuse expert, the most important determinant appears to be *the absence of biological parents.* In other words, while children do risk abuse at the hands of biological parents, they are much more likely to be sexually abused by a cohabiting or other male who is not biologically related to them. One 1997 study by authority David Finklehor found that 7.4 percent of children with a single parent had been sexually abused, compared to 4.2 percent of children living with both biological parents.[30] Any number of other studies confirm that from the point of view of avoiding sexual abuse, children and teenagers are far better off with their biological parents than with substitutes.

This is the meaning of British psychiatrist Theodore Dalrymple's particularly arresting formulation: "He who says single parenthood and easy divorce says child sexual abuse."[31] One 2001 article on child sexual abuse among low-income families studied the question of perpetrator identity, that is, who exactly was preying on the children. As David Blankenhorn observed at the time, "Only 10 percent of the perpetrators were biological fathers and only 4 percent were strangers. Which means 86 percent of the perpetrators were known to the family, but were someone other than the child's father." In short, "the presence of the biological father in the home in actuality is a protective factor against child sexual abuse. . . . The most likely perpetrators of such abuse are adult males known to the victim, often residing within the household, at least for a portion of the time of the abuse."[32] Reviewing the evidence, he concludes, "The best prevention program . . . for child sexual abuse is this: 'Have two loving parents in a stable home, at least one of whom is not working for long periods of time outside the household, and who do not drink excessively or commit crime.'"

As this example suggests, the benefits of a present and protective biological father are not only self-evident but increasingly a focus of social science itself. Less noted elsewhere in the literature, however, is this related point: In order for predatory males to abuse (and they are almost always males), they must first have access. The increasing absence from home of biological mothers as well as fathers obviously increases exactly that.

WHAT WE SAY VERSUS WHAT WE DO

In sum, in two areas of real as opposed to virtual sex—STDs and child sexual abuse—today's children and teenagers once again compare disadvantageously with the generation of their parents; and in another area, that of pheromones, there is reason to wonder whether absent fathers are not a factor in the younger ages at which girls have sex. Moreover, even the one positive indicator to which progressive-minded people cling—somewhat lower teen pregnancy rates—does not prove their all-is-well point. The very technologies that have made that dip possible, in particular the long-term contraceptives that amount to temporary sterilization, have also given teenagers even less reason to think seriously before having sex.

In the statistics on teenage STDs lurks one of the saddest stories in this book. Here is a clear-cut example that laissez-faire parenting has caused real harm to millions of teenagers, most seriously the girls whose bodies now carry viruses latent with short- and long-term problems—everything from infertility to increased risks of various cancers. Many of them do not even know what they have, and neither do their happy-talk parents who continue on in their enlightened happy-talk way—responsibly buying their responsible adolescents birth control, all the while clinging to ideological reassurances about "responsible" teenage sex.

Moreover, the story on teen sex is poignant in another way that may be difficult to quantify but is nevertheless real. The promiscuity that has created this epidemic signals a desperation, a craven bid for affection that points up the emotional emptiness of at least some of these kids' worlds. Casual sex on their scale surely suggests a profound need for love not met elsewhere, starting at home.[33]

Like other payments neglected and allowed to grow overdue, this one will be steep when it comes, at least for some of those girls. Their organs pummeled for decades by HPV and/or chlamydia, they will not know till they try to become pregnant and can't. Some will suffer complications of pregnancy itself, and some will contract STD-linked cancers—perhaps even as a new generation of optimists continues to cheerlead for value-neutral adolescent sex. Some will pass genital warts and worse onto their babies. And to note the eerie generational twist on all this, some of those well-meaning parents buying their teenager contraceptives today will not become grandparents one, two, or three decades from now, on account of what some daughters will have contracted under the regimen they are supposedly handling so well.

To say that absent parents make teenage sex more likely is not to say they are the only factor, but it is easier to rage at the screen or other abstractions—corporate America, music videos, and the rest—than do the more tedious work of actually supervising the kids. In a fascinating essay called "The Contradictions of Parenting in a Media Age," Kay S. Hymowitz of the Manhattan Institute calls attention to the "dissonance between what parents say about popular culture and what they actually do about it."[34] As she observes, American parents tell every survey and outlet available about their disgust with popular culture, and yet toddlers watch more hours of television year by year; some 65 percent of kids eight to eighteen have television sets in their bedrooms, and some 58 percent of households watch television during dinner. Does that circle really square?

In drawing attention to Hymowitz's point—that many of us are not putting our money where our mouths are, at least not when it comes to our electronic babysitters—I do not mean that efforts at resistance are beside the point. I say that not only as an author but also as a mother as sick as any other of the Happy Meal dollies dressed like streetwalkers, of the thong underwear fashioned for eight-year-olds, of the video games for boys of all ages laced not only with violence but also simulated pornography. *Yes*, the parents and professionals who police and attack such corruption are on the right side of a generally thankless cause. *Yes*, the corporate excuses—such as MTV president Judy McGrath's droll horror over those "five seconds none of us knew anything about"—ought to be grounds for dismissal. Many parents feel a stab of guilt over not doing more in the way of boycotting, channel blocking, and other domestic activism, and likely we should.

Yet more attention should also be given to this question: How does a lack of supervision allow many teenagers to dive headfirst into cybersex and Internet pornography, both of which are believed by Meeker and others to be fueling real-life experimentation? One of her case studies involves a young teenager suffering depression and panic attacks, which, it turned out, were the result of obsessive pursuit of pornography. The verdict of social science on the causal relationship between fake sex and real sex isn't in yet, perhaps because the clinical phenomenon of pornography addiction is too new. Even so, Dr. Meg Meeker's larger point stands: More teenagers today are more intimately familiar with smut than any preceding generation, and we don't need longitudinal data to suspect a problem here. As a professor remarks to her: "[W]hat about these young kids now? Cybersex is shaping their sex lives. Twelve- and 13-year-old teens are having cybersex before they have real sex. It is shaping their expectations, it changes their relationships. It will even begin shaping their sexuality." How could it not?

Even so, the front lines of today's teen sex scene are not to be found on the screen or tube that gives them the ideas for sex but, rather, in the empty homes and bedrooms where they actually have it. A lot of corrective thinking is overdue on this subject, and it starts by getting certain adults to first do no harm. Some might need to stop cheerleading on the sexual sidelines and start learning about what today's kids risk that baby boomers did not. Some parents might need to do more to keep a warm body in the house, especially after school. Above all, let the facts about STDs put a stop to all the happy talk of how glorious it is to be young in this sexual dawn. If tobacco were doing to teenage girls' lungs what intercourse and oral sex are now doing to their ovaries and other female organs, there would be no more adult talk of "safe sex" than there is talk of "safe cigarettes." The difference is that one can always stop smoking, whereas some of the STDs are for keeps.

8

Specialty Boarding Schools:
Tough Love or Ultimate Outsourcing?

A FEW YEARS AGO, CURIOUS ABOUT A BOOK RECEIVING RAVE RE-
views from my older children and several of their friends, I read Louis
Sacher's 1998 runaway hit novel for teenagers and preteens called *Holes*.[1]
Winner of both the Newberry and National Book awards, it is the story
of a boy who is unjustly packed off to a military-style institution for
teenagers, ironically called Camp Green Lake. That's ironic because the
place is more like a jail than a camp, nothing is green, and there is no lake.
Though sometimes effectively played for laughs, Camp Green Lake
struck me as a truly frightening creation—an institution run by sadistic
authorities whose main activity, in the name of building character, is
forcing thirsty and exhausted teenagers to dig holes in rock under the
blazing Texas sun.

Sacher's tale has a happy ending—luckily for younger readers who
otherwise would find it too dark. Yet as it turns out, and as I did not know
on first reading the story, Camp Green Lake is far from being pure fic-
tion. It is actually more descriptive of reality for some American teenagers
than most people realize. For among other transformations that might tell
us something about how children and adolescents are faring today, one
surely worth noting is the tenfold expansion during this last decade in
specialty institutions delivering round-the-clock, out-of-the-house care
and supervision for better-off troubled teenagers.

Unlike previous generations, American parents today who decide
that their teenagers will be better off living elsewhere have a truly wide,
albeit very costly, array of institutions from which to choose, including

therapeutic boarding schools, emotional growth schools, residential treatment schools, boot camps, and wilderness programs. These specialty
schools are not to be confused with the traditional boarding schools,
which emphasize academic and other standard achievements. To the contrary: They have been created and designed precisely to fill a need that
traditional prep and private schools do not and cannot: out-of-home,
24/7, behavior-modifying care for adolescents with emotional and other
problems.[2] This is a newly minted, quite unprecedented phenomenon. As
reporter Sara Rimer put it in a 2001 *New York Times* article, it is a "multi-
billion-dollar industry that has surged in the last 10 years to satisfy what
many say is a booming market in parental desperation."[3]

A tenfold growth in any industry in as many years is a remarkable
fact in itself, if only commercially. But a tenfold growth in this particular industry has obvious and immediate bearing on one question raised
repeatedly in these pages: Are some American adolescents in worse shape
than adolescents before them? Here again, in the case of the specialty
schools, is suggestive evidence that the answer for certain teenagers is
yes. To put that tenfold growth another way is to observe this corollary:
Roughly ten times as many teenagers are now being labeled "troubled"
and sent away to behavior-modifying boarding schools than was done a
decade ago.

Where does this spectacular industry growth come from? Why now,
and what does it tell us? These questions are different from the more
data-driven inquiries of some other subjects taken up in this book—as
they must be because the adolescent reality represented by the specialty-
school system is itself unique. It is, for example, markedly smaller than
other trends previously described, involving only thousands rather than
millions of teenagers. It is also darker in the sense that much light remains to be shed on it. Despite numerous detailed investigative accounts,
only one book-length treatment of the subject yet exists, and that one is a
partisan polemic. Yet it is a story offering incontrovertible evidence of one
more singular connection between absent parents and obviously damaged
and messed-up kids.

A BOOM MARKET

The first thing to be said of the specialty schools is also the least controversial: Business is booming. In 1991, Sara Rimer wrote in her *Times* piece, there were "perhaps two dozen" such programs for troubled teenagers. Ten years later, 250 such schools were considered reputable enough to be listed by the Independent Educational Consultants Association (IECA), which also estimated that there were hundreds more operating that are not yet accredited. New schools, Rimer further reported, are opening at a rate of three per month.

Other, more indirect measures of the specialty-school industry confirm this stunning growth. As of 2001, for example, the IECA itself—one of several professional referral-type organizations that have grown apace with specialty schools—included 365 members, "more than double" the total of a decade before, according to its executive director. Again, as with the schools themselves, hundreds more agents also operate unofficially outside the IECA. Similarly, the National Association of Therapeutic Schools and Programs (NATSAP), another organization brought into existence by the schools, was created in January 1999 "to serve as a national resource for programs and professionals assisting young people beleaguered by emotional and behavioral difficulties," in the words of its Web site. NATSAP literature also emphasizes how fast the field has grown.[4]

So far it is agreed that there is a thriving demand for institutions that provide day care and night care for teenagers. To venture beyond this point about the schools, however, is to enter a vitriolic swamp in which ferociously opposed camps of observers employ utterly different vocabularies to describe what is going on. To administrators and some grateful parents, a specialty school like Casa by the Sea in Mexico is a lifesaving intervention in a problem teen's life, to say nothing of a "foreign experience [that] results in a stronger appreciation for home and family" (as one brochure puts it). To other people, including some former residents, it is a hellhole of deprivation and brainwashing overseen by cruel guards and behavior modification practices that would be imprisonable offenses in the United States. Similarly, to the desperate parents who employ them for $1,500 and up, the burly men who take their teenagers by force to far-away schools (usually without saying good-bye at home) are "trained escorts," known also as "friendly gorillas," without whom these lifesaving interventions could not even begin. To at least some of the former residents so conveyed, the gorillas are instead abductors, brutes, and kidnappers. To cut to the ultimate dispute about specialty institutions, some residents and their families credit the programs with saving their lives, others with having destroyed them.

The depth of controversy over these institutions can't even be captured in a few short pages, let alone adjudicated. But to begin to understand what is genuinely new here is to recognize at least this much: The aggressively cheerful promotional literature put out by the schools and referral agencies reads very oddly alongside the harsh details about daily life in some schools as chronicled by former residents and investigative reports.

The *New York Times* article quoted earlier was followed by several other detailed investigative pieces on the same phenomenon by another reporter, Tim Weiner (also in the *Times*).[5] Based on his account of hundreds of interviews with participants on all sides of the specialty-school equation, Weiner's articles (which have been vehemently disputed by some parents and school administrators) amount to a particularly harrowing account of this new form of adolescent institutionalization, at least as it is relayed by some parents and former residents.

"Ryan Fraidenburgh was 14 when he was brought here [to a specialty school in Mexico] shackled, kicking and screaming" begins one of the scores of stories related by Weiner.[6] "Two men carrying handcuffs and leg irons came for him at his mother's house in Sacramento, Calif., shoved him into a van and bound him hand and foot. They drove him 12 hours south, over the Mexican border, into a high-walled compound near here called Casa by the Sea."

There, Ryan encountered what some would call "behavior modification"; his parents later decried it as treatment like "an animal in a cage." Punishments for infractions included lying on the floor in an isolation room, sometimes for days, or standing with his nose to the wall for several hours. Talking was discouraged apart from speaking when spoken to, and affection was forbidden. Under the interesting if arguably problematic power structure on which the school prides itself, discipline was imposed in part by older juveniles who had "ascended" to levels where they could now do to other, younger residents what had once been done to them— such as inflicting punishments of isolation and physical discomfort (some say pain) for days on end.

In one way, Ryan's story turns out to be unusual; his parents, unlike many, removed him from the institution ahead of schedule and went on record as regretting having put him there. In most other ways, however, his case appears prototypical of others that Weiner relates—and therein hangs the real investigative tale. Like many other teenagers sent to reside in them—and markedly unlike those of previous generations sent to traditional reform schools—Ryan Fraidenburgh was not a criminal or protocriminal. Essentially, he was a truant whose parents had other things to do.

Many of the youths in these schools, Weiner explains, "have never had encounters with the police, or with drugs"; numerous other sources in his reports and others back that claim.[7] One administrator told Weiner of his own institution that "about 70 percent" of the residents are "not hard-core," but kids who "cannot communicate at home."[8] Similarly, a referral service called teencrisissolutions.com describes the typical candidate for specialty schools in these terms: "Upon entering, students generally have a history of poor decision making, disrespect and blaming others for what happened in their life. There may have been little or no honest communication with parents." Note what is not being said here: violence, suicidal or homicidal tendencies, criminal record, and other such red-flag words. The fascinating fact, well documented by Weiner especially, is that it is not criminality and hard cases that drive the boom in specialty schools but, rather, the gray-area cases whose common denominators include some things outside of any teenager's control: "divorce, adoption, drugs, sex, low self-esteem, ADD/ADHD symptoms, and death of a parent."

Like many adolescents whose stories are told by Weiner and others, Ryan Fraidenburgh was also emblematic of the specialty-school population in another way: His parents were "in the middle of a bitter divorce and custody battle," during which they decided to handle their truant teenager by sending him to one school he could not skip while they fought things out. In fact, just about every account from these schools comes sooner or later to the d-word, *divorce*. It is so common to the pool of would-be residents that some educational consultants also offer "custody counseling" upon request. And, finally, Ryan is typical of many other stories that Weiner relates in one other way: The Fraidenburghs are well-off.

That is not to say that all the adolescents now detained in the specialty system represent better-off families. At least one mother reported by Weiner had to mortgage the house to raise the tuition, and the fact that financial incentives are offered by many institutions suggests that it is a burden for some families. (Typically, one gets a tuition break for successfully recommending someone else's troubled teenager.) Even so, the overwhelming majority of the parents and kids appear to be at least middle- and, more likely, upper-middle-class families that might be known as the socioeconomic cream of the crop. Indeed, they would have to be because tuition at most of these specialty institutions runs between $40,000 and $80,000 per year.

Weiner's articles zero in on another troubling aspect of the specialty-school trend: The institutions are proliferating in places far removed from the American scene and from American law. Specialty boarding schools in the United States, he explains, "have faced increasing legal and licensing challenges over the years." Thus, "more and more are moving abroad—some to Mexico, Central America, or the Caribbean—where they operate largely under the regulation radar and where they employ minimum-wage custodians more than teachers or therapists." Weiner further quotes Ron Woodbury, publisher of a report that rates troubled-teen programs, as acknowledging that American programs have moved abroad "to avoid the laws and regulations of the States." Tuition also tends to be cheaper at the out-of-country institutions. No wonder that the overseas schools, according to Weiner, are "growing so fast that United States consular officials in overseas embassies say they have no idea how many such programs exist."

A third point made clear by Weiner's articles and others is that despite the attempt to minimize frictions by moving the schools offshore and farther from legal reach, accusations of abuse against specialty institutions abound. The World Wide Association of Specialty Schools, or WWASP—the largest of the specialty-schools organizations, which handles around twenty-five hundred children and teenagers—is a particular lightning rod. "Over the past seven years local governments and State Department officials have investigated WWASP-affiliated programs in Mexico, the Czech Republic, and Samoa on charges of physical abuse and immigration violations," Weiner writes.[9] Some schools have imploded under rather dramatic circumstances (as when Costa Rican authorities shut down one behavior-modification school, Dundee, on human-rights grounds). Yet, as the schools themselves make very clear, lawsuits are a two-way street. According to its Web site, which lays out a very different view of the reasons for student disgruntlement, WWASP has sued certain critics for "defamation, conspiracy, and business interference."

Quite apart from questions of lawsuits and what might technically qualify as "abuse," certain reported practices that may be perfectly legal are troublesome in their own right. Consider examples from one WWASP institution, Spring Creek Lodge Academy in Montana. One former matriculant tells Weiner: "There are girls on so many antidepressants given out by the program that they can't move. They can't get out of bed. They are like dead animals." A mother reports of her son that "he came out thirty pounds lighter, acting like a zombie. . . . He was worse, far worse." A former staff member relates: "They take kids down to the Vermilion Bridge at night, blindfold them, and push them off into the river; they come back into the woods, and they come back hurt. . . . They claim it's a mind-increaser. I think it breaks the kids down—breaks their will down. Mentally, they do damage. Emotionally, too."[10]

In sum, what some schools call "tough love" is very obviously what some people (and arguably some laws, too) consider physical and mental abuse. For that reason it is all the more striking that Spring Creek's associate director echoes what "37 parents, children and staff members" interviewed by Weiner also report: "Few Spring Creek Lodge children are delinquents."[11]

SAVIORS OR SADISTS?

Another investigative reporter who dissected the American specialty-school phenomenon, this time in a lengthy two-part article for the British *Observer Magazine* in 2003, is Decca Aitkenhead.[12] She focuses on one particularly rigid school, Tranquility Bay in Jamaica (where she was the first journalist allowed access in five years). Aitkenhead, who literally stumbled onto the story of specialty schools after passing by the walled Tranquility compound on the beach during a trip to Jamaica, makes many points similar to Weiner's.

The "typical Tranquility parent," she reports, is "busy, wealthy," and often en route to a second family; a "messy divorce and remarriage are the norm among these parents." As for the students, though many have experimented with drugs or used them routinely, truly acute drug problems actually disqualify one for membership. Tranquility, like most other catchall problem-behavior schools, does not accept real addicts. And although some students have landed at the school by first landing in court, many have not been in trouble with the law but were sent there instead for low-level orders of dysfunction: "running away from home, sleeping around, or being expelled from school . . . wearing inappropriate clothes, using bad language, or hanging around with the wrong sorts of friends," in Aitkenhead's words.

Like Weiner, Aitkenhead also details behavior-modification practices that are surely extreme by just about anyone's standards—whether or not they violate U.S. or Jamaican law:

> Guards take them (if necessary by force) to a small bare room and make them (again by force if necessary) lie flat on their face, arms by their sides, on the tiled floor. Watched by a guard, they must remain lying face down, forbidden to speak or move a muscle except for 10 minutes every hour, when they may sit up and stretch before resuming the position. Modest meals are brought to them, and at night they sleep on the floor of the corridor outside under electric light and the gaze of a guard. At dawn they resume the position. . . . One boy told me he'd spent six months in OP [observation

placement]. I didn't think this could be true, but it transpired it was not even exceptional. "Oh no," says [the American owner of Tranquility Bay]. "The record is actually held by a female." On and off, she spent 18 months lying on her face.

In addition to these and other forms of dramatic behavior modification, Tranquility Bay, like many other specialty schools, also discourages contact between student and home, and instructs parents to discount complaints about treatment (on the grounds that the students can be expected to lie). In effect, the strategy of these programs is to improve communication between parent and student by first rendering the student incommunicado. Tranquility Bay, by the way, accepts children as young as eleven.

If the details of the investigational stories such as Weiner's and Aitkenhead's raise questions about some specialty institutions, they also make clear that many parents and administrators earnestly and passionately believe the schools are as tough as nails because they have to be. Their real business is saving adolescent lives. In fact, many or even most of the children and teenagers who have been residents appear to have real and awful problems. Some have tried to leave home, many have been involved with sex or drugs or both, and others have had problems such as eating disorders or histories of self-mutilation. A fair number seem also to have records of two particular parental abominations: failing and dropping out of school. Moreover, the stiff price of admission speaks poignantly to the fact that for many parents these schools are the last resort and hope. After all, practically no one, however rich, spends $40,000 to $80,000 a year without serious reason.

A high number of those formerly desperate parents report the schools a godsend. "With my son it worked," one father related. "[I]t's not going to work for everyone. When you send your kid there, you're giving them the last chance to turn their lives around." "They are very physically severe at [a school in Jamaica]," acknowledges one mother whose son had two teeth knocked loose by a staff member and spent eight months in the "isolation room." "[But] I do think the program helps a lot of families that are desperate and don't know where to turn." Aitkenhead similarly quotes one Tranquility Bay father who speaks for many: "People who say this place is too harsh, they've never had their own troubled kids. If you criticize it, you don't know what the hell you are talking about."[13]

Parent gratitude is also a major theme of the Web sites and promotional literature for the schools, which abound with personal testimonials like this one: "This program has not only helped our son, but it has also helped the family to stay together, help each other to deal with life in a better way, fighting the important battles, and being firm when the need arises. This program has been the best experience in our lives, and we thank God each day that we came across teen help." Student testimonials sound similar notes of gratitude. Here is one from Spring Creek Academy, one of the U.S. schools about which serious questions have been aired: "I am home now, and I've done great. I am in high school in the graduating class of 2001. I am playing Varsity Football, running Varsity Track and very involved in my church youth group. I am a person that others can look up to now. I even chose to spend my summer working at one of the program schools. It was wonderful to be there and a way of showing my gratitude by giving back. Without these programs, I would most certainly not be here. I wouldn't get to accomplish all these things that my family and I never thought would happen. You truly have saved my life." Another testimonial from a former student in Tranquility Bay says simply what all the desperate parents reading the literature yearn to hear: "Dad, I never thought I would say this, but thanks for sending me here."

With a few exceptions, administrators and staff members, present and former, tend also to back the programs forcefully. One particularly interesting example was a first-person essay for *Salon* in 2000 called "I Was a Hired Thug for Tough Love."[14] In it, writer Sheerly Avni, who spent two years helping to run a therapeutic wilderness program, takes on a question asked of her by a former graduate of the specialty system: "How the hell do you sleep at night, knowing what you did to kids?" Easy, her answer appears to be. For one thing, readers need to understand just what kind of kids end up being "begged, bribed, tricked and sometimes physically dragged from their beds to get to us." These are no mere angels with dirty faces but "out-of-control, drug-using, sleeping-around, disrespectful, underachieving, overmedicated, underappreciated, blue-haired, multi-pierced, ADHD, ADD, OCD, dyslexic and usually damned unhappy kids."

Avni also describes what some on the administrative side of these schools hope to effect, dramatic positive events longed for and sometimes achieved under the rigors of extreme personal tests. These she calls "the miracles," the moments when hardened teenagers, bending finally under the intended pressures of the program, have their moments of epiphany or self-realization. After detailing the experience of one particular teenager, Karen, Avni explains just why she can sleep at night: She saw personally what parents and promoters of the programs depend on—the idea that "out in the canyons, Karen was the rule, not the exception."

Yet, not surprisingly, beneath the flowery testimonials seethes an underground of hatred and vituperation. To certain former matriculants the specialty-school network is known as "the gulag" (of which they consider themselves survivors). Their opposition is also increasingly institutionalized—in lawsuits and on Web sites where former students share terrifying tales of their experiences. One leader of this opposition is a former *Washington Post* reporter named Alexia Parks. Her 2000 book, *American Gulag: Secret P.O.W. Camps for Teens*, details her attempts to rescue a niece from one such institution; this experience apparently transformed Parks into a crusader. To her and to many former students who offer their own bitter antitestimonials in her book and elsewhere, specialty schools are not heaven-sent, but hell-bound. They represent the "fast-growing rise of a child abuse industry . . . where the tools of war, brainwashing and torture are used on captive children"—a world set in motion by what Parks calls "desperate parents who can afford to pay for the private incarceration of their child."[15]

Some parents have come to agree. One told an Associated Press reporter that Tranquility Bay's $30,000-a-year program turned her two teenage sons into "Stepford children" and that she withdrew them after a surprise visit that found them thin, infected with ringworm, scarred with chemical burns, and displaying "terror in their faces."[16] Similarly, a lawyer representing ten families in legal actions against Teen Help programs summarized it this way: "What they call therapy I call child abuse. My clients were stripped of their identities. . . . They've destroyed some of these kids."[17] Many other resentful former residents appear to agree. If the testimonials of the grateful are authentic, so, too, is the hatred. To read the quotes, message boards, and other postings of the survivors is in one sense much like reading the parent testimonials: They are too deeply felt to be anything but authentic. In other words, there is no denying that some kind of serious suffering has indeed been visited on at least some of these teenagers.

Do the programs work? Empirically speaking, no one really knows, at least not yet. Weiner observes, "No long-term studies of the 1,500 youths who have been to Tranquility Bay, or the 300 who have graduated, have been done," and the same appears true of the other born-yesterday institutions. As for predictions, the programs' defenders point to a high parent-satisfaction rate—95 percent, according to one key industry figure. Detractors predict instead the advent of "a new generation of sadists," as one critic put it. Some families glow with praise for the strict behavior-changing treatment that returned their children to them, and others cite a terrifying world of abandoned and suffering teenagers in which abusive adults rule by force.

Both sides, to judge by the record, can claim part of the truth. On the one hand, in story after story, the abject grief of mothers and sometimes fathers seeps through. What they typically describe would break any parent's heart: the unfathomable, unwanted transformation of yesterday's affectionate baby into today's surly, distant, out-of-control, and often self-destructive teenager. The fact that many of those same parents are simultaneously tearing up their own emotional worlds with divorce and the rest, or having them so torn up by other adults, only adds to the sadness of their stories. For many who feel driven to the specialty system, the radical decision to send a child away represents a dual loss: not only an exiled teenager but often a departing spouse as well.

On the other hand, and just as unmistakably, their chosen last resort causes its share of suffering, too. For just as "tough love" and manifold deprivations obviously do work for certain kids, so also do they manifestly traumatize and stigmatize others. These include the teenagers (sometimes preteenagers) who have ended up in the specialty system not because of drugs or crime or violence, but because of a very different order of adolescent failing: *They were in the way of what adults needed or wanted to do.*

These walking wounded, these faithful correspondents of the flaming Web bulletin boards, are right to want to put a name to this hitherto nonexistent chain of related institutional islands created for troubled and troublesome teens. They are wrong, however, to call it a "gulag"; that is unfair to those who praise the system. More accurately, this new thing is a detention archipelago—the 24/7 version of what used to take twenty or thirty punitive minutes off an erring juvenile's day.

THE REAL TROUBLE WITH TEENAGERS: THEY NEED US

As we have seen on several occasions in this book, the polite consensus of the times goes something like this: There is nothing really new under the American sun about child and teenage problems. The kids are really all right, or at least not worse off than before. And, anyway, absent parents are not to blame for teenagers' problems. The specialty-school explosion refutes these claims handily. It is an obviously fertile petri dish offering evidence of our much larger national experiment in family-child separation, and its evidence is suggestive in the extreme.

Here is a solid real-life example—as opposed to the studies and analyses in which debate is usually framed—of exactly the point that much of current thinking denies: The profound ties between absent or absentee parents, on the one hand, and seriously fouled-up kids on the other. To say this is not to say that all the parents driven to the system fit that description. As the record of their anguish shows, that claim would be unfair. Moreover, some children do have awful problems, and some are better off cared for or corralled by others if their parents are not up to the job. Nonetheless, it is striking—no, it is stunning—just how obvious the absent-parent connection is to almost everyone who has weighed in on the specialty-school scene, whether inside the system or out of it.

If there is one thing about which the legally and morally opposed will agree, it is this: *Off-site parenting is the main force driving all that growth.*

The founder of WWASPs himself cites "the breakdown in the family" as what gave rise to his industry. ("When the family is not functioning, society suffers," he adds.) The executive director of the National Association of Therapeutic Schools and Programs told ABC News, "Many successful parents have invested more time in their businesses than in their children, contributing to the rapid growth of these programs."[18] Antischool crusader Alexia Parks likewise identifies single and dual-income parents as two main causes of the industry's growth.[19] Reporter Tim Weiner's own summary after months of investigation reads the same: "The reasons that the parents, children, staff members and program officials cite are the crises common to American family life: fractured marriages, failing schools, frantic two-job couples with no time to devote to children."[20] Sara Rimer similarly observes, "Some [experts] also say that their emergence partly reflects the failures of a generation of permissive, distracted parents. And many of the parents interviewed for this article would agree."[21]

Divorce and dual income, dual income and divorce: The refrain hums like a mantra throughout the literature. That is why these schools cannot be written off as just the latest creation of problem rich kids. The teenagers ending up in them—surly, disaffected, malfunctioning, blue-haired, and the rest—are surely only the tip of what has become a real iceberg of resentment and estrangement between significant numbers of absent or preoccupied parents and *their* teenagers. Certainly the referral literature, with its reference to a teen "epidemic," understands as much. If more people could afford them, likely a great many other teenagers would also be spending their last years before adulthood out of the house. To put the point rhetorically: What does it tell us about the ferocity of demand that despite lawsuits, critical investigative reports, and accusations of abuse, the schools aren't being built fast enough? As another journalist observed of the phenomenon, "Ironically, every national television piece about Teen Help programs, however critical, produces a rush of inquiries from parents."[22]

Taking issue with the dominant view that today's kids are really all right is beginning to feel like shooting whales in a barrel, but the example of specialty schools drives the point home as perhaps no other. Virtual parents cause real problems for at least some real-life kids. Seen this way, the schools amount to one more new social institution, unknown on anything like today's scale only a decade ago, created to cushion the blow of hands-off parenting.

In that sense, they resemble day care institutions. Like day care, they may not cause long-term harm to many or even most of the juveniles passing through them. Also like day care, the better institutions may even be an improvement over having a parent or parents do the job. But like day care, too, the specialty schools are surely inflicting immediate suffering and perhaps worse on at least some children and adolescents. Though the literature may emanate from the extreme emotional end of the specialty experience, it seems fair to say that other teenagers along a continuum are suffering lesser but still real ill effects, just as babies and toddlers adversely affected by day care also appear to fall along a continuum, from obvious hard cases on down.[23]

To return to where we started, the question in the end remains: Why now? What is it about our own time and place that accounts for these schools' remarkable growth? Has there been, for example, a revolution in psychological knowledge such that we now know much better how to handle such teenagers, and behavior modification boarding schools are it? This is not a claim that the schools themselves make. Though some do specialize in ADD/ADHD and other recently designated psychological disorders, many more are behavioral catchalls for adolescents with a varied set of problems, and most further disdain traditional therapy. Indeed, the system's critics frequently complain that most staff do not have psychological credentials or expertise.

Is it simply that enough Americans have become rich enough to do what many parents would have liked to do earlier—send problem teenagers off to someone else? Americans certainly are richer today on the whole than ever before, so there is surface appeal to this answer. At the same time, just having more money doesn't explain it, either. After all, previous bouts of widespread wealth creation produced no such thing. As Harvard child psychology professor and *Raising Cain* author Dan Kindlon told reporter Sara Rimer, what is different is that "we look now to institutions to do this stuff."[24] Sending problem teenagers away from home is hardly a historical rarity, as popular culture indicates at least from, say, Huck Finn on up to the 1990s hit television show *Fresh Prince of Belair* (a situation comedy based on exactly that). But sending them away to nonfamily settings in which their letters are typically censored and their other communications with home strictly reduced—that is new indeed and is not explained simply by having the money to do it.

What about the refrain of many parents that the stresses on kids today are so extreme and the problems they face so novel that only separating them from their own adolescent culture will do? This, too, is a chord that rings sympathetically with any parent who has ever tried to supervise the Internet, let alone try to find out what the latest recreational drug potentially available at a teenage party might be. The fact is that if pressures like these are the problem, then there is all the more reason that more parental attention is required: Take away the car keys, check the hard drive, be on hand at the end of the school day, and home-school or hire a GED tutor for truants. The point is that the appeal to novel pressures simply doesn't explain the existence of the specialty schools. Most of the behaviors for which the students are sent there—sex, drugs, alcohol, truancy—are as old as the bucolic hills in which the institutions are set.

No, the answer to the question of "Why now?" is something else, and it is as plain as the nose ring on a teenager's face. These schools are inadvertent monuments to one of the most mistaken assumptions in our time, namely, the idea that today's uniquely neglected generation of adolescents is doing just fine. It isn't. These teenagers are the first fruits of the generation in which, demographically speaking, paid outside work for mothers of infants and small children became the statistical norm. They are the kids who grew up at a time when divorce was so common, and politesse about it so pronounced, that the idea of "staying together for the kids" was mentioned with derision if at all. This was the generation that was supposed to take care of itself, and some members of it apparently couldn't. And if certain of the better-off of the children raised under that regimen look like those who populate the specialty schools, what does that tell us about what some of the *worse-off* are going through?

What the specialty-school example exposes in the end is not so much the shortcomings of their residents, but the shortcomings of an adult world that has shrunk by leaps and bounds the amount of time that children and teenagers are allowed to command. After all, we live in a society that regards staying home with one's babies and toddlers as a daunting personal sacrifice. By definition, such is also a society in which the time-intensive needs of those same children ten years later are almost certainly not going to be served—not as the norm, anyway, and not without a lot of parental resentment.

The truth is that not only adorable babies and toddlers but also some difficult and obnoxious adolescents need their mothers and fathers around an awful lot more than some appear to have them. No one wants to lift up that social rock because no one really wants to know what is under it. And yet throughout the detention archipelago, from one Camp Green Lake to another, certain troubled and unlucky teenagers dig it up every single day.

9

Conclusion: Beyond the Blame Game

MORE MENTAL AND BEHAVIORAL PROBLEMS, MORE MIND-altering pills, more STDs, more obese, unhappy, and institutionalized children of all ages—these poignant facts either did not exist a quarter century or so ago or were markedly less prevalent than they are now. It has been change for the worse for many American kids. Thus we come full circle to the query raised at the beginning of this work: What is responsible for the specific, novel problems seen in children and teenagers today?

That question has not been neglected in current talk about American family life, but it has been widely misunderstood. Faced piecemeal with the evidence accumulated in this book, observers from the kitchen table to the academy have asked what might account for one or another of these new and different problems, and over the years the list of purported culprits has grown and grown. Included are vaccines, PCBs (polychlorinated biphenyls), growth hormones in milk, fast food, school bullies, television, video games, and rap music. Like Pinocchio's nose, only without the humor, the list lengthens with every asking of the question. From bad news about day care to bad news about behavior drugs, child fat, mental problems, and STDs, commentators have offered a bounty of explanations for why the kinds of problems discussed in this book either aren't problems or are not due to the chronic absence from many homes of many parents.

In short, the prevailing prohibition against raising the question of parents and home life has operated as an intellectual gag rule. Under cultural pressure to suppress what is up with kids today, most commentators have offered a wild and varied assortment of theories pointing in all directions—everywhere but at the home. In so doing, they have inadvertently become like a lawyer with six arguments too many for whatever he or she is up to—in a word, unconvincing.[1]

For example, if our skeptical reader were to discuss the various problems and issues raised in these pages, each one would have a different explanation, and the result would run something like this. If I ask about the upswing in mental and behavioral disorders, he blames it on PCBs or vaccines, or growth hormones in cow's milk, or better screening and higher awareness of such problems. If I ask about children who are overweight or obese, he points to television and fast food. If I mention that day care seems to increase aggression in some kids, he counters that it isn't really aggression or it is only affecting some of the kids. Or he might say that maybe what is called aggression is more good than bad, and that you have to weigh the increase in aggression against the benefits of early socialization. If I add that many teachers and principals think that kids today are worse behaved than they used to be, he says the culprits are class size, violent video games, awful rap music, and too much sugar and refined food.

That kind of grimly determined attempt to deflect attention from where it belongs—a move known as *denial*—tells us something important. Multiple causes of all kinds of human phenomena do exist, of course, including for the problems examined in this book, but not all causes are created equal. Some are more essential than others, as is clearly shown by a closer look at the prevailing and, for the most part, diversionary purported causes now being offered for those same problems.

JUMPING THROUGH THE HOOPS

Consider, for example, an explanation for a child problem described earlier that has increased dramatically of late: autism. For years professionals and lay observers alike have noted a steep rise in the number of children who fit the description of autistic spectrum disorder—meaning that they have symptoms ranging from obvious and serious social impairment to more subtle forms of what used to be considered behavioral traits such as introversion, bossiness, or rudeness. In seeking to explain the increase in such behavioral traits, most observers have looked for an underlying cause somewhere other than the child's home life.

Thus, many doctors have looked inward, at the "brain wiring." Many other people have looked outward at a variety of other inanimate suspects such as PCBs and other environmental toxins, and vaccines.[2] Very few observers have asked whether autism (and, by extension, related juvenile mental problems) might be related to other trends affecting many children including life without Dad, seeing little of Mom, enjoying fewer siblings and extended family, and other aspects of modern home life.

The fervor with which the inanimate suspects are pursued—in particular the theory of vaccines as the cause of autistic spectrum disorder—does show one thing: exactly how hard some people will work to avoid mentioning any of the family trends. In study after study the magnifying glass taken to vaccines has turned up nothing. A May 2004 *New York Times* headline put it plainly in the latest summary of the scientific evidence: "Panel Finds No Evidence to Tie Autism to Vaccines."[3] That article explained how a committee of experts appointed by the Institute of Medicine—one of the most authoritative medical organizations in the country—concluded at the end of a four-year investigation that the vaccine theory of autism was a red herring. The committee's report further urged that research on autism should focus on "more productive" areas such as genetic and "environmental [that is, home life] factors." This highly unusual admonishment in a document issuing from establishment medicine itself speaks to the frustration that doctors and researchers feel when faced with the persistence of the vaccine theory.[4]

And yet experience suggests that this latest disproof will be no more effective in defusing the passionate conviction that something like vaccines "explains" autism. Why? Because the vaccine theory of autism is just one manifestation of a powerful cultural urge to find the source of today's unique child problems someplace other than in the child's immediate surroundings, which is to say his home, parents, and family or lack thereof.

To repeat a point made earlier, I am not saying that the mental and behavioral problems burdening many of today's kids are all caused by absent parents. I'm not a doctor or lab researcher, and I don't doubt that "real" mental illness can exist in children as well as in adults. What I am saying is that the passionate desire to attribute today's behavioral and mental problems to inanimate suspects such as vaccines *despite* serious evidence to the contrary shows us how reflexively our society fastens on to some explanation, any explanation, that does not involve parents.

A second example showing the gravitational pull of nonparental or nonfamilial explanations for today's child problems can be seen in the current consensus about another of the issues examined earlier: the rise in child obesity. To many commentators the culprits behind the child fat epidemic are obvious enough: sedentary lifestyles and fast food. Both factors are explanatory up to a point. As we saw in the chapter on obesity, both answer one part of the question: "how," in a mechanical sense, kids (and adults) get fat. But they are not explanations for the "why" question that underlies them both: Why are kids allowed to do all this sitting around and eating in the first place? The answer to that question can only be that children are less supervised around these temptations than they used to be. Often no one is around to say the things that protected other generations of kids from overeating the way today's do, such as "Go out back and play" or "Get out of the cupboard and wait for dinner" or "Finish your homework, and I'll take you to the park." Surely one unintended consequence of parent-child separation is that it has reduced the number of meals supervised by parents, the very adults who have the deepest personal interest in a child's long-term health. Yet for all the publicity given to juvenile obesity these last couple of years, this obvious explanation has been the least sounded. This is, again, the force of our social prohibition against raising questions about adult absence and the fallout to kids.

Consider a third example of how that prohibition distracts attention from another problem: the STD epidemic. Experts have repeatedly suggested what one does not need an expert to figure out: that some of today's teens are having lots of casual sex because effective (and especially long-term) contraception makes it easy. This explanation is surely right in the limited sense that contraception provides a certain way of answering the "how" question (that is, how casual sex became possible). But the "why" of teen sex, which is a different question, can only be answered this way: The STD explosion is as high as it is in considerable part because many teenagers are not supervised, especially after school. Of the various studies and reports mentioned in this book, among the most arresting to my mind was the one in *Pediatrics* cited in the chapter on STDs, which indicated *where* most of the kids were having sex: somebody's (presumably adult-empty) home. But are "parents" and "STD" even mentioned in the same sentence when the subject of those diseases does come up? Hardly ever.

Another diversionary tactic, effectively if not intentionally, is the ongoing argument over another favored culprit for children's problems: television and related electronic entertainments. Many concerned adults, including many doctors and teachers, believe that the apparent rise in behaviorally troubled kids—including and especially ADD/ADHD cases—is connected to widespread electronic gorging from babyhood on up. Moreover, those critics have evidence on their side. Though orthodox thinking about ADD/ADHD vigorously rejects the connection, that particular disorder has been repeatedly linked to extra time spent watching television.[5] Even if it is not in fact "creating" ADD/ADHD or other specifically labeled problems, most television programming is still cheap, violent, and debasing, to say nothing of smutty, unwholesome, and dumb. And some children do try to imitate what they see on it. For both reasons, most people who give it some thought agree that the tube stinks.

But here again, in the case of television, we are looking at a "how" explanation, not a "why" one. After all, TV, the Internet, and other passive entertainment wouldn't be the problems and influences they are if mothers and fathers did not rely on them. Why do millions of kids have televisions in their bedrooms even when their parents deplore what they watch (at least in surveys)? Because there is something in it for the parents. Television and the rest of the electronic ensemble keep kids occupied. As Judith Shulevitz put it with admirable candor for *Slate*, in a piece criticizing pediatricians for a recent recommendation to limit children's TV time, "Television makes the dual-career or single-parent family possible."[6]

A STANDARD OR A SLOGAN?

This brings us to the most intellectually sophisticated evasion of the central point, the polemical trump card that always gets played whenever someone says the kids aren't all right. "Whoa there," this line of reasoning can be paraphrased. "I'm willing to acknowledge that some or even many kids today face certain serious problems that we didn't, but those problems only *correlate* with the empty-parent home. That doesn't mean absent parents are the *cause* of them. Don't you know the first rule of social science, that correlations don't prove causality?"

"Correlations don't prove causality" is the ultimate rhetorical stratagem in the service of home-alone America. Every so often, over the years, someone has raised a hand when day care, latchkey children, father absence, behavior pills, or mental problems were being discussed and said, in effect, *Look, there's evidence here that parental absence is harming kids.* And every time somebody has said that, the same thing has happened next: An army of white-coated statistical warriors has looked up from its collective spreadsheets and orthogonal factor rotations and regression analyses, slid down its collective reading glasses, and chanted with a frown: *So what? After all, correlations don't prove causality.*[7]

But what exactly does this formulation mean?[8] At one level—the most transparent—it represents the innocent enough logical fact that just because some things seem to go together doesn't mean one of them is causing the other.[9] For instance, as Judith Rich Harris explains the point, it might be the case that rich people eat more broccoli than others, but that doesn't mean eating broccoli has made them rich. As a simple matter of logic, that is one way of explaining what that phrase means.

The more pertinent question, given its prominence in today's debates about the family, is just how this formulation is used. Interestingly enough, at least in the contemporary literature of child-parent separation, it is invoked for only one purpose: to dismiss the idea that any new study or survey or other argument has really "proved" that absent parents damage kids in any way.[10] That is why anyone following certain long-running controversies these last couple of decades—the mommy wars, the day care wars, the literature on fatherlessness and divorce—will already have heard this scholarly catchphrase several times over. It is, as I said, a trump card, or so believe the advocates who have come to use it that way.

In fact, however, this fancier way of dodging the issue of responsibility, like the others, also flunks the credibility test. Consider this important counterexample from elsewhere in life: smoking. For years the beleaguered tobacco industry has argued, in essence, exactly what some enlightened people do today about child problems—that the correlations between smoking and certain health problems are just that, correlations, and correlations do not prove causality. In other words, according to the tobacco companies' frequent refrain, just because people who smoke tend to have more health problems doesn't mean the problems are "caused" by tobacco. Has that argument from "correlation" aided Big Tobacco? Have people nodded vigorously and said, in effect, *that's great*, and since nothing has really been "proven" about tobacco causing health problems, we can all go on smoking as before?

That isn't what has happened at all, of course. To the contrary: Regulations and laws of all kinds have been changed, and smoking has been dramatically taxed, reduced, and stigmatized. Why? Because when they are being reasonable and not ideological about things, most people, given the evidence of their senses, suspect that smoking causes physical harm. In exactly the same way, most people can connect the dots between parental absence and child problems, and they do not need a regression analysis or other social-scientific device in order to do it.[11]

The fourth edition of *Father Facts*, a compendium mentioned earlier that summarizes empirical data from all over on the problems of fatherless homes, states the limitations of social science nicely: "While no single study can *prove* that father absence hurts children (social science is messier than mathematics), the evidence that it does is abundant and compelling. Even after researchers control for socioeconomic variables such as race and income, children who grow up without their fathers *still* consistently score lower on measures of well-being."[12] Surely only a social scientist would argue that the growth in all those problems has nothing to do with the growth in the number of kids who have no one under the same roof called Dad.

THE "DEFAULT" BIAS: ADULTS

Another symptom of our cultural denial is this: When faced with the empirical fact that many mentally and behaviorally troubled kids come from troubled families, our delegated authorities routinely assume it's the kids rather than the families that are the cause of those troubles even though the reverse could just as well be true.

Numerous expert sources have observed that families with children who are diagnosed bipolar, ADD, autistic, and so on have very high divorce rates.[13] They further universally draw the following connection between those facts: Because a mentally or behaviorally troubled child places a serious strain on the rest of the family, therefore his parents are more likely to break up. That way of explaining things might be true in any number of cases. After all, since even normal and healthy children can strain marriages (as feminists tirelessly insist and many women's magazines regularly complain), the burden of a child with intense problems is indeed unimaginable to anyone who does not have to bear it. But look closely at the assignation of responsibility that is automatically being made here. It emphasizes that parental action in any form is not the problem, whereas something about the kids is (their brains, genetics, or other "wiring"). But couldn't the opposite way of interpreting that connection also be true? Might something about a troubled set of parents be part of what influences the behaviors later diagnosed as bipolar, ADD, or whatever—at least for some kids? To ask that question is not to deny that mental problems do exist. It's just to inquire about the commonsensical possibility that family problems might be a two-way street.

We don't know as much about that fallout from parents to kids as we ought to. The reason we don't know is that our social prohibition against raising the question of parents acts as a powerful disincentive to this sort of research. To my limited knowledge, nobody at all asks whether the apparent high marital breakup rate of parents whose children are diagnosed with these new labels means that the parents have problems which are rubbing off on those kids, rather than vice versa.[14]

The same stifling effect also explains professional neglect of a related inquiry: the connection in a significant number of cases between chaotic home lives and ADD/ADHD. Here, too, researchers should be asking questions about environment that are not being asked now even though they are obvious to anyone who reads the professional literature. For example, it has been documented that in addition to being more likely to divorce, parents of children diagnosed as having ADD/ADHD are also more likely to be alcoholics or other substance abusers than adults generally. Once again, virtually everyone addressing those kinds of facts says something similar: that having a problem child (that is, one with ADD/ADHD) is what drives parents to such behavior.[15] It may well be true in a given case, but, once again, that "default" explanation makes the child rather than the family responsible. Common sense fairly demands an airing of this question: Why is the higher rate of turmoil in these families automatically assumed to be something the child is doing to the parents rather than vice versa?

Like other attempts at sidestepping the question of what adult choices might have to do with child problems, the scholarly-sounding phrase that "correlations don't prove causality" is not the rhetorical or intellectual trump card advocates wish it to be. There is a double standard governing its uses—one suggesting that what began as a philosophical principle is now being deployed as an ideological device.

BEING THERE

In the end, all these exercises in avoiding the obvious fall apart for the same reason: They mislead us into looking at the wrong things. Brain chemistry, bullying in high school, mercury in fish, refined sugar, classroom size, video games like Doom—all these and other figurative whipping boys may deserve a turn at the public post, but as the problems examined in this book show over and over, what ails many children and teenagers is something more immediate and elemental than the likes of these. Their own music and literature as well as other proofs affirm this.

What we need more than any new longitudinal study or chart is a sharper focus on the short-term and pedestrian facts of life—something like an adult Warm Body Standard. Put aside for the moment all the questions about the influence of parents on long-term personality, career prospects, cognitive development, and the rest. The fact remains that a parent or other adult in the home aids kids in the critical *short* term for two reasons: That presence exercises a day-to-day emotional gain, and it has an important chilling effect on certain child and adolescent impulses. These are the common truths that the frantic search for outside culprits has obscured.

If we really want to talk about the evidence, empirical data from any number of exercises in social science affirm what common sense already knows: The presence of parents acts as a protective factor for children from earliest childhood on up. One particularly dramatic and recent illustration comes from a study of nine thousand American babies, published in the May 2004 issue of *Pediatrics*.[16] That study showed a striking difference in infant mortality between breast-fed babies and others, with the former apparently 20 percent less likely to die in the first year of life than the latter (meaning, in the authors' guesstimates, that some 720 infant deaths would be prevented every year if more babies were breast-fed).

Yet even more arresting than those numbers was the interpretation of this difference offered by the researchers. Not all of it, they hypothesized, was due to the immunological and other benefits of human milk. Some of it was attributed to a more prosaic factor, something obviously related to the likelihood of serious accidents in that first year of life: maternal presence. As one of the researchers put it, "It may be something as simple as physical proximity. *Breast-fed kids are closer to Mom* [emphasis added]."

Similarly, and moving up the age chain, one much-publicized study a few years back by the Council of Economic Advisors found that "significant differences were noted between teens who eat dinner with their parents at least five times a week and teens who do not." Those with parent(s) at the table were said to have half the risk for drinking, somewhat less the risk for smoking, half the risk for marijuana use, half the risk for suicide attempts, and so on. It is absurd to infer (as some commentators dutifully did) that eating dinner as a family confers talismanic benefits, whether to teenagers or anyone else, but it is equally absurd to ignore the elementary meaning of those results. What the dinner-eating statistics mean is that somebody—an adult somebody whose mere presence in the place makes certain activities more problematic than they would be otherwise—is actually there to exercise such influence, however tacit or even unintentional it may be.

One fine way of putting this homely point appeared in a 2003 op-ed column in the *New York Times* by a veteran New York City police officer.[17] Reporting on a well-publicized local incident at a roller rink frequented by teenagers in which four people were stabbed and five police officers were injured, he observed: "Though evidence suggests that the stabbings may be linked to gangs, the underlying cause is likely to be far more complicated. Those investigating the incident would do well to keep in mind that the most important principle of detection is, as Sherlock Homes might have put it, 'to look for what should be there.' As I watched the young teenagers leaving the club early Sunday morning, it was easy to figure out the missing element: parents."

Look for what should be there. There is no more simple summary of what we really do know or ought to: There is an immediate emotional and behavioral importance to most children and teenagers of having mothers and fathers, however imperfect, just plain showing up as much as they can.

KNOWING IT WHEN WE SEE IT

In the end, the deepest problem with current explanations for child and adolescent problems is this: They distract us from the evidence of our own senses. They make us think that the answer to the question of what's right for children will be found somewhere, sometime, in some column of numbers—that if we just get the latest longitudinal data lined up or rotate all the inputs and outputs in some new way, we'll know what to think and decide. But what "meta-analytic" could possibly measure, say, the emotional hole in today's teenage music? What data do we use to capture the chronic low-intensity sadness of a yearning baby who just plain misses her mother day in and day out? What instruments can we apply to what teachers from across the country tell us is the evidence of *their* senses—that they are seeing more behavioral problems with children than they used to? Something has indeed run amok in the American experiment with separationism. Understandably, some adults, including well-meaning and responsible people influenced by the ideological happy talk of the last few decades, really don't want to face it. Yet even the clichés about kids that are mouthed unthinkingly these days inadvertently give the game of desensitization away.

We say *children are resilient*, but what we mean is that we needn't worry about them as much as we ought. We say *it takes a village to raise a child*, ignoring the fact that in any real village that child has other supporting adults, many of them related to him; they are in addition to his mother and father, not instead of them. We say *teenagers are rebellious*, but what we mean is that there must be some hardwired, parent-exonerating explanation for not seeing our own adolescent minus a headset or away from a computer for several weeks.

We're very good at taking a grain of anything—PCBs, vaccines, hormones, advertising, corporations, entertainment, television, the Internet, brain chemistry—and growing from it some large explanation that adults can hide behind. We say, "Look there! Look there!" What we mean is, "Look anywhere but here." That is the standard ruling our home-alone world, and it is past due for a serious realignment.

EPILOGUE

AND SO WE COME INEVITABLY TO THE QUESTION POSED IN ONE way or another by the problems dissected in these pages: *What is to be done?*

What, for example, are we to do about the shortcomings of day care in a world where some people absolutely must use it? If medication isn't the answer to all those sad and disaffected kids, what is? What might reduce STD rates—abstinence programs, or more and better sex education courses? And how about those uncivilized elementary school children that teachers report about? Won't smaller class sizes help or perhaps more charter schools? In short, to put the point generally, if our experiment in parent-child separation really has run amok, what specifically should we do now?

Unlike many other contemporary treatments of social problems, this one does not end with a bulleted how-to list armed with snappy answers to those and other questions. This simply isn't that kind of book. That is not to say that debates over the Family Medical Leave Act, say, or tax credits or vouchers or other policy "fixes" are not important. They are, and the argument of these pages does weigh in, however tacitly, on some of those political discussions.[1] In the end, however, those debates can't really be adjudicated by the evidence accumulated here because that evidence is about something different: our ongoing radical experiment in parent-child separation, an experiment driven not so much by policies as by the more intractable forces of ideas, intellectual trends, and hardened opinions.

In other words, and at the risk of dissatisfying some readers, this epilogue is pretty much lacking in sound bite solutions. I say that with some misgiving; we all want happy endings to our stories even when we suspect none is forthcoming. But as the evidence of these pages shows, there are no quick fixes for the chronic deficit of parental attention that is now the norm for a great many American kids. Pretending otherwise does a disservice to just how serious their problems are.

Yet our review of the evidence does suggest one other kind of answer to the question of what is to be done. Just as ideas are part of what got us into these problems, a change of ideas will be needed to get out of them. What this investigation of child and adolescent problems strongly suggests is this: We need a different set of ideas to measure and practice nurture. In particular we need a higher and better standard by which to judge the moral claims of children and teenagers on the adult world—a more humane understanding of that balance than the one we have recently descended to.

What might this better standard look like? Nothing more or less than a change of social heart, a new public consensus: *It would be better for both children and adults if more American parents were with their kids more of the time.* That is to say, it would be better if more mothers with a genuine choice in the matter *did* stay home and/or work part-time rather than full-time and if more parents entertaining separation or divorce did stay together for the sake of the kids.

Certainly from the point of view of today's children and adolescents, as their own plaintive expressions make clear, having more adults on the premises would be a social and emotional improvement over today's situation. This is the real consensus about parents and children that we have come to need—not more calls for universal day care and other self-defeating fixes aimed at enabling even more parent-child separation but, rather, the adoption of a higher standard that acknowledges what has too long gone unacknowledged: the benefits of increasing the number of intact adult-supervised homes.

How might such a major realignment of opinion come about? The answer, both theoretical and practical, is too deep to plumb in full here, but I will try to at least sketch its most obvious requirements.

To begin with the most abstract point, we need a revised common understanding about that most dreaded word in the parental vocabulary: *guilt*. For years now the phenomenon of parental guilt has been interpreted in only one, not very sophisticated way: as a trump card thrown down whenever the bad news about American kids has been linked to absent parents. That way of using guilt has abetted the wider desensitization of the adult world. By serving to stop discussion just when it needs to start, this reflexive rhetorical misuse has obscured several other, more important points.

One such point is that when we cannot choose otherwise, we have nothing to feel guilty about. Though this might seem a rather elementary observation—that there is no meaningful guilt without the freedom to make it possible—it is one that our current discussion of child-rearing customarily overlooks. The single mother who works because she must, the father who endures a long commute to make money for tuition at the Catholic school because the public school stinks, the cleaning lady married to the busboy who works just to pay the rent—these actors are not part of the drama of guilt as it has come to be played out because they do what they must. In other words, when critics complain that bad news only adds to the load of parental guilt, they are *not* talking about the experience of all parents but, rather, about the subset of parents who enjoy that thing without which guilt makes no sense: meaningful choice.

Well, what about those parents who do have a choice? Under our current separationist-inspired understanding of what children are allowed to need, we are not supposed to ask that question. Yet asking it raises an interesting point: Perhaps continuing complaints about the guilt felt by absent mothers says more than we think it does—that those mothers feel the need to spend more time with their children whether they have bought into the separationist experiment or not.[2] Perhaps their well-publicized feelings of guilt are further proof of a social experiment run amok.

To put that point more directly, some readers might wonder whether they have stayed away from home too much and might even feel that twinge of guilt familiar to all parents who take their responsibilities seriously. Any real mother or father knows that feeling by heart; after all, to be a parent is to make scores of decisions on behalf of one's children day in and day out, any one of which might be wrong and many of which—to sound a personal note—definitely will be. But is it really the worst thing in the world for mothers and fathers to feel such things? Surely it would be worse for children if they did not.

As much as we run from it, the fact is that there are things even more important than parental sensitivities about guilt, things important enough to trump those sensitivities. The problems examined in this book—problems that either did not exist a generation ago or did not exist in anything like today's extreme forms—are only some examples. Why speak frankly of a subject like child fat when so many adults might find it embarrassing or offensive? Because the obesity problem, so clearly related to the absent-parent home, is impairing millions of kids both physically and emotionally. Why draw attention to the bad data on day care when some families absolutely must rely on institutions and others laud their benefits? Because the babies and toddlers who are adversely affected by such care, too young to speak for themselves, deserve advocates, too. Why emphasize the link between absent parents and teenage sex when the teen pregnancy rate has been falling for the last couple of years? Because some of the diseases those unsupervised kids are contracting, particularly girls, will mar their lives, destroy their fertility, and perhaps give them incurable cancers.

But wait, the skeptical reader might say. How can you state that American parents need to be more attentive to children when we live in the most child-indulgent society on earth? Isn't it true that parents today feel more anxiety and spend more money on child-rearing than ever before—from the bookshelves full of how-to tomes to expensive educational toys to all that standardized test preparation and other forms of child enrichment?

The answer is yes. The separationist experiment has indeed coincided with and has, in fact, given rise to the ultraconsumerism of contemporary parenthood. But that very phenomenon is just one more symptom of what ails us. All those success-oriented toys, all those pamphlets and manuals, are material outsourcings in themselves. We buy more books to tell us how to rear our children instead of just sitting on the floor with them a lot and figuring it out for ourselves. We seek electronic devices to jump-start their development because, consciously or unconsciously, we realize we are not around enough to do the trick. The depth of our nervousness gives us away, signaling what numerous commentators have observed— namely, how psychologically unbalanced American child-rearing has become.[3]

And yet, fixated as we are on exorcising guilt rather than meditating on what it tells us, we resist understanding exactly what gives rise to that imbalance, which is the core fact of this book. Too many parents are absent from too many homes, and in addition to the toll this takes on children, one can also discern a certain psychological tax on many adults. If hypocrisy is the homage that virtue pays to vice, then an excess of anxiety is the homage that the consciences of many of today's parents pay to absence.

Fair enough, some readers may be thinking by now. Maybe we do need an intellectual overhaul in certain departments, but that's a very abstract point to leave us with. What about the more immediate one? How might the social move toward a new standard of nurture affect decisions by real mothers and fathers who must operate in the real, complicated, and difficult world?

As mentioned in the beginning, this book is not about what any one parent or family has chosen to do. How could it be? Only individuals have the information about their own lives to know what they personally are free and not free to decide. Only they know what specific trade-offs and pressures shape their domestic situations. Can a mother who is also responsible for indigent parents afford to stay home with her toddler? Only she is in a position to know—not I, not the reader, not any other armchair theorist. There really is no "one size fits all" answer here.

Thus, the answer to the question of what comes next is not as simple as "All mothers should stay home" or "All biological parents should be forced to live together until their children are grown."[4] Maternal out-of-the-house employment is not always and everywhere bad for children; many mothers do have to work; a great deal depends on whether Dad or other family is around; in addition, at-home mothering is no guarantee of child-rearing success.[5] Also, some couples grow to hate the sight of each other and are measurably happier living apart (a different issue from that of how their children feel about it). Any number of other facts of life affect these kinds of decisions, too—the presence or absence of other family, a given child's gifts or problems, school demands, earning the money that means the difference between a poor school or neighborhood and a safer or nicer one.

But it is also true, as we have seen, that from the point of view of many children and adolescents, there are simply not enough grown-ups—meaning attentive, nurturing parents—to go around, and that fact also demands a place at the social table, whether it makes some adults uncomfortable or not. We all need to step back from our own stories and cases, fascinating though we undoubtedly find ourselves, and return to the formulation being weighed here. It is not about anecdotes but about evidence and argument: *We need to replace our current low moral bar regarding nurture with a more humane standard acknowledging that individuals and society would be better off if more parents spent more time with children.*

This proposition does not require that any particular family or individual choose one way rather than another (the ideological mire in which the "mommy wars" and "day care wars" remain trapped). Rather, it calls for something else: a swing of the social pendulum from which society overall would benefit. In fact, even parents who are unable or unwilling to spend more time with their children can get behind the idea that we need this new way of looking at things because, and as the chapters in this book all bear out in one way and another, having more parents on the child and adolescent scene benefits everyone.

That is what these pages finally amount to: the missing empirical link between today's unique child and adolescent problems and the new public consensus we need in order to prevent further damage. Thus, for example, you might not be able to avoid a full-time demanding career, but you would be better off, and so would your child, if more parents were around to know what the kids are up to, if more "eyes were on the street" in all senses, as Ehrenhalt put it. Similarly, I might not be around after school when my teenager heads over to her boyfriend's house, but if that boyfriend has a mother, father, grandparent, or other adult at home, then the possibilities for, say, drinking, drugging, or contracting something awful through sex are limited, if only for the hours of that afternoon and even if I personally am not around to diminish them. The point is that *somebody else is*, and that's good for me whether I'm participating in the effort or not.

Likewise, your neighbor's son might not be spared, say, his parents' divorce, but wouldn't it be better for him if *other* fathers in the neighborhood were not similarly out of the picture, if just a few more were around to help pick up the slack left by the ones who are absent? That might mean one less kid who grows up "play[ing] catch by [him]self," in Tupac Shakur's perfectly awful image of the fatherless boy. In the same way, it may be that John's father, who lives two states away, can't coach the local basketball team for obvious reasons, but if his friend's father or mother can, because one or the other can make the sacrifice of leaving work early two days a week, that sacrifice is good not only for their son but also for John and his family.

That a social realignment along lines like these would benefit many people besides the offspring immediately involved is true from the smallest examples—such as whether there are enough chaperones for a school trip to the museum—on up. More adults on urban and suburban playgrounds in the late afternoon would mean more kids who are free to do something besides sit in front of a screen after school. More children who could go to someone else's home after school—including those of friends who have a warm adult body around during those hours—might just mean more children who are less institutionalized and a little happier as a result.[6] In millions of small but interlocking ways, children generally stand to benefit from an increase in the number of adults who are on the scene—whether their own parents are included or not.

In other words, just as widespread parental *absence* reverberates to create the kind of large problems described in this book, so would more parental *presence* on the child and adolescent scene ameliorate some of the fallout. Moreover, these reverberations would extend beyond the immediate world of playgrounds and classrooms to some of the more rarefied places visited in these pages, including medicine and psychology. More adults present and attending to children might just increase adult empathy and sensitivity to the wide range of what is normal for various age groups. That enhanced adult experience might in turn reduce some of the need to pathologize and medicate children for their behavior—again, even if not all parents are able to participate in redrawing the lines.

This is not to say, of course, that all the problems discussed in these pages would be ameliorated if more adults were back in children's lives. The homework problem, for example, springs eternal. Those children who have parents or other family to help and support them will benefit, and those who do not, barring the most driven and ambitious, will simply continue falling behind. Similarly, the emotional turmoil that divorce and unwed motherhood inflict on so many kids—powerfully presented in their music, as we have seen—is just what it is: for many and perhaps most, a scarring and profoundly unwanted experience, no matter what the grown-ups in their lives feel and say about it.

Even so, our real focus needs to be on the fact that adopting a less radical version of today's separationist experiment would benefit many people and especially many children, whether their parents are able to be around or not. Surely this is something with which reasonable adults everywhere can agree, whatever personal baggage or misgivings we may carry with us.

So far I have tried to sketch what a significant realignment of opinion might require, but what about another fundamental question: Is such a social changeover toward a more child-beneficial standard even possible given the facts of our world?

The answer depends on the fate of the deeper trends outlined in the beginning of this book: divorce/illegitimacy (the absent-father problem), maternal employment (the absent-mother problem), and, smaller but still significant, the absence for many of the extended family. In at least the first two cases the bad-news story of this book may be ameliorated by recent and perhaps hopeful soundings. As today's high rates of family breakup, absent parents, and the rest continue to take their toll, there are signs of serious revisionism afoot. At the levels of scholarship and journalism, at least, real reevaluation about what might be called the root causes of family life appears to be under way.

Consider the example of divorce and unwed parenthood. The news about absent fathers is indeed very bad—in some ways even worse than we have reviewed. For many children, having a father out of the home also means having him out their lives completely. Scholars say that half of all children who do not reside with their father have never even been in that father's present home; and studies also have shown that a hefty percentage of the children of divorce—roughly one-third—have not seen their biological father in the preceding year.

Fathers are not always the ones responsible for family breakups, of course. It has often been pointed out that women are now more likely to initiate divorce than men. But regardless of who starts it, divorce/separation almost always results in the father's taking up residence elsewhere and seeing less and less of his children year by year. Many children will encounter this outcome at some point in their growing-up years, and a rising number will also live with unmarried parents.

And yet, in both the intellectual and practical spheres, there are signs that an increasing number of observers are uncomfortable with this situation. To begin with the matter of theory, here is a remarkable fact: Today, unlike ten years ago, "fatherlessness" is understood to be not just another social issue but a real and serious problem that many children and teenagers experience as damaging. Conservatives and liberals, Republicans and Democrats alike are largely agreed that so many children growing up without fathers is a social problem of the highest order. That consensus is new.

Moreover, there has been a concomitant dip in divorce rates over the past few years, a fact that several noted scholars of American family life think is significant.[7] Perhaps that statistical change—small but still moving down and not up—reflects the renascence of an old idea: that mothers and fathers, barring cases of gross abuse, should strive mightily to make marriages work for "the sake of the kids." For most of the last two decades those words have been used ironically, if at all. Today, with increasing frequency, they are used in earnest. That, too, is a positive change, if only emblematically.

Similarly, recent revisionist writing and thinking about maternal separation from children, particularly young children, may herald a real change of opinion further down the social road. As current literature mentioned elsewhere suggests, more better-off women have lately made a public issue of staying home for some or all of their children's growing-up years. Once again this change in the wind of opinion is accompanied by a statistical dip, slight but real, in the proportion of better-off women in the full-time workforce. As everyone knows, much passion reigns over the question of mothers maintaining outside jobs and careers. It always will because mothers, even those who are self-declared partisans of the separationist experiment, nevertheless feel ambivalent about being apart from their children, especially when they are young. Yet from the point of view of children, by contrast, more time spent in the company of their mothers is undeniably a big emotional plus.

And so, both theoretically and actually, events of the last several years suggest a few grounds for cautious optimism—perhaps the first evidence of what might later prove to be a social change for the better.

In weighing the ultimate fate of the separationist experiment, we must realize that there is nothing deterministically fixed about the current high rates of institutionalized and separated Western children. It is true, as the fatalists among us often observe, that the genies of modernity will not go back into their bottles, but it is also true that we Western men and women are not helpless victims of historical machinations beyond our control. People change their minds about social and other experiments—as sociologists say, they "renorm"—all the time. Perhaps this separationist experiment of ours, so counter not only to history but also to what we know of human nature, will ultimately prove unsatisfactory not only to children but to some critical mass of Western adults, too.

To acknowledge the kernel of truth inside two decades of advocacy on behalf of that experiment, children can't always get what they want. That is indeed a fact of life. But in hardening ourselves against asking when they rightly should, we miss something important about them and about ourselves: The most important measure of any society is not the standard that its strongest members set for themselves, but rather where they fix the moral bar for the weakest. In the end this book is a modest attempt to raise that bar, to redress some of the imbalance in discussion so far, and to give adults who do have choices some evidence and argument about it all that they might not otherwise have possessed.

NOTES

INTRODUCTION

1. For example, Susan Faludi (*Backlash*, 1991), Joan K. Peters (*When Mothers Work*, 1997), Susan Chira (*A Mother's Place*, 1998), Ann Crittenden (*The Price of Motherhood*, 2001), and Susan J. Douglas and Meredith W. Michael (*The Mommy Myth*, 2004).
2. For example, Carolyn Graglia's *Domestic Tranquility* (1998), Danielle Crittenden's *What Our Mothers Didn't Tell Us* (1999), Wendy Shalit's *A Return to Modesty* (1999), and Susan Venker's *7 Myths of Working Mothers* (2004).
3. These include Daphne de Marneffe's 2004 *Maternal Desire* and numerous recent magazine-length renditions of the same theme, including Lisa Belkin's much-discussed October 26, 2003, *New York Times Magazine* cover story and *Time* magazine's related March 22, 2004, cover on "The Case for Staying Home."
4. See, for instance, Allison Pearson's emblematic 2002 best-selling novel, *I Don't Know How She Does It.* Even in another 2002 best-seller not told from the mother's point of view, *The Nanny Diaries* by Emma McLaughlin and Nicola Kraus, the perspective remains that of the adult female caretaker rather than any other character.
5. William Damon, *Greater Expectations: Overcoming the Culture of Indulgence in America's Homes and Schools* (New York: Free Press, 1995), p. 7.
6. "Event Summary: Measuring Child Well-Being: A New Index," Brookings Institution, March 24, 2004.
7. Alan Ehrenhalt, *The Lost City: The Forgotten Virtues of Community in America* (New York: Basic Books, 1995).

CHAPTER 1: THE REAL TROUBLE WITH DAY CARE

1. Joan K. Peters, *When Mothers Work: Loving Our Children Without Sacrificing Ourselves* (Reading, MA: Perseus Books, 1998), pp. 3–4.
2. Brian C. Robertson, *Day Care Deception: What the Child Care Establishment Isn't Telling Us* (San Francisco: Encounter Books, 2003).
3. Bryce Christensen, "A Schoolhouse Built by Hobbes," in *The Child-Care "Crisis" and Its Remedies, Family Policy Review* 1, no. 2 (Fall 2003).
4. See, for example, Allan Carlson, "The Fractured Dream of Social Parenting," ibid.

5. Quoted in Kathleen Curry, "Children's Ear Infections Rampant Across Country," *Lexington Herald-Leader,* November 2, 1993.

6. Robert A. Hoekelman, "Day Care, Day Care: May Day, May Day!" *Pediatric Annals* 20 (1991): 403. As the editorial further pointed out, it is not only the children in such centers but also their pregnant mothers and their pregnant day care providers who are at risk—in the case of pregnant women, for fetal infections and for stillbirths.

7. Jody Heymann, *The Widening Gap: Why America's Working Families Are in Jeopardy— and What Can Be Done About It* (New York: Basic Books, 2000), p. 61.

8. Ibid., p. 62.

9. Arlie Russell Hochschild, *The Time Bind: When Work Becomes Home and Home Becomes Work* (New York: Metropolitan Books, 1997).

10. NICHD Early Child Care Research Network, "Child Care and Mother-Child Interaction in the First Three Years of Life," *Developmental Psychology* 35 (1999): 1399–1413. See also Jay Belsky's discussion of this study in "The Politicized Science of Day Care," *Family Policy Review* 1, no. 2 (Fall 2003): 23–40.

11. National Institute of Child Health and Human Development, Early Child Care Research Network, "Does Amount of Time Spent in Child Care Predict Socioemotional Adjustment During the Transition to Kindergarten?" *Child Development* 74, no. 4 (July/August 2003): 976–1005.

12. Robert Karen, *Becoming Attached: First Relationships and How They Shape Our Capacity to Love* (New York: Oxford University Press, 1994), chapter 22, "A Rage in the Nursery: The Infant Day-Care Wars." See also Jay Belsky, "The Politicized Science of Day Care," in *The Child-Care "Crisis" and Its Remedies, Family Policy Review* 1, no. 2 (Fall 2003).

13. Robertson, *Day Care Deception,* p. 79.

14. Kathy Tout et al., "Social Behavior Correlates of Cortisol Activity in Child Care: Gender Differences and Time-of-Day Effects," *Child Development* 69 (1998): 1247–62.

15. Susan Chira, *A Mother's Place: Choosing Work and Family Without Guilt or Blame* (New York: HarperPerennial, 1998), p. 117.

16. Susan Faludi, *Backlash: The Undeclared War Against American Women* (New York: Random House, 1991), p. 43.

17. "Colds with a Silver Lining," Abraham B. Bergman, *Archives of Pediatrics & Adolescent Medicine* 156 (2002): 104.

18. Caitlin Flanagan, *Atlantic,* April 2004. In her previous cover story in the same pages, Flanagan also shrewdly observed another interesting fact of our day care wars—that some of the most passionate advocates do not use institutional care themselves. Many have instead in-the-house, one-on-one paid help.

19. For examples of how this callousness permeates so-called Third Wave feminism, see my "Feminism's Children," *The Weekly Standard* (November 5, 2001).

20. Stanley Kurtz, "The Guilt Game," nationalreview.com (April 26, 2001).

21. Peters, *When Mothers Work,* p. 73.

22. Thanks to Stanley Kurtz for the observation about Belkin's essay. E-mail communication, October 2003.

23. Kay S. Hymowitz, *Ready or Not: Why Treating Children As Small Adults Endangers Their Future—and Ours* (New York: Free Press, 1999). According to the progressive and

neoprogressive theories dominant in education, children are self-motivated, inherently cooperative learners who will invent their own strategies on impulse. The idea of the self-sufficient child—even the self-sufficient baby and toddler—is also ingrained in current psychology. Experts from Piaget onward have stressed the rational, competent, information-processing of the child, writing off any friction with this happy scenario to "developmental stages." Influenced partly by such theories, forward-looking legal theorists—Hillary Rodham Clinton, among many others—have also stressed the autonomy and rights of the child against those of the parents (a movement driven particularly, as Hymowitz argued, by the political desire to allow minors easy access to abortion).

24. See my "Putting Children Last," *Commentary* (May 1995).

25. For a representative list, see Arlie Russell Hochschild, *The Time Bind*, pp. 226–28.

26. See, for example, Skip Thurman, "Day Care Becomes Night Care in Era of Busy Work Schedules," *Christian Science Monitor* (October 23, 1997), and "A 24-Hour Day Care Trend?" CBSNews.com, November 13, 2003.

27. Skip Thurman, "Day Care Becomes Night Care in Era of Busy Work Schedules," *Christian Science Monitor* (October 23, 1997).

28. See Leet Smith and Elaine Rivera, "Turning Librarians into Babysitters," *Washington Post*, February. 2, 2004. See also Kellie Patrick, "Libraries: Public Safety Isn't Assured," Philly.com (February 10, 2004).

CHAPTER 2: THE FURIOUS CHILD PROBLEM

1. David Lohr, "Ted Bundy: The Poster Boy of Serial Killers," *Crime Magazine*, October 6, 2002. Available online at http://crimemagazine.com/serial.htm.

2. Brian C. Robertson, *Day Care Deception: What the Child Care Establishment Isn't Telling Us* (San Francisco: Encounter Books, 2003), p. 21.

3. One famous scholarly example of such resiliency is Anna Freud's study of children in London living next to a bomb shelter, most of whom not only went on to lead normal lives but also showed little in the way of pathological problems at the time.

4. Jonathan Kellerman, *Savage Spawn: Reflections on Violent Children* (New York: Ballantine Books, 1999), p. 70.

5. See, for example, Kellerman, *Savage Spawn*. See also James Q. Wilson, "The Family Way," *OpinionJournal*, wsj.com, January 7, 2003. As he summarizes the research, "Family disorganization is more important than either race or income in explaining violent crime."

6. See, for example, "Teen Homicide, Suicide, and Firearm Death," *Child Trends DataBank*, 2001. Available at http://www.childtrendsdatabank.org/indicators/70Violent Death.cfm.

7. James Q. Wilson, "Gore, Bush, and Crime," Slate.com, August 25, 2000.

8. See, for example, Jeffrey Butts of the Urban Institute quoted in Ana Radelat, "Drop in Juvenile Crime Confounding the Experts," *Salt Lake Tribune*, April 28, 2002, http://www.sltrib.com.

9. "Teen Homicide, Suicide, and Firearm Death," *Child Trends DataBank*.

10. Between 1960 and 1998, for example, suicide rates for fifteen- to twenty-four-year-old men doubled in England and Wales, while rates for twenty-four- to thrity-five-year-olds

rose 60 percent. See "Age-Specific Suicide Rates," National Electronic Library for Health, http://www.nelmh.org. See also World Health Organization Fact Sheet Euro/02/03, "Children's and adolescents' health in Europe," noting that "European countries experience some of the highest rates of suicide in the world" and that "some countries have recently shown a secondary peak in the age group 15 to 24 years."

11. See Émile Durkhiem, *Suicide: A Study in Sociology,* reissue edition (New York: Free Press, 1997).

12. Robert D. Putnam, *Bowling Alone: The Collapse and Revival of American Community* (New York: Simon and Schuster, 2000), p. 264.

13. Barbara Schneider and David Stevenson, *The Ambitious Generation: America's Teenagers: Motivated but Directionless* (New Haven, CT: Yale University Press, 1999).

14. Ibid., p. 192.

15. Eric Fombonne, "Suicidal Behaviors in Vulnerable Adolescents: Time Trends and Their Correlates," *British Journal of Psychiatry* 173 (1998): 154–59.

16. See, for example, pages 48–50 of *Father Facts,* which summarize some of the studies documenting higher rates of emotional and psychological problems among children of divorce.

17. David Lester, "Time-Series Versus Regional Correlates of Rates of Personal Violence," *Death Studies* (1993): 529–34.

18. Claudia Wallis, "Does Kingergarten Need Cops?" *Time* (December 15, 2003). Thanks to Steven Menashi for the reference.

19. Greg Toppo, "School Violence Hits Lower Grades," *USA Today* (January 12, 2003).

20. Joshua Kaplowitz, "How I Joined Teach for America—and Got Sued for $20 Million," *City Journal* (Winter 2003). Available at http://www.city-journal.com.

21. The last three quotes are from the aforementioned *Time* essay "Does Kindergarten Need Cops?"

22. Correspondent Thalia Assuras, "Kids Getting Violent at School," CBS Evening News, January 10, 2004. Available at CBSnews.com.

23. Richard Rothstein, "Add Social Changes to the Factors Affecting Declining Test Scores," *New York Times*, October 25, 2000.

24. Francis Fukuyama, *The Great Disruption: Human Nature and the Reconstitution of Social Order* (New York: Free Press, 1999), p. 134.

25. The fact that Japanese women are typically home with their children is much remarked upon, both in scholarly literature and by foreigners familiar with Japan. For an interesting comparison of Singaporean versus Japanese mothers, see Soh Ping Ling, "Full-Time Mother or Full-Time Career Woman?" The Asahi ShimbuAsia Network (April 12, 2002), available at http://asahi.com/English/asianet/column/eng_020412.html.

26. Jody Heymann, *The Widening Gap: Why America's Working Families Are in Jeopardy—and What Can Be Done About It* (New York: Basic Books, 2000), pp. 56–57.

CHAPTER 3: WHY DICK AND JANE ARE FAT

1. Rob Stein, "Obesity Passing Smoking as Top Avoidable Cause of Death," *Washington Post*, March 10, 2004.

3. Julie Magno Zito et al., "Psychotropic Practice Patterns for Youth, a 10-Year Perspective," *Archives of Pediatric & Adolescent Medicine* 157, no. 1 (January 2003): 17–25.

4. Vedantam, "More Kids Receiving Psychiatric Drugs."

5. Cheryl Gay Stolberg, "Children's Use of Prescription Drugs Is Surging, Study Shows," *New York Times*, September 19, 2002.

6. Leon Kass et al., *Beyond Therapy: Biotechnology and the Pursuit of Happiness: A Report by the President's Council on Bioethics* (New York: ReganBooks, 2003), p. 82.

7. Coyle, J. T., "Psychotropic Drug Use in Very Young Children," *Journal of the American Medical Association* (February 23, 2000): 1059–60.

8. Marc Kaufman, "FDA Cautions on Antidepressants and Youth: Doctors Warned About Potentially Higher Suicide Risk for Those Under 18 on the Drugs," *Washington Post*, October 28, 2003.

9. Since such drugs can also have significant side effects, more drugs are often needed to control the consequences of the primary medication. Children taking methylphenidate, for example, sometimes need sleeping pills to battle the insomnia it causes; children taking SSRIs often need other medicines to counter other side effects. Thus, where one psychotropic medication goes, another often follows.

10. Michael Fumento, "Trick Question: A Liberal Hoax Turns Out to Be True," *New Republic*, February 2, 2003.

11. Malcolm Gladwell, "Running from Ritalin," *New Yorker*, February 2, 1999. Gladwell's remark brings up a point often made by advocates: Psychiatric drugs are needed to fix the faulty "hardwiring" of some people, just as eyeglasses are needed to fix nearsightedness. If that is true, then it is hard to explain why normal people react the same way. Methylphenidate (Ritalin), for example, acts the same way on the physiologies of all people, regardless of whether they are diagnosed with ADD or hyperactivity. As physician Lawerence Diller puts it in his *Running on Ritalin*, methylphenidate "potentially improves the performance of anyone—child or not, ADD-diagnosed or not." Writing in the *Public Interest* in 1998, psychologist Ken Livingston provided a similar summary of the research, citing well-known National Institute of Mental Health studies conducted during the mid-seventies to early eighties by Judith Rapaport. These studies clearly showed, in Livingston's and others' views, "that stimulant drugs improve the performance of most people, regardless of whether they have a diagnosis of ADHD, on tasks requiring good attention." ("Indeed," he comments further in an obvious comparison, "this probably explains the high levels of 'self-medicating' around the world" in the form of "stimulants like caffeine and nicotine.")

 The same is true of SSRIs. According to Peter Kramer's 1997 afterword to *Listening to Prozac*, "There is still no large-scale, definitive research on that topic [of whether SSRIs affect people with no psychiatric problem]. . . . The small studies that have come to my attention all point in one direction: these medications do have the power to affect 'normals'—people without any psychiatric diagnosis."

 What these facts point up is the fallaciousness of the eyeglass analogy for the most commonly prescribed psychiatric drugs taken by children today. The analogy is wrong. If I wear glasses for nearsightedness, they are useless to someone with 20/20 vision.

12. In 1999 an essay of mine published in *Policy Review* called "Why Ritalin Rules" outlined what seemed then (and still seems) a rather glaring social paradox: In the United States, where students from preschool onward can recite the "anti-drug" catechism by heart, millions of middle- and upper-middle-class children and teenagers are being *legally* drugged with mind-altering substances, including stimulants such as Ritalin that are chemically interchangeable with cocaine. Certain themes in this chapter, including the pharmacological similarities between Ritalin and cocaine and the subjectivity of the ADD/ADHD diagnosis, are explored at greater length in that essay. See Mary Eberstadt, "Why Ritalin Rules," *Policy Review* (April–May 1999), available at policyreview.org.

13. Kaufman, "FDA Cautions on Antidepressants and Youth."

14. *Teacher*, November/December 1996.

15. Sally Satel as quoted in Fumento, "Trick Question."

16. *Teacher*, November/December 1996.

17. "CHADD Expresses Disgust at Inaccurate, Sensational Depiction of ADHD on Montel Williams Show," press release, April 16, 2003, available at chadd.org.

18. Methylphenidate was already in vogue as a kind of poor man's cocaine when I was a college student just over twenty years ago, and it was snorted at parties almost as frequently as crystal methedrine. At the time it was marketed less as a child stimulant (though that idea was in commercial development) than as a medication for cardiac patients, which is how most users then described it. Whatever its stated purpose, the chemical effect of chop-and-snort would have been the same.

19. "Wonder Drugs Misused: Teens Abusing and Selling Ritalin," ABCnews.com, February 25, 2003.

20. Christopher Tennant, "The Ritalin Racket," available at student.com.

21. DEA Congressional Testimony, statement by Terrance Woodworth, deputy director, Office of Diversion Control, Drug Enforcement Administration, before the Committee on Education and the Workforce: Subcommittee on Early Childhood, Youth and Families, May 16, 2000. Available online at dea.gov.

22. The question of whether prescribed stimulants might lead to future abuse of related substances such as cocaine remains unsettled. On one side is evidence that the two substances act on the brain in much the same way; see, for example, Brian Vastage, "Pay Attention: Ritalin Acts Much Like Cocaine," *Journal of the American Medical Association*, 286 (2001): 905–6. For the opposing interpretation, that Ritalin and the rest actually prevent future illicit drug abuse, see T. E. Wilens et al., "Does Stimulant Therapy of Attention-Deficit/Hyperactivity Disorder Beget Later Substance Abuse? A Meta-analytic Review of the Literature," *Pediatrics* 111, no. 1 (2003): 179–85.

23. For a picture of Ritalin Man (who is also sometimes available for sale on eBay), see http://www.toymuseum.com/inside/c3/3265044.html.

24. Karen Thomas, "Back to School for ADHD Drugs," *USA Today*, August 21, 2001.

25. Kass, *Beyond Therapy*, p. 85.

26. Lawrence Diller, "An End Run to Marketing Victory: Drugmakers Find Ways to Circumvent an Advertising Ban and Promote Psychiatric Drugs for Children," Salon.com, October 18, 2001.

27. Ibid.

28. See Dennis Boyle, "The Syndrome That Became an Epidemic," *New Statesman*, October 6, 2003. For an account of the rise in Ritalin abuse in England, see Sue Reid, "The Curse of Kids Cocaine," *Daily Mail*, May 31, 2003.

29. Several lawsuits have been brought of late against Novartis, manufacturer of Ritalin. They accuse Novartis and CHADD of conspiring to create the phenomenon of ADD. Thus far each has been dismissed.

30. See Annette Lansford, M.D., "ADHD and the Military: Can Our ADHD Patients Get in (and Stay in) the Military?" American Academy of Pediatrics. Pediatric Development and Behavior home page, Fall 1998.

31. Ibid.

32. Eileen Bailey, "ADHD in the Military: Ritalin Is Not Welcome in the Armed Services," interview on about.com. Search the site for "ADHD military."

33. Sergeant First Class Mike Westphal of the Kansas State University ROTC, quoted in James Hurla, "Building a Soldier: Military Standards Restrict Enlistment," *Kansas State Collegian*, February 19, 2003.

34. Note that the National Medical Association, which consists of more than twenty thousand black doctors, is one of the few professional health organizations to have expressed public skepticism about current levels of psychotropic drug-taking among children.

35. Charles Cross, *Heavier Than Heaven* (New York: Hyperion, 2001), pp. 19–20.

36. Adam Matthews, "Eminem Opens Up," *Rolling Stone*, April 27, 1999. Thanks to Steven Menashi for the reference.

37. Thanks to Rick Eberstadt for the *Simpsons* reference.

38. Jon Popik, "Go Ahead and Have a Cow, Man," an interview with Nancy Cartwright, *City*, Rochester's alternative newsweekly, October 23, 2002.

39. Elizabeth Wurtzel, "Adventures in Ritalin," *New York Times*, April 1, 2000.

40. Walter Kirn, "Revving Up on Ritalin," *GQ*, December 2000.

41. Francis Fukuyama, *Our Posthuman Future: Consequences of the Biotechnology Revolution* (New York: Farrar, Straus and Giroux, 2002), pp. 51–52.

42. As it turns out, even seeing psychotropic drugs through this benevolent lens raises uncomfortable questions. The President's Commission on Bioethics closes its examination of child enhancement with these troubled observations: "It would be paradoxical, not to say perverse, if the desire to produce 'better children,' armed with the best that biotechnology has to offer, were to succeed in its goal by pulling down the curtain on the 'childishness' of childhood. And it would be paradoxical, not to say perverse, if the desire to improve our children's behavior or performance inculcated shorter-term and shallow notions of success at the expense of those loftier goals and finer sensibilities that might make their adult lives truly better."

43. In 2001, Connecticut approved a first-of-its-kind law prohibiting teachers and other officials from recommending psychotropic drugs.

CHAPTER 6: "OZZIE AND HARRIET, COME BACK!":
THE PRIMAL SCREAM OF TEENAGE MUSIC

1. Ironically, Ehrlich was speaking at a conference on domestic violence.

2. By "popular music" I mean the secular, commercial, rock and rock-descended songs that dominate FM airwaves, MTV, VH1, and the rest. Christian rock and country music, though also popular genres, are subjects in their own right and not under discussion here.

3. Special thanks to Rick and Kate Eberstadt, whose insights about contemporary music inform this chapter throughout.

4. In 1985, to take a particularly well-known example, the wives of several congressmen on both sides of the aisle formed a committee led by Tipper Gore known as the Parents Music Resource Center, or PMRC, to educate parents about what it called "alarming trends" in popular music—violence, crime, drug use, suicide, and the rest. In 1995 another coalition led by William J. Bennett and C. DeLores Tucker, head of the National Political Congress of Black Women, put public pressure on media giant Time Warner to modify some of its gangsta rap.

5. As to the pragmatic success of these efforts, results varied. The PMRC did effect one hoped-for innovation: Some records were marked with a label (known as the "Tipper sticker") that advised parents about what the PMRC called "explicit content," and some record stores agreed to carry those records (though many did not). The Bennett-Tucker effort resulted in a moral victory of sorts: a promise by Time Warner executives that the company would be more assiduous in its own moral policing of the product. Even so, the phenomena of violence and other unwanted themes in current music, which both groups set out to battle, has only grown larger in the years since.

6. In 2000 the American Academy of Pediatrics, the American Medical Association, the American Psychological Association, and the American Academy of Child & Adolescent Psychiatry all weighed in against contemporary lyrics and other forms of violent entertainment before Congress with a first-ever "Joint Statement on the Impact of Entertainment Violence on Children." As the last-named group explained the collective worry in a subsequent policy statement: "A concern to many interested in the development and growth of teenagers is the negative and destructive themes of some rock and other kinds of music, including best-selling albums promoted by major recording companies."

7. William Shaw, "Why Are America's Rock Bands So Goddamned Angry?" *Blender* [the Ultimate Music Magazine], August 2002, available online at http://blender.com/articles/article362.html.

8. Gabriella, "Interview with Mark Hoppus of Blink 182," *NY Rock*, August 2001.

9. "Miss Pink: This Pop Star Speaks the Universal Language of Teenage Rebellion," ABCnews.com, November 6, 2003.

10. Allan Jones, interview with Eddie Vedder, *Melody Maker*, May 21, 1994.

11. Shaheem Reid, with reporting by Sway Calloway, "Jay-Z: What More Can I Say," MTV.com, November 12, 2003.

12. Donna Britt, "Stats on Teens Don't Tell the Whole Story," *Washington Post*, January 23, 2004.

13. John Metzger, review of "Eminem: the Marshall Mathers LP," *The Music Box* 8, no. 6 (June 2001), available at http://www.musicbox-online.com.

14. Allan Bloom, *The Closing of the American Mind* (New York: Simon & Schuster, 1987), p. 73.

CHAPTER 7: THE RAVAGES OF "RESPONSIBLE" TEENAGE SEX

1. "Viacom's Porn Channel," editorial, *Wall Street Journal*, February 4, 2004.

2. Joan Walsh, "Good News from Teen America," Salon.com, April 30, 1999.

3. Gregg Easterbrook, *The Progress Paradox: How Life Gets Better While People Feel Worse* (New York: Random House, 2003), p. 54.

4. Hillard Weinstock, Stuart Berman, and Willard Cates Jr., "Sexually Transmitted Diseases Among American Youth: Incidence and Prevalence Estimates, 2000," *Perspectives on Sexual and Reproductive Health* 36, no. 1 (January/February 2004): 6–10.

5. J. R. Cates, N. L. Herndon, S. L. Schultz, and J. E. Darroch, *Our Voices, Our Lives, Our Futures: Youth and Sexually Transmitted Diseases*, School of Journalism and Mass Communication, University of North Carolina, 2004.

6. Debra Kalmuss et al., "Preventing Sexual Risk Behaviors and Pregnancy Among Teenagers: Linking Research and Programs," *Perspectives on Sexual and Reproductive Health* 35, no. 2 (March/April 2003): 87–93.

7. Nicholas Eberstadt, American Enterprise Institute, private communication, March 7, 2004.

8. To give one example of such neglect, a major statistical compendium on children and adolescent health, "America's Children, Key National Indicator of Well-Being 2003," does not even follow the problems of child sexual abuse and STDs. Instead, it tracks teen pregnancy rates as if these were the only measure of sexual well-being.

9. N. Brener et al., "Trends in Sexual Risk Behaviors Among High School Students— United States, 1991–2001," *Morbidity and Mortality Weekly Report*, September 27, 2002.

10. Committee on Prevention and Control of Sexually Transmitted Diseases, Institute of Medicine, *The Hidden Epidemic: Confronting Sexually Transmitted Diseases*, ed. Thomas R. Eng and William T. Butler (Washington, D.C.: National Academy Press, 1997).

11. Fifteen years ago a pediatrician in Washington, Dr. Ronald Bashian, told me during a routine baby visit that sexually transmitted diseases in adolescents were the worst health problem that pediatricians faced, and that politically correct notions of "sexual freedom" were keeping the bad news from the publicity it deserved. In retrospect, his words were remarkably prescient.

12. Committee on Prevention and Control of Sexually Transmitted Diseases, *The Hidden Epidemic*, p. 60.

13. Ibid., p. 38.

14. Ibid., p. 36.

15. Ibid., p. 37.

16. Ibid., p. 37.

17. Ibid., p. 37.

18. The *Salon* Web site, for example, has now run so many stories on this subject that a special category on oral sex exists in its archives.

19. Ibid., p. 20.

20. Meg Meeker, M.D., *Epidemic: How Teen Sex Is Killing Our Kids* (Washington, D.C.: Lifeline Press, 2002), p. 12.

21. Ibid.

22. Ibid., p. 98.

23. See, for example, R. W. Blum, T. Beuhring, and P. M. Rinehart. *Protecting Teens: Beyond Race, Income and Family Structure* (Minneapolis: Center for Adolescent Health, University of Minnesota, 2000).

24. Deborah A. Cohen, M.D., M.P.H. et al., "When and Where Do Youths Have Sex? The Potential Role of Adult Supervision," *Pediatrics* 110, no. 6 (December 2002): 66–72.

25. Kalmuss et al., "Preventing Sexual Risk Behaviors and Pregnancy Among Teenagers."

26. Bruce J. Ellis et al., "Quality of Early Family Relationships and Individual Differences in the Timing of Pubertal Maturation in Girls: A Longitudinal Test of an Evolutionary Model," *Journal of Personality and Social Psychology* 77, no. 2 (August 1999): 387–401.

27. Bruce J. Ellis and Judy Garber, "Psychosocial Antecedents of Variation in Girls' Pubertal Timing: Maternal Depression, Stepfather Presence, and Marital and Family Stress," *Child Development* 71, no. 2 (March/April 2000): 485–501.

28. Robert J. Quinlan, "Father Absence, Parental Care, and Female Reproductive Development," *Evolution and Human Biology* 24 (2003): 376–90.

29. Andrea J. Sedlak, Ph.D., and Diane D. Broadhurst, M.L.A., "Executive Summary of the Third National Incidence Study of Child Abuse and Neglect," U.S. Department of Health and Human Services, September 1996.

30. David Finklehor et al., "Sexually Abused Children in a National Survey of Parents: Methodological Issues," *Child Abuse and Neglect* 21 (1997): 1–9.

31. Theodore Dalrymple, "Our Great, Societal Neverland," *National Review*, December 22, 2003, p. 31.

32. David Blankenhorn, "Commonsense Article About Abuse," National Fatherhood Initiative, February 6, 2001.

33. Thanks to P. J. O'Rourke for this insight. Private communication, March 2004.

34. Kay S. Hymowitz, "The Contradictions of Parenting in a Media Age," in *Kid Stuff: Marketing Sex and Violence to America's Children*, ed. Diane Ravitch and Joseph P. Viteritti (Baltimore: Johns Hopkins University Press, 2003).

CHAPTER 8: SPECIALTY BOARDING SCHOOLS: TOUGH LOVE OR ULTIMATE OUTSOURCING?

1. Louis Sacher, *Holes* (New York: Farrar, Straus and Giroux, 1998).

2. This point is reiterated throughout the referral literature. As one service called Parent Help explains: "There are hundreds of boarding schools in the United States but a lot of them are NOT geared toward helping troubled teens."

3. Sara Rimer, "Desperate Measures: Parents of Troubled Youths Are Seeking Help at Any Cost," *New York Times*, September 10, 2001.

4. "Many different types of programs," its Web site explains, "have evolved over the past decade to serve the growing needs and numbers of struggling young people." It adds a point also made frequently by critics, that "since the profession of therapeutic schools and programs is relatively new, there are currently no national standards for several categories of these programs."

5. See Tim Weiner, "Parents, Shopping for Discipline, Turn to Tough Schools Abroad," *New York Times*, May 9, 2003; "Parents Divided over Jamaica Disciplinary Academy," *New York Times*, June 17, 2003; and "Program to Help Youths Has Troubles of Its Own," *New York Times*, September 6, 2003.

6. Weiner, "Parents, Shopping for Discipline, Turn to Tough Schools Abroad."

7. Weiner, "Parents Divided over Jamaica Disciplinary Academy."

8. Weiner, "Program to Help Youths Has Troubles of Its Own."

9. Weiner, "Parents, Shopping for Discipline, Turn to Tough Schools Abroad."

10. Weiner, "Program to Help Youths Has Troubles of Its Own."

11. Ibid.

12. Decca Aitkenhead, "The Last Resort," *Observer Magazine*, June 29, 2003.

13. Ibid.

14. Sheerly Avni, "I Was a Hired Thug for Tough Love," Salon.com, August 30, 2000.

15. Alexia Parks, *An American Gulag: Secret P.O.W. Camps for Teens* (Eldorado Springs, CO: The Education Exchange, 2000).

16. " 'Behavior Modification': Salvation for Problem Teens or Brainwashing?" *Associated Press*, June 14, 1999.

17. Martha Shirk, "Kid Help or Kidnapping?" *Youth Today*, June 1999, p. 1.

18. Erika Brown, "When Rich Kids Go Bad: The Desperate but Lucrative Business of Putting Self-Destructive Kids Back Together," ABCnews.com, October 10, 1993.

19. Parks, *An American Gulag*, pp. 76–77.

20. Weiner, "Program to Help Youths Has Troubles of Its Own."

21. Rimer, "Desperate Measures."

22. Shirk, "Kid Help or Kidnapping?," p. 4.

23. For a discussion of the continuum of adverse effects in day care, see Stanley Kurtz, "The Guilt Game," nationalreview.com, April 26, 2001.

24. Quoted in Rimer, "Desperate Measures."

CHAPTER 9: CONCLUSION: BEYOND THE BLAME GAME

1. In sophisticated parlance, they violate the philosophical principle known as Occam's razor—the idea that if two explanations are competing for favor, the one requiring fewer premises is to be preferred.

2. According to the vaccine theory, autism is the result of an adverse reaction to measles, mumps, and/or rubella vaccination.

3. Sandra Blakeslee "Panel Finds No Evidence to Tie Autism to Vaccines," *New York Times*, May 19, 2004.

4. Pediatricians in particular worry that parents will not have their children inoculated on schedule because of it, thus increasing the children's risks for diseases that vaccination has hitherto practically wiped out.

5. Dimitri Christakis, M.D., M.P.H., et al., "Early Television Exposure and Subsequent Attentional Problems in Children," *Pediatrics* 113, no. 4 (April 2004): 708–13.

6. Judith Shulevitz, "I Want My Electronic Babysitter!" *Slate*, August 5, 1999.

7. As Susan Chira, among a few thousand others, has formulated the point: "It is also crucial to remember that studies may find a 'correlation,' but that does not prove cause and effect. A study may demonstrate that there is a connection stronger than random chance would dictate between, say, a mother's work and a child's test scores, but that does not prove that her work affected the child's scores." Chira, *A Mother's Place*, p. 115.

8. One meaning comes from the history of philosophy. Something like "correlation does not prove causality" was the rallying cry of eighteenth-century Scottish philosopher David Hume, who invoked a related insight to challenge the metaphysics of his own time. Hume's best-known example was the humble fact that the sun rises and sets every day. Most people, he argued, draw an incorrect inference from this fact—namely, that the sun will rise tomorrow because it has risen each previous day. But an unfailing pattern does not prove causality; it merely shows what Hume called the "constant conjunction" of events.

9. And so, in our current context, their rhetoric would run something like this: Do children of divorce show higher rates of drug and alcohol consumption than do others? Maybe so, but that doesn't tell us *why* they do; after all, correlations don't prove causality. Do some infants whose mothers are employed full-time outside the home perform worse on educational testing at age three than other children? (They do.) Maybe so, but that doesn't mean that mother absence per se is responsible; after all, there are many other "confounding variables" at work. Do teenage boys without biological fathers in the home exhibit more behavioral trouble and violence and worse educational outcomes than other boys? Yes, they do, but we can't say that absent fathers are the reason; plenty of other factors, such as low incomes and frequent moves, might be implicated, too.

10. Such was the argument of Judith Rich Harris's controversial 1998 best-seller, *The Nurture Assumption*, a particularly sophisticated exercise in showing that correlations don't prove causality. Essentially, Harris took that skeptic's bludgeon—correlations don't prove causality—to a large stack of literature from the preceding century, which asserted the influence of parents over children's long-term development. Using recent studies of separated twins and other attempts to measure the influence of genetics on behavior, she argued in part that much of what we think of as "nurture" is actually heredity in disguise. She further found a great deal of social science commonly cited in support of the nurture assumption "worthless" for a variety of reasons: It fails to take intrinsic qualities of children into account; it fails to disentangle the effects of parents on children from the effects of children on parents (the "causal vector" problem); and it customarily overlooks the difference between behavior in the home and behavior in the outside world. She also presented evidence from a variety of sources—linguistics in particular—to suggest that whereas parents are not the formative influences on children, peers are.

11. Here is a second reason for such skepticism, and it sheds further light on how selectively the point is used. That correlation doesn't prove causality is true enough, but it doesn't *disprove* causality, either. Yet this corollary is typically traduced by the

people who invoke it as the gold standard of judging evidence. For example, when children of divorce, say, are shown to have a higher likelihood of psychological and behavioral problems, advocates point out that since correlations don't prove causality, we can't attribute those problems to divorce. Formulation declared; case closed. This is the way contemporary debate about the family has become calcified. At some point someone reminds the rest of us that "correlation doesn't prove causality," and that reminder is assumed to be the end of the argument. It shuts discussion down.

But should it? Look again at the words in quotation marks. They imply that the cause of the problems *might* be something else other than the correlation in question, but they don't prove that it *is* something else. Equally important, they don't rule out that the correlation is causally connected, only that we can "prove" that much just by looking at them in isolation. In other words, the fact that two phenomena appear alongside each other—such as fatherlessness and earlier sexual activity, as was mentioned in the chapter on STDs—does not by itself prove anything about a causal relationship. But it doesn't mean they are randomly coinciding, either, and it also doesn't mean that we're entitled to rule out one correlation (fatherlessness) as the cause of the other (earlier sexual activity). Yet such ruling out is how advocates routinely dismiss highly suggestive findings about the relationship between absent parents and child and adolescent woes.

12. *Father Facts*, pp. 177–78.

13. On the divorce rate, see Linda Lamb, "Autistic Spectrum Disorders: An Interview with Author-Advocate Mitzi Waltz," http://www.patientcenters.com/news/waltz_2002_interview.html.

14. Psychoanalyst Bruno Bettelheim long argued that autism was a disorder caused by mothers who did not want their children. This "mother-blaming" theory has made him a figure of utmost derision in current thinking.

15. As the National Institutes of Health connects the causal dots on marital trouble: "Families who have children with ADHD, *as with other behavioral disorders and chronic diseases*, experience increased levels of parental frustration, marital discord, and divorce [emphasis added]." Also, see "What Is the Impact of ADHD on Individuals, Families and Society?" in Diagnosis and Treatment of Attention Deficit Hyperactivity Disorder, NIH Consensus Statement Online 16, no. 2 (November 16–18, 1998): 1–37.

16. Aimin Chen, M.D., Ph.D., and Walter J. Rogan, M.D., "Breastfeeding and the Risk of Neonatal Death in the United States," *Pediatrics* 113, no. 5 (May 2004): 435–39.

17. Donald J. McHugh Jr., "Parental Guidance Required," *New York Times*, July 12, 2003, p. 16.

EPILOGUE

1. To give just one example, the wisdom of welfare reform as we know it, which essentially took children without fathers and further deprived them of a mother much of the time, seems highly debatable in light of links mentioned earlier in this book between maternal employment and an increase in sedentary pursuits as well as obesity.

2. As Stanley Kurtz has put the point, "Many of us have forgotten the inescapable necessity of some reasonable sense of guilt to any human flourishing. Mothers cannot forget." See "The Guilt Game," nationalreview.com, April 26, 2001.

3. For an intricate historical account of child-rearing theories over the last hundred years, see Ann Hulbert, *Raising America: Experts, Parents and a Century of Advice About Children* (New York: Knopf, 2003).

4. Nor is it a call to "return to the 1950s," a decade that I, like many readers, never lived in anyway.

5. At the same time there are real limits to the argument that every single household in an era of unprecedented prosperity needs two paychecks just to make ends meet. As David Gelernter put this point sharply several years ago in a *Commentary* essay called "Why Mothers Should Stay Home," "The economic-necessity argument hits home with a nice solid thunk. Yet ultimately it makes no sense: as a nation we used to be a lot poorer, and women used to stay home."

6. This point has been hammered home to me and other at-home mothers day after day. Many of us share the experience of showing up at school to pick up our own children and getting importuned, sometimes tearfully, by other children in after-care asking if they could please, please come to our house instead of having to stay at school until six. Over the years I have heard many variations on this theme. It is an odd but interesting fact that the social pecking order of children and preteens largely reverses the commercial and social order of adults; in the former, unlike the latter, the child with the at-home mother is the envy of many peers.

7. See, for example, David Popenoe and Barbara Defoe Whitehead, "Marriage and Children: Coming Together Again?" National Marriage Project, June 2003, available at http://www.marriage.rutgers.edu.

BIBLIOGRAPHY

ARTICLES

ABCNews.com. "Miss Pink: This Pop Star Speaks the Universal Language of Teenage Rebellion," November 6, 2003.

——. "Wonder Drugs Misused: Teens Abusing and Selling Ritalin," February 25, 2003.

"Age-Specific Suicide Rates." National Electronic Library for Health. http://www.nelmh. org.

Aitkenhead, Decca. "The Last Resort." *Observer Magazine*, June 29, 2003.

Anderson, Patricia M., Kristin F. Butcher, and Phillip B. Levine. "Maternal Employment and Overweight Children." NBER Working Paper No. W8770 (February 2002). http://ssrn.com/abstract=299814.

Armstrong, J., J. J. Reilly, and the Child Health Information Team. "Breastfeeding and Lowering the Risk of Childhood Obesity." *Lancet* 359 (June 8–9, 2002): 2003–4.

Assuras, Thalia. "Kids Getting Violent at School." CBSNews.com, January 11, 2004.

Avni, Sheerly. "I Was a Hired Thug for Tough Love." Salon.com, August 30, 2000.

Bailey, Eileen. "ADHD in the Military: Ritalin Is Not Welcome in the Armed Services." About.com September 16, 2001.

Beard, Steve. "Childhood Divorce Fuels Fire of New Rock." *Washington Times*, October 4, 2002.

Belkin, Lisa. "The Opt-Out Revolution." *New York Times Magazine*, October 26, 2003.

Belsky, Jay. "The Politicized Science of Day Care," in *The Child-Care "Crisis" and Its Remedies*, special issue of *Family Policy Review* 1, no. 2 (October 28, 2003).

Bergman, Abraham B. "Colds with a Silver Lining." *Archives of Pediatrics & Adolescent Medicine* 156 (2002): 104.

Bernstein, Nina. "Daily Choice Turned Deadly: Children Left on Their Own." *New York Times*, October 19, 2003.

Blakeslee, Sandra. "Panel Finds No Evidence to Tie Autism to Vaccines." *New York Times*, May 19, 2004.

Blankenhorn, David. "Commonsense Article About Abuse." National Fatherhood Initiative, February 6, 2001.

Boyle, Dennis. "The Syndrome That Became an Epidemic." *New Statesman*, October 6, 2003.

Brener, N., et al. "Trends in Sexual Risk Behaviors Among High School Students—United States, 1991–2001." *Morbidity and Mortality Weekly Report*, September 27, 2002.

Britt, Donna. "Stats on Teens Don't Tell the Whole Story." *Washington Post*, January 23, 2004.

Brown, Erika. "When Rich Kids Go Bad: The Desperate but Lucrative Business of Putting Self-Destructive Kids Back Together." ABCnews.com, October 10, 2002.

Burke, K. C., et al. "Comparing Age at Onset of Major Depression and Other Psychiatric Disorders by Birth Cohorts in Five U.S. Community Populations." *Archives of General Psychiatry 1991* 48 (September): 789–95.

Burton, Thomas M. "Advisory Issued on Antidepressants: FDA Action Follows Reports About Suicidal Thinking Among Young Users in Trial." *Wall Street Journal*, October 28, 2003.

Butcher, Kristin F., Patricia M. Anderson, and Phillip B. Levine. "Maternal Employment and Overweight Children." FRB of Chicago Working Paper No. 2002–10 (August 2002). http://www.ssrn.com/abstract-327060.

"California Cries '273% Increase in Autism and We Don't Know Why!'" *Los Angeles Times*, April 15, 1999.

Carlson, Allan. "The Fractured Dream of Social Parenting," in *The Child-Care "Crisis" and Its Remedies*, special issue of *Family Policy Review* 1, no. 2 (October 28, 2003).

Carr, Martha Randolph. "My Son's Disability, and My Own Inability to See It." *Washington Post*, January 4, 2004.

Cates, J. R., N. L. Herndon, S. L. Schultz, and J. E. Darroch. *Our Voices, Our Lives, Our Futures: Youth and Sexually Transmitted Diseases.* School of Journalism and Mass Communication, University of North Carolina, 2004.

CBSNews.com. "A 24-Hour Day Care Trend?," November 13, 2003.

———. "U.S.: A Nation Reared on Drugs," January 13, 2003.

"CHADD Expresses Disgust at Inaccurate, Sensational Depiction of AD/HD on 'Montel Williams Show.'" chadd.org, April 16, 2003.

Chakrabarti, Suniti, and Eric Fombonne. "Pervasive Developmental Disorders in Preschool Children." *Journal of the American Medical Association* 285 (2001): 3093–99.

Chen, Aimin, M.D., Ph.D., and Walter J. Rogan, M.D. "Breastfeeding and the Risk of Neonatal Death in the United States." *Pediatrics* 113, no. 5 (May 2004): e435–39.

"Childhood Obesity: Screening and Prevention." Published in French under the title "Obesité, dépistage et prévention chez l'enfant." *Editions Inserm*, 2000, 180FRF.

Christensen, Bryce. "A Schoolhouse Built by Hobbes," in *The Child-Care "Crisis" and Its Remedies*, special issue of *Family Policy Review* 1, no. 2 (Fall 2003).

Cohen, Deborah A., et al. "When and Where Do Youths Have Sex? The Potential Role of Adult Supervision." *Pediatrics* 110, no. 6 (December 2002): 66–72.

"Columbine Shooter Was Prescribed Anti-depressant." http://www.cnn.com/HEALTH/9904/29/luvox.explainer, April 29, 1999.

Coontz, Stephanie. "What Will Last?" *Washington Post*, January 4, 2004.

Coyle, Joseph, T. "Psychotropic Drug Use in Very Young Children." *Journal of the American Medical Association* (February 23, 2000): 1059–60.

Curry, Kathleen. "Children's Ear Infections Rampant Across Country." *Lexington Herald-Leader*, November 2, 1993.

D'Agenio, P., et al. "Obesity and Overweight Among Pre-adolescents." *Bollettino epidemi-ologico nazionale* 14, no. 1 (January 2001). http://www.epicentro.iss.it/ben/precedenti/gennaio/2_en.htm.

Dalrymple, Theodore. "Our Great, Societal Neverland." *National Review*, December 22, 2003.

Diller, Lawrence. "The Business of ADHD." Interview with Frontline, 2001. http://www.pbs.org/wgbh/pages/frontline/shows/medicating/experts/business.html.

———. "An End Run to Marketing Victory: Drugmakers Find Ways to Circumvent an Advertising Ban and Promote Psychiatric Drugs for Children." Salon.com, October 18, 2001.

———. "Just Say Yes to Ritalin!" Salon.com, September 25, 2000.

Eberstadt, Mary. "Feminism's Children." *Weekly Standard*, November 5, 2001.

———. "Putting Children Last." *Commentary*, May 1995.

———. "Why Ritalin Rules." *Policy Review*, April 1999.

Edelhart, Courtenay. "Lilly Doing Spin Control After News Oregon Shooter Took Prozac." *Indianapolis Star*, www.starnews.com, May 23, 1998.

Ellis, Bruce J., et al. "Quality of Early Family Relationships and Individual Differences in the Timing of Pubertal Maturation in Girls: A Longitudinal Test of an Evolutionary Model." *Journal of Personality and Social Psychology* 77, no. 2 (August 1999): 387–401.

——— and Judy Garber. "Psychosocial Antecedents of Variation in Girls' Pubertal Timing: Maternal Depression, Stepfather Presence, and Marital and Family Stress." *Child Development* 71, no. 2 (March/April 2000): 485–501.

Event Summary: "Measuring Child Well-Being: A New Index." Brookings Institution, March 24, 2004.

Finklehor, David, et al. "Sexually Abused Children in a National Survey of Parents: Methodological Issues." *Child Abuse and Neglect* 21 (1997): 1–9.

Flanagan, Caitlin. Letters column. *Atlantic*, April 2004.

Flegal, K. M., M. D. Carrol, C. L. Ogden, and C. L. Johnson. "Prevalence and Trends in Overweight Among U.S. Children and Adolescents." *Journal of the American Medical Association* 288, no. 14 (October 9, 2002): 1928–32.

Fombonne, Eric. "Suicidal Behaviors in Vulnerable Adolescents: Time Trends and Their Correlates." *British Journal of Psychiatry* 173 (1998): 154–59.

Fumento, Michael. "Trick Question: A Liberal Hoax Turns Out to Be True." *The New Republic*, February 2, 2003. See also his exchange with me in the letters column, *The New Republic*, March 17, 2003.

Gelernter, David. "Why Mothers Should Stay Home." *Commentary*, February 1996.

Gladwell, Malcolm. "Running from Ritalin." *New Yorker*, February 15, 1999.

Griffith, Gail. "The Fear of No Right Answer." *Washington Post*, November 9, 2003.

Groopman, Jerome. "O.C.D." *New Yorker*, April 10, 2000.

Hoekelman, Robert A. "Day Care! Day Care! May Day! May Day!" *Pediatric Annals* 20(1991): 403.

Horn, Wade F. "Commonsense Article About Abuse." National Fatherhood Initiative, February 6, 2001.

Hurla, James. "Building a Soldier: Military Standards Restrict Enlistment." *Kansas State Collegian*, February 19, 2003.

Hymowitz, Kay S. "The Contradictions of Parenting in a Media Age," in *Kid Stuff: Marketing Sex and Violence to America's Children*, Diane Ravitch and Joseph P. Viteritti, eds. Baltimore: Johns Hopkins University Press, 2003.

Jaeger, Elizabeth. "Child Care and Mother-Child Interaction in the First Three Years of Life." NICHD Early Child Care Research Network. *Developmental Psychology* 35 (1999): 1399–1413.

Jellinek, Michael, et al. "Pediatric Symptoms Checklist at Massachusetts General Hospital." http://www.mgh.harvard.edu.

Johnson, Ellen, Ruth E. K. Stein, and Mark R. Dadds. "Moderating Effects of Family Structure on the Relationship between Physical and Mental Health in Urban Children with Chronic Illness." *Journal of Pediatric Psychology* 21, no. 1 (February 1996): 43–56.

Jones, Allan. Interview with Eddie Vedder. *Melody Maker*, May 21, 1994.

Juvenile Bipolar Research Foundation. "Frequently Asked Questions About Early-Onset Bipolar Disorder." http://www.jbrf.org/juv bipolar/faq.html.

Kalies, H., J. Lenz, and R. von Kries. "Prevalence of Overweight and Obesity and Trends in Body Mass Index in German Pre-school Children, 1982–1997." *International Journal of Obesity* 26, no. 9 (September 2002): 1211–17.

Kalmuss, Debra, et al. "Preventing Sexual Risk Behaviors and Pregnancy Among Teenagers: Linking Research and Programs." *Perspectives on Sexual and Reproductive Health* 35, no. 2 (March/April 2003).

Kaplowitz, Joshua. "How I Joined Teach for America—and Got Sued for $20 Million." *City Journal*, Winter 2003.

Kaufman, Marc. "FDA Cautions on Antidepressants and Youth: Doctors Warned About Potentially Higher Suicide Risk for Those Under 18 on the Drugs." *Washington Post*, October 28, 2003.

Kirn, Walter. "Revving Up on Ritalin." *GQ*, December 2000.

Kurtz, Stanley. "The Guilt Game: The Truth About Day Care." nationalreview.com, April 26, 2001.

———. "A Mother's Love: If It Takes a Village to Raise a Child in Africa, Why Not Here?" nationalreview.com, May 12–13, 2001.

Lamb, Linda. "Autistic Spectrum Disorders: An Interview with Author-Advocate Mitzi Waltz." patientcenters.com, July 9, 2002.

Land, Celeste. "Autism and the Breastfeeding Family." *Leaven* 37, no. 2 (February/March 2001): 10–11.

Lansford, Annette. "ADHD and the Military: Can Our ADHD Patients Get in (and Stay in) the Military?" *American Academy of Pediatrics* (Fall 1998). dbpeds.org.

Lemke, Tim. "House Panel Toughens Fines for Broadcast Smut." *Washington Times*, March 4, 2004.

Leonard, Andrew. "School of Hard Knocks." Salon.com, February 23, 1998.

Lester, David. "Time-Series Versus Regional Correlates of Rates of Personal Violence." *Death Studies* (1993): 529–34.

Levine, Arthur. "Tomorrow's Education, Made to Measure." *New York Times*, December 22, 2000.

Lewin, Tamar. "SAT Test Changes Disability Policy." *New York Times*, July 15, 2002.

———. "Study Links Working Mothers to Slower Learning." *New York Times*, July 17, 2002.

Ling, Ping. "Full-time Mother or Full-time Career Woman?" Asahi ShimbuAsia Network, April 12, 2002. http://www.asahi.com/English/asianet/column/eng_020412.html.

Livingston, Ken. "Ritalin: Miracle Drug or Cop-Out?" *Public Interest*, Spring 1997.

Lohr, David. "Ted Bundy: The Poster Boy of Serial Killers." *Crime Magazine*, October 6, 2002. http://www.crimemagazine.com/serial.htm.

McHugh, Donald J. Jr., "Parental Guidance Required." *New York Times*, July 12, 2003.

McTigue, Kathleen, Joanne M. Garrett, and Barry M. Pokin. "The Natural History of the Development of Obesity in a Cohort of Young U.S. Adults Between 1981 and 1988." *Annals of Internal Medicine* 136, no. 12 (June 18, 2002): 857–64.

Matthews, Adam. "Eminem Opens Up." *Rolling Stone*, April 27, 1999.

May, Meredith. "Welfare Reforms Not Ending Poverty." *San Francisco Chronicle*, April 16, 2002.

Meikle, James. "Overweight Children Get Diabetes Warning." *Guardian*, February 21, 2002.

Metzger, John. "Eminem: the Marshall Mathers LP." *Music Box* 8, no. 6 (June 2001). http://www.musicbox-online.com.

Miller, Marian. Letter to the Editor. *New York Times*, February 2, 2004.

Moore, Michael Scott. "Buying Time." Salon.com, February 9, 2000.

Moynihan, Daniel Patrick. "Defining Deviancy Down." *American Scholar* (Winter 1993).

Munro, Neil. "Brain Politics." *National Journal*, February 3, 2001.

National Center for Health Statistics. "Teen Birth Rate Continues to Decline; African-American Teens Show Sharpest Drop," press release, December 17, 2003.

National Institute of Child Health and Human Development. Early Child Care Research Network. "Does Amount of Time Spent in Child Care Predict Socioemotional Adjustment During the Transition to Kindergarten?" *Child Development* 74, no. 4 (July 2003): 976–1005.

National Institute of Mental Health. "Treatment of Children with Mental Disorders." http://www.nimh.nih.gov/publicat/childqa.cfm, September 2000, updated June 18, 2001.

Newby, Jonica. "Early Menarche." Report interviewing Dr. Bruce Ellis and Dr. Julie Quinlivan. ABC-TV. http://www.abc.net.au/catalyst/stories//s958787.htm, October 2, 2003.

Ollivier, Debra. "Whose Crisis Is This, Anyway?" Salon.com, November 5, 2003.

O'Reilly, Bill. "Poverty-inducing Entertainment." townhall.com, January 18, 2003.

Ortiz, Michelle Ray. "Boot Camps for Wayward Youths Offer Hope, Help, Hell." Associated Press, June 13, 1999.

Patrick, Kellie. "Libraries: Public Safety Isn't Assured." Philly.com, February 10, 2004.

Pell, Sheila. "Family Dinner, Minus Family." *Washington Post*, January 11, 2004.

Picard, Andre. "Fat Children Outweigh Fat Adults, Statscan Says." *Globe and Mail*, October 19, 2002.

Pollitt, Katha. "Good News for Women." *Nation*, December 24, 2003.

Popenoe, David, and Barbara Defoe Whitehead. "Marriage and Children: Coming Together Again?" National Marriage Project, June 2003. http://www.marriage.rutgers.edu.

Prober, Charles G., M.D., F.A.A.P. "Evidence Shows Genetics, Not MRR Vaccine, Determines Autism." *AAP News* (December 1999): 24.

Quinlan, Robert J. "Father Absence, Parental Care, and Female Reproductive Development." *Evolution and Human Behavior* 24, no. 6 (2003): 376–90.

Radelat, Ana. "Drop in Juvenile Crime Confounding the Experts." *Salt Lake Tribune*, April 28, 2002.

Reibstein, Larry, with Thomas Rosenstiel. "The Right Takes a Media Giant to Political Task." *Newsweek*, June 12, 1995.

Reid, Shaheem, with reporting by Sway Calloway. "Jay-Z: What More Can I Say." MTV.com, November 21, 2003.

Reid, Sue. "The Curse of Kid's Cocaine." *Daily Mail*, May 31, 2003.

Richters, John, and Dante Cicchetti. "Mark Twain Meets DSM-III-R: Conduct Disorder, Development, and the Concept of Harmful Dysfunction." *Development and Psychopathology* 5 (1993): 5–29.

Rimer, Sara. "Desperate Measures—Parents of Troubled Youth Are Seeking Help at Any Cost." *New York Times*, September 10, 2001.

Rothenberg, Ben. "Extra Time Policies Are an Unfair Advantage." *Bulldog News*, St. Albans School, Washington, D.C., November 12, 2003.

Rothstein, Richard. "Add Social Changes to the Factors Affecting Declining Test Scores." *New York Times*, October 25, 2000.

Rubenstein, Judith L., et al. "Suicidal Behavior in Adolescents: Stress and Protection in Different Family Contexts." *American Journal of Orthopsychology* 68 (1998): 274–84.

Schemo, Diana Jean. "Study Finds Mothers Unaware of Children's Sexual Activity." *New York Times*, September 5, 2002.

Sedlak, Andrea J., Ph.D., and Diane D. Broadhurst, M.L.A. "Executive Summary of the Third National Incidence Study of Child Abuse and Neglect." U.S. Department of Health and Human Services Administration for Children and Families Administration on Children, Youth and Families National Center on Child Abuse and Neglect, September 1996.

Shaw, William. "Why Are America's Rock Bands So Goddamned Angry?" *Blender* (the "Ultimate Music Magazine"), August 2002. http://blender.com/articles/article 362.html.

Shugart, Margaret A., and Elda M. Lopez. "Depression in Children and Adolescents: When 'Moodiness' Merits Special Attention." *Postgraduate Medicine* 112, no. 3 (September 2002).

Shulevitz, Judith. "I Want My Electronic Babysitter!" Slate.com, August 5, 1999.

Smith, Leet, and Elaine Rivera. "Turning Librarians into Babysitters." *Washington Post*, February 2, 2004.

Stein, Rob. "Obesity Passing Smoking as Top Avoidable Cause of Death." *Washington Post*, March 10, 2004.

Stepp, Laura Sessions. "Infants Now Murdered as Often as Teens." *Washington Post*, December 10, 2002.

Stolberg, Cheryl Gay. "Children's Use of Prescription Drugs Is Surging, Study Shows." *New York Times*, September 19, 2002.

Surgeon General's Conference on Children's Mental Health: A National Action Agenda, January 3, 2001. Office of the Surgeon General. http://www.surgeongeneral.gov/topics/cmh/childreport.htm.

Sylvester, Tom. "Day Care May Hurt Kids . . . but Don't Worry!" nationalreview.com, July 28, 2003.

Takahashi, E., K. Yoshida, H. Sugimori, M. Mikayawa, T. Izuno, T. Yamagami, and S. Kagamimori. "Influence Factors on the Development of Obesity in 3-Year-Old Children Based on the Toyama Study." *Preventive Medicine* 28, no. 3 (March 1999): 293–96.

Tanoue, Y., and S. Oda. "Weaning Time of Children with Infantile Autism." *Journal of Autism and Developmental Disorders* 19, no. 3 (September 1989): 425–34.

Taylor, Stephanie K. "TV ADDs to Student Woes." *Washington Times*, August 27, 2003.

"Teen Homicide, Suicide, and Firearm Death." *Child Trends Data Bank*, 2001. http://www.childtrendsdatabank.org/indicators/70ViolentDeath.cfm.

Tennant, Christopher. "The Ritalin Racket." http://articles.student.com/article/ritalin.

Thomas, Karen. "Back to School for ADHD Drugs." *USA Today*, August 28, 2001.

Thurman, Skip. "Day Care Becomes Night Care in Era of Busy Work Schedules." *Christian Science Monitor*, October 23, 1997.

Tout, Kathy, et al., "Social Behavior Correlates of Adrenocortical Activity in Daycare: Gender Differences and Time-of-Day Effects." *Child Development* 99, no. 5 (1998): 1247–62.

Toppo, Greg. "School Violence Hits Lower Grades." *USA Today*, January 12, 2003.

Twenge, Jean M. "The Age of Anxiety? Birth Cohort Change in Anxiety and Neuroticism, 1952–1993." *Journal of Personality and Social Psychology* 79, no. 6 (December 2000): 1007–21.

Vastage, Brian. "Pay Attention: Ritalin Acts Much Like Cocaine." *Journal of the American Medical Association* 286, no. 8 (August 22/29, 2001): 905–6.

Vedantam, Shankar. "FDA Approves ADHD Drug Offering Fewer Side Effects." *Washington Post*, November 27, 2002.

———. "More Kids Receiving Psychiatric Drugs: Question of 'Why' Still Unanswered." *Washington Post*, January 14, 2003.

Wallis, Claudia. "Does Kindergarten Need Cops?" *Time*, December 15, 2003.

———. "The Case for Staying Home." *Time,* March 22, 2004.

Walsh, Joan. "Good News from Teen America." Salon.com, April 30, 1999.

Wang, Guijing, and William H. Dietz. "Economic Burden of Obesity in Youths Aged 6 to 17 Years: 1979–1999." *Pediatrics* 109, no. 5 (May 2002): 81.

Weiner, Tim. "Parents Divided over Jamaica Disciplinary Academy." *New York Times*, June 17, 2003.

———. "Parents, Shopping for Discipline, Turn to Tough Schools Abroad." *New York Times*, May 9, 2003.

———. "Program to Help Youths Has Troubles of Its Own." *New York Times*, September 6, 2003.

Weinstock, Hillard, Stuart Berman, and Willard Cates Jr. "Sexually Transmitted Diseases Among American Youth: Incidence and Prevalence Estimates, 2000." *Perspectives on Sexual and Reproductive Health* 36, no. 1 (January/February 2004).

Weiss, Kenneth R. "Regents Order Review of Extra Time on SAT Test." *Los Angeles Times*, January 20, 2000.

Welsh, Patrick. "Young, Male, White—and Confused." *Washington Post*, December 14, 2003.

"What Is the Impact of ADHD on Individuals, Families and Society?" in "Diagnosis and Treatment of Attention Deficit Hyperactivity Disorder," NIH Consensus Statement Online 16, no. 2 (November 16–18, 1998): 1–37.

Wilens, T. E., et al. "Does Stimulant Therapy of Attention-Deficit/Hyperactivity Disorder Beget Later Substance Abuse? A Meta-analytic Review of the Literature." *Pediatrics* 111, no. 1 (2003): 179–85.

Williams, Marjorie. "Propriety Malfunction," *Washington Post*, February 5, 2004.

Wilson, James Q. "Gore, Bush, and Crime." Slate.com, August 25, 2000.

———. "The Family Way." *OpinionJournal*, wsj.com, January 7, 2003.

"Wonder Drugs Misused: Teens Abusing and Selling Ritalin." ABCNews.com, February 25, 2003.

Wood, Peter. "Crippling Thoughts: The ADA's Powerful Psychological Hold." nationalreview.com, June 5, 2001.

Woodworth, Terrance, deputy director. Office of Diversion Control, Drug Enforcement Administration, before the Committee on Education and the Workforce: Subcommittee on Early Childhood, Youth and Families. dea.gov, May 16, 2000.

World Health Organization Fact Sheet Euro/02/03. "Children's and Adolescents' Health in Europe."

Wurtzel, Elizabeth. "Adventures in Ritalin." *New York Times*, April 1, 2000.

Zinsmeister, Karl. "The Problem with Day Care." *The American Enterprise*, May 1, 1998.

Zito, Julie Magno, et al., "Psychotropic Practice Patterns for Youth: A 10-Year Perspective." *Archives of Pediatric & Adolescent Medicine*, 157, no. 1 (January 2003).

BOOKS

Armstrong, Thomas. *The Myth of the ADD Child*. New York: Plume, 1997.

Belkin, Lisa. *Life's Work: Confessions of an Unbalanced Mom*. New York: Simon & Schuster, 2002.

Blankenhorn, David. *Fatherless America: Confronting Our Most Urgent Social Problem*. New York: Perseus Books, 1995.

Bloom, Allan. *The Closing of the American Mind*. New York: Simon & Schuster, 1988.

Blum, R. W., T. Beuhring, and B. M. Rivehart. *Protecting Teens: Beyond Race, Income, and Family Structure*. Minneapolis: Center for Adolescent Health, University of Minnesota, 2000.

Chira, Susan. *A Mother's Place: Choosing Work and Family Without Guilt or Blame*. New York: Perennial, 1999.

Coontz, Stephanie. *The Way We Never Were: American Families and the Nostalgia Trap*. New York: Basic Books, 2000.

Critser, Greg. *Fat Land: How Americans Became the Fattest People in the World*. Boston: Houghton Mifflin, 2003.

Crittenden, Ann. *The Price of Motherhood: Why the Most Important Job in the World Is Also the Least Valued*. New York: Metropolitan Books, 2001.

Crittenden, Danielle. *What Our Mothers Didn't Tell Us: Why Happiness Eludes the Modern Woman*. New York: Touchstone, 2000.

Cross, Charles. *Heavier Than Heaven.* New York: Hyperion, 2001.

Damon, William. *Greater Expectations: Overcoming the Culture of Indulgence in Our Homes and Schools.* New York: Free Press, 1995.

Decter, Midge. *An Old Wife's Tale.* New York: HarperCollins, 2001.

DeGrandpre, Richard. *Ritalin Nation.* New York: W.W. Norton & Company, 1999.

de Marneffe, Daphne. *Maternal Desire: On Children, Love, and the Inner Life.* New York: Little, Brown, 2004.

Demitri, F., and M. D. Papolos. *The Bipolar Child: The Definitive and Reassuring Guide to Childhood's Most Misunderstood Disorder.* New York: Broadway Books, 2002.

Diller, Lawerence. *Running on Ritalin: A Physician Reflects on Children, Society, and Performance in a Pill.* New York: Bantam Books, 1999.

Douglas, Susan J, and Meredith W. Michael. *The Mommy Myth: The Idealization of Motherhood and How It Has Undermined Women.* New York: Free Press, 2004.

Easterbook, Gregg. *The Progress Paradox.* New York: Random House, 2003.

Ehrenhalt, Alan. *The Lost City: The Forgotten Virtues of Community in America.* New York: Basic Books, reprint 1996.

Ellkind, D. *The Hurried Child: Growing Up Too Fast Too Soon,* 3rd ed. New York: Perseus Books, 1988.

Eng, Thomas R., and William T. Butler, eds. *The Hidden Epidemic: Confronting Sexually Transmitted Diseases.* Committee on Prevention and Control of Sexually Transmitted Diseases, Institute of Medicine. Washington, D.C.: National Academy Press, 1997.

Faludi, Susan. *Backlash: The Undeclared War Against American Women.* New York: Random House, 1991.

Fukuyama, Francis. *Our Posthuman Future: Consequences of the Biotechnology Revolution.* New York: Farrar, Straus and Giroux, 2002.

———. *The Great Disruption: Human Nature and the Reconstitution of Social Order.* New York: Free Press, 1999.

Graglia, F. Carolyn. *Domestic Tranquility: A Brief Against Feminism.* Dallas, TX: Spence, 1998.

Harris, Judith Rich. *The Nurture Assumption.* New York: Free Press, 1998.

Hewlett, Sylvia Ann. *Creating a Life: Professional Women and the Quest for Children.* New York: Talk Miramax Books, 2002.

Heymann, Jody. *The Widening Gap: Why America's Working Families are in Jeopardy—and What Can Be Done About It.* New York: Basic Books, 2000.

Hochschild, Arlie Russell. *The Time Bind: When Work Becomes Home and Home Becomes Work.* New York: Metropolitan Books, 1997.

Horn, Wade F., and Tom Sylvester. *Father Facts,* 4th ed. National Fatherhood Initiative, 2002.

Hulbert, Ann. *Raising America: Experts, Parents, and a Century of Advice About Children.* New York: Alfred A. Knopf, 2003.

Hymowitz, Kay S. *Ready or Not: Why Treating Children as Small Adults Endangers Their Future—and Ours.* New York: Free Press, 1999.

Karen, Robert. *Becoming Attached: First Relationships and How They Shape Our Capacity to Love.* New York: Oxford University Press, 1994.

Kass, Leon, et al. *Beyond Therapy: Biotechnology and the Pursuit of Happiness.* Foreword by Leon Kass, M.D. New York: ReganBooks, 2003.

Kellerman, Jonathan. *Savage Spawn: Reflections on Violent Children.* New York: Ballantine Books, 1999.

Kirn, Walter. *Thumbsucker: a Novel.* New York: Anchor Books, 1999.

Kramer, Peter. *Listening to Prozac.* New York: Penguin Books, 1997.

Kraus, Nicola, and Emma McLaughlin. *The Nanny Diaries.* New York: St. Martin's Press, 2002.

McLaughlin, Emma, and Nicole Kraus. *The Nanny Diaries: A Novel.* New York: St. Martin's Press, 2002.

Meeker, Meg, M.D. *Epidemic: How Teen Sex Is Killing Our Kids.* Washington, D.C.: Regnery Publishing, 2002.

Parks, Alexia. *An American Gulag: Secret P.O.W. Camps for Teens.* Eldorado Springs, CO: The Education Exchange, 2000.

Pearson, Allison. *I Don't Know How She Does It.* New York: Random House, 2002.

Peters, Joan K. *When Mothers Work: Loving Our Children Without Sacrificing Our Selves.* Reading, MA: Perseus Books, 1998.

Pierre, DBC. *Vernon God Little.* London: Faber and Faber, 2003.

President's Council on Bioethics. *Beyond Therapy: Biotechnology and the Pursuit of Happiness.* New York: ReganBooks, 2003.

Putnam, Robert D. *Bowling Alone: The Collapse and Revival of American Community,* New York: Simon & Schuster, 2000.

Ravitch, Diane, and Joseph P. Viteritti, eds. *Kid Stuff: Marketing Sex and Violence to America's Children.* Baltimore: Johns Hopkins University Press, 2003.

Robertson, Brian C. *Day Care Deception: What the Child Care Establishment Isn't Telling Us.* San Francisco: Encounter Books, 2003.

Sacher, Louis, *Holes.* New York: Farrar, Straus and Giroux, 1998.

Satel, Sally. *P.C.M.D.: How Political Correctness Is Corrupting Medicine.* New York: Basic Books, 2002.

Schneider, Barbara, and David Stevenson. *The Ambitious Generation: America's Tennagers: Motivated but Directionless.* New Haven, CT: Yale University Press, 1999.

Shalit, Wendy. *A Return to Modesty.* New York: Free Press, 1999 (paperback ed.).

Sommers, Christina Hoff. *The War Against Boys: How Misguided Feminism Is Harming Our Young Men.* New York: Simon & Schuster, 2000.

Venker, Susan, *7 Myths of Working Mothers.* Dallas, TX: Spence, 2004.

Vicusi, Kip. *Smoking: Making the Risky Decision.* New York: Oxford University Press, 1992.

Warren, Elizabeth, and Amelia Warren Tyagi. *The Two-Income Trap: Why Middle-Class Mothers and Fathers Are Going Broke.* New York: Basic Books, 2003.

Wilson, James Q. *The Marriage Problem: How Our Culture Has Weakened Families.* New York: HarperCollins, 2002.

INDEX